WHAT PEOPLE

DO YOU

Unlike so much written on religion, this book isn't slyly trying to push you into a faith. It is, simply, humbly and honestly informative. I don't think I need a God, but I like and appreciate this book.
Matthew Parris

An original approach to a remarkable variety of the world's religions.
Professor Carl Harline of Brigham Young University, Utah, USA

A fine general introduction to the world's major faiths for the curious and enquiring, expressed with clarity and some essential humour.
Rabbi Dr Charles Middleburgh, Director of Studies at Leo Baeck College, London and Rabbi to the Cardiff Reform Synagogue

Do You Need God?

Exploring different paths to spirituality
even for atheists

Do You
Need God?

Exploring different paths to spirituality
even for atheists

Rory J.Q. Barnes

CHRISTIAN
ALTERNATIVE

Winchester, UK
Washington, USA

First published by Christian Alternative Books, 2014
Christian Alternative Books is an imprint of John Hunt Publishing Ltd.,
Laurel House, Station Approach,
Alresford, Hants, SO24 9JH, UK
office1@jhpbooks.net
www.johnhuntpublishing.com
www.christian-alternative.com

For distributor details and how to order please visit the 'Ordering' section on our website.

Text copyright: Rory J.Q. Barnes 2013

ISBN: 978 1 78279 380 9

A CIP catalogue record for this book is available from the British Library.

Design: Lee Nash

Printed and bound by CPI Group (UK) Ltd, Croydon, CRO 4YY

We operate a distinctive and ethical publishing philosophy in all areas of our business, from our global network of authors to production and worldwide distribution.

CONTENTS

Read this book if

- you would like to find meaning in your own apparent insignificance,

- you seek a reason for acting in accordance with a moral code,

- you feel a need for some religious system but don't know what to believe,

- you are curious about other people's religions,

- you want to know how religions compare,

- you are an atheist or agnostic but have a nagging desire for a spiritual life of some sort,

- you think religion is rubbish but would like to be better informed about what you don't believe in.

I would like to thank the following for their advice. Note that any mistakes are my own.

On Christianity: Professor Craig Harline of Brigham Young University, USA and Professor Norman Tanner of the Gregorian University, Rome, Italy.

On Islam: Professor Wael Hallaq of Columbia University, USA and Dr Jan-Peter Hartung of the School of African and Oriental Studies London University (SOAS), UK.

On Judaism: Rabbi Dr Charles H Middleburgh Director of Studies at Leo Baeck College, London, UK and Rabbi to the Cardiff Reform Synagogue.

On Zoroastrianism: Dr Almut Hintz, Head of Zoroastrian Studies at SOAS, UK.

On Buddhism: Dr Tadeusz Skorupski, Reader in Buddhism at SOAS, UK and Professor Richard Gombrich of Oxford University, UK

On Taoism: Dr. Louis Komjathy, Assistant Professor of Chinese Religions and Comparative Religious Studies, Department of Theology and Religious Studies, University of San Diego, USA.

On Sikhism: Professor Hew McLeod of Otago University, New Zealand.

On Confucianism: Professor Xinzhong Yao, Director of the Kings China Institute, Kings College, London, UK.

Part I

Part I

Chapter I

What is Religion?

Are you religious? If you think you aren't, could you be? What does religion involve? Could you be religious without even knowing it?

An Oxford professor once said to me that he thought it fatuous to attempt to define religion. However, it is no good writing a book explaining and comparing religions without considering what religion is. It is quite correct that there is no universally agreed definition of religion. There are a number of definitions. These are not competitive statements of eternal truth. Rather, they are essentially working tools, each fulfilling a function according to the purpose of the user.

If you are a sociologist or anthropologist you will be more interested in a definition which centers on people's culture, rituals and social behavior. If you are interested in psychology that will color your definition. If you are of no religion, that will affect your definition.

There are many different ideas of what religion is about. That religion is a means of political oppression. That its purpose is to enable people to share a social identity. That its purpose is simply to give meaning to that which has no meaning. That it is an aspect of culture. That it is a form of neurosis. That its essential element is a sense of awe. That it must involve worship. Above all; that it is to do with a belief that we can move to a higher plane of existence. It has been said that a definition of religion tells you more about the person proposing it than about religion.

Thus definitions of religion are functional. They depend on your perspective, your purpose, what you want to use them for. This is a book comparing the core ideas of the current major world religions. So for our purpose perhaps we need a definition which describes just what those core ideas have in common.

All current world religions seek to put our individual lives in a context, to relate our lives to the universe and eternity and to draw conclusions as to how we should behave.

Now, if you are going to tell people how to behave you have to have some thing which is the basis of 'ought', some thing which enables a view to be taken as to what is 'good' and what is not.

That brings us to the issue of absolute or universal values. These are moral values which are unlimited in time and space, which go beyond mere standards of sensible behavior for humans to adopt in dealing with one another. You could explain the idea by asking if good would still exist if there were no human beings at all.

However, there's a bit more to the idea of universal values. If they exist they must be underwritten by something; they can't just be arbitrary rules hanging in philosophical air. All world religions have the idea of universal values, but different religions have different ideas about what it is that puts the foundation under them. Some say it's God, but others say it's something else entirely, some sort of natural law perhaps.

Let me give you a taste of how different religions deal with this issue. In the Abrahamic religions (Christianity, Judaism and Islam), Sikhism and the Baha'i Faith universal values are underwritten by God, they are God's revealed will and command, evidenced in scripture. For Zoroastrianism universal values arise from a combination of scripture (some of which is said to be the word of God) and Asha, the cosmic principle of order, justice, righteousness and truth. Hinduism, or most of it, has a creator God, albeit with many faces, but for many Hindus it is not a revealed religion. Its values are embedded in dharma, right action, part of existence, natural law, the way of things. The dharma of fire is to produce heat, the dharma of humans is to follow the principles of love, detachment, honesty, selfless work and a desire to get closer to God. Buddhism's values are under-written by the requirements of the path to Nirvana, which leads away from the unsatisfactoriness and suffering of daily life. Jainism's values are underwritten by the principle that spirit has an innate nature, which it should follow. Confucianism's values are underwritten either by our inner nature or by natural law, which naturally harmonize with the Way. Taoism's values are whatever is required to bring earth, Heaven and humankind into harmony. Shinto's, by what brings benign harmony in nature and humanity. Universal values are the reason why we should behave in a certain way. Thus, for Christianity, Islam, Judaism, Sikhism and Zoroastrianism 'good' is what God says it is, and for the Eastern religions it is what is consistent with the path to closeness to a universal principle. There's a lot more about this in the chapters on individual religions.

Another idea which all world religions have is the idea that there exists energy and consciousness which cannot be scientifi-cally identified or proved, which we can refer to as 'spirit'.

So, if you wonder about your place in the universe, believe in good and not good, and are prepared to think that there may be energy and consciousness which we cannot prove exists, then I would suggest that you can be religious. In fact you may be religious without even having realized it.

You will have plenty of company. These basic elements of religion are common to most societies in recorded history and spiritual belief seems to be a widespread desire.

This book attempts to describe the veins of thought, of ideas, that run through each current major religion. And that brings us to that thing called faith, which is the most potent element of religious choice. Faith turns a mere belief into a self-evident and overpowering truth. If this book describes veins of thought, then faith is the blood that brings them to life. To give another analogy, this book is a map. Looking at the map is one thing.

Traveling, if that is what you want to do, is quite another.

Some believers say that if you lack faith in a religion you cannot understand it. That can't be an argument against at least trying. Others say that the desire for spiritual belief is hardwired into us, like ants building a complex nest through mere instinct. Yet others say that this need for belief is a psychological need, for comfort, security, hope.

People argue whether this need to believe is benign or malign, and you will have to make your own mind up about that. On the malign side there are those who point to religious conflict and the deaths and harm that that has caused. Others reply that in the twentieth century there were those without religious belief who caused millions and millions of deaths: for example, Stalin, Mao and Pol Pot.

Some may say that if you detach the need for belief from religion that need may attach itself to something else, perhaps some political ideology. Or that if you do away with the need altogether you may just have unrestrained self-interest. A question to be answered is whether a humanism which dispenses with spiritual belief can be the building block of civilization, or whether it is a mere product of a civilization originally built on a foundation of belief.

Indeed, an issue raised by this book is the relationship between the basis of secular humanism and the basis of world religions and whether they are as far apart as secular humanists seem to suggest. Moral theology starts from human experience.

There is evidence that many people in the West have some sort of nagging desire or need for spirituality, but have no specific belief system to hang it on. They believe but they do not belong.

It may be helpful to see religions as consisting of a substructure of idea and beliefs with a superstructure of traditions, rituals, art, buildings, customs and so on. In religions which have a strong regional connection this superstructure often blends in with local culture and custom. Sometimes the superstructure has elements of another religion or of local primitive religions that have been absorbed and taken over. Sometimes it can be difficult to identify the dividing line between a religion's practices and local cultural traditions. Followers of less education may blend the practice of their religion with folklore and custom. For many people the super-structure is the most important part of their religion. Sociologists, anthropologists, historians and others may define religion and categorise religions by reference to the super-structure. Finally, note that in practice followers of a religion may choose to suit themselves and not accept this or that part of its ideas or practice.

So, this book tries to give guidance about choices of spiritual belief. Remember that spiritual belief systems don't all require a belief in God. There are non God systems and there will be many options here for the atheist or agnostic who would like some sort of spiritual life. Also, if you do not seek some belief but merely are curious as to the beliefs of others, there will be plenty for you here. For those who do seek belief, this book sets out decisions which have to be taken before you make your choice of belief system, or which are involved in your choice.

Some religions do not readily explain all their most basic beliefs. There is a tendency for words such as 'God', 'soul', 'worship', and many others, to be used without explaining what particular meaning the religion in question gives them. You can't properly understand a religion from the outside without such explanation, any more than you can properly use a recipe book without understanding how to fry, or a carpentry manual without knowing how to hold a saw.

I would suggest that if you have a desire for specific belief you start very simply. When you have taken your basic decisions, and those will be set out below, then you can proceed to the superstructure of your belief system, but not before.

It may be that you are not interested in the basics, but only in the superstructure, that you want a belief system that you feel comfortable with, that provides a spiritual cocoon of ritual, that gives companionship, an unthinking security, an unenquiring certainty. That is a perfectly reasonable point of view, and if it is the case, don't stop reading. There will be more for you later on.

Most seekers will probably prefer a set of beliefs that do not conflict with what is presently accepted as scientific fact. But it doesn't seem to worry a lot of people, and it is a matter for you to choose. However, to exercise choice you must be aware what the choice is and put yourself to the question.

Sometimes a consideration of the range of available belief (and I include both religious and secular belief systems) can lead to a feeling that it doesn't matter what you believe. Can tolerance and commitment be reconciled? Perhaps the analogy of the mountain can do that. It goes as follows. Imagine that the meaning of life is to be found at the top of a mountain. And imagine that there are a number of paths up to the top of that mountain. Lots of people are trying to climb up each path. Are all the paths important? Of course they are. They all lead to the top. Is any path less important than another? No. For they all lead to the top. But if someone is climbing to the top of the mountain is any path more important to them than another? Of course. It's the one they are walking along, or perhaps climbing or struggling along. That path is more important to them because it's the one which may get them to the top. They have to pay close attention to it. Otherwise they may fall down or get lost and never get anywhere near the top at all.

To say that you need to look at a religion's underlying beliefs before you consider the superstructure is not to reduce the importance of the superstructure. Yet if you are choosing a religion, you need to be clear as to what are the basic ideas that you have to take on, and what elements form a superstructure which comes with the religion but is not necessarily essential to its basic belief. If you are born to a religion you take what you are given. If you choose it, you have the responsibility to be aware of just what it is that you are accepting. And remember, religion isn't just something people believe. It's something they do.

Chapter 2

One Idea and One Word

I shall attempt to capture each major world religion in one idea and one (or two) words.

The main idea of **Christianity** is that, in your single life, you should behave in a way which ensures that your soul is close to God after your death, and that such closeness has been made possible by God's sacrifice of his son aspect Jesus Christ, whose teachings are to be followed, together with those of God's prophets.

For Christianity the word is **'love'**. God sent Christ out of love for us. We love God for sending Christ. Loving our neighbors as ourselves ensures we can all become a 'we' with God, remaining ourselves yet becoming one.

The main idea of **Islam** is that in your single life you submit to God's rules as revealed by his greatest prophet Muhammad so that you may join God (Allah) in Paradise after your death.

For Islam the word is **'tawhid'**, which is the oneness of God. It is through God that everything is interconnected. And it is we who are the trustees of God's creation. Our task in this is to try to ensure that everything is in a state of harmony and grace, to bring about a moral order on earth by doing what is permitted and not doing what is not permitted. In doing this we are being obedient to our inner and innate nature.

The main idea of **Sikhism** is that in your many lives you use your free will with the assistance of God's grace to overcome I-am-ness and become God-centered rather than man-centered, so that you may end your cycle of reincarnation and merge with God.

Others might disagree, but for Sikhism I would choose the word **'haumi'** or I-am-ness. This is putting yourself at the center of life. Sikh scripture says that if haumi is understood the door of liberation can be found.

The main idea of **Judaism** is that in your single life you should obey an agreement made between God and the Jews. By doing this you are showing your obedience to God and he will deal with your spirit appropriately when you die.

So for Judaism the one word is '**covenant**'. This is a binding agreement entered into by the Jewish people and God. By this agreement the Jews agreed to keep God's laws as revealed to them and so to bring holiness into every aspect of their lives.

The main idea of mainstream **Hinduism** is to end your cycle of reincarnation and so get as close as possible to the universal principle. Karma ensures that all actions performed with a desire for their results will affect this journey.

Hinduism has such a wide range of belief that I cannot think of a word that will cover all of it. I could choose the word 'dharma', a sort of natural law, but it isn't something to be explained briefly. So instead I will have the words '**Brahman**' and '**atman**'. Brahman is the universal principle which you may call God and atman is something of that principle found in us. The relationship resembles that of salt (atman) in water (Brahman).

The main idea of **Zoroastrianism** is that in your single life you should embrace good and reject evil, reflect the creative spirit of God, support his spiritual creation and enlarge his material creation, and take your positive part in the battle of good against evil, so that you may join God in a creation restored to its natural purity and perfection.

Perhaps the best expression to choose for Zoroastrianism is '**Angra Mainyu**' or the Devil, for if you understand the nature of the Devil that will tell you much of how Zoroastrianism works. The Devil is an uncreated spirit who has spoiled creation. Our task is to help God defeat him. When that is done creation will be restored to its perfect state, including our perfected bodies.

The main idea of **Buddhism** is that at any one moment our

spiritual being is in a process of change, of becoming. It does not exist in the sense of a constant eternal soul. Our object in life should be to steer this process so we can be free from the cycle of death and rebirth and to be in a position where we can, if we wish, achieve the blissful, permanent but unknown non state of Nirvana.

It is difficult to decide on the word for Buddhism. After much thought I would go for '**sunyata**' translated as '**emptiness**', and sometimes '**void**'. It's a difficult concept. The idea of emptiness is that things have no unchanging self-nature, they only exist in relation to one another. We ourselves are but a flow of energies and appearances. We cling to and desire permanence but so long as we do so we can only have an unsatisfactory experience. If we can grasp that there is no independent permanent existence for ourselves or anything, we can find our way to the understanding of how things are that is Nirvana.

The main idea of **Jainism** is that you should conduct yourself in such a way as to tend to release your soul from material ties, and so end the cycle of reincarnation so that your self can experience the bliss and omniscience of being its true self.

So for Jainism let's take the word '**karma**'. Jainism sees karma as matter. It adheres to the jiva/soul. A jiva freed of karma is a jiva self-realized, in a state of energy, omniscience and bliss.

The main idea of the **Baha'i Faith** is of the unity of humanity and of religion, under one God, who periodically sends a messenger, such as Abraham, Christ, Krishna, Muhammad, and so on.

For the Baha'i Faith the word is '**unity**': unity of mankind, religion and science.

The main idea of **Shintoism** is that nature is governed by spirit entities and that there is a harmony inherent in human nature and nature itself. You will seek to behave in a way which helps this harmony and which is consistent with it. You will seek favors from the spirits. The religion is more interested in this world than the next, as are Confucianism and Taoism.

So Shintoism's word is '**wa**' or benign harmony.

The main idea of **Taoism** is that there is a principle, a force, which flows through everything, and that your goal is to harmonise with this force, which is called the Tao.

So Taoism's word has to be the '**Way**', the pathway of a communication which governs the relationship between Earth, Heaven and Humankind, and which is the spontaneous power behind things which goes into every part so every part has something of the whole.

The main idea of **Confucianism** is that there is a cosmic order, that the world should be brought into harmony with this order, that humans should lead their lives so as to increase this harmony and that the starting point for this is self-cultivation within a specified network of social relationships.

Picking a word for Confucianism is really difficult, but I would go for '**Li**'. In practical terms Li is proper conduct between parties. If we follow Li then we follow the Way and then the world will be in harmony as we reach out, in and from our personal life into society in a spiritual and moral union.

You can see from all this that a common theme in the major world religions seems to be for us to get close to and or submit to a universal principle of some kind. There is an emphasis on the ultimate unity of all things and a concentration on the idea of achieving a higher, transcendent state, sometimes in this life.

As for secular **humanism**, its main idea is that human ethics and morality are based on what is good for humans, an idea which contains buried assumptions about human nature. It can be argued that this idea is not that structurally different from that of some religions albeit without the idea of spirit.

As to the word for secular humanism, I would choose **humanness** as a deliberate echo of, say, Confucianism.

Chapter 3

Who was First?

Generally, current world religions seem to have largely developed from ancient traditions of worship based on **sacrifice**. This idea was that if you gave up something or gave something to powerful spirit beings you would gain or avoid something. It appears that in time this idea became ritualised to the point where it was sometimes believed that the sacrifice was bound to work and that if it didn't the ritual must not have been performed properly.

Of current world religions, **Zoroastrianism** might be seen as the earliest. Its founder, Zoroaster, lived sometime between 1500 and 1200 BCE. He came from a network of tribes called Aryans and in some areas Indo-Europeans. Some Aryans had already spread from the southern Russian steppes into Europe. Later other Aryans spread into India between 1500 BCE and 1000 BCE, and into Iran in about 1000 BCE. The Aryans had a religion of sacrifice to the gods. Zoroaster moved beyond this idea. His vision was that there was only one god, God. Evil, the spoiling of creation, was the product of another uncreated powerful spirit, the destructive spirit, the Devil. Zoroaster said humans had to choose which one they followed. Zoroastrianism became the largest world religion and remained so for centuries, centered on the Persian Empire.

In India the Aryan religion developed into what is called the Vedic religion. This was initially still a religion of sacrifice but over centuries developed the idea of a universal spirit/Brahman/God, and a soul or atman which had a close identity with God. It also developed the ideas of reincarnation and of karma. The attention of the devotee was thus turned from looking outside to the sacrificial gods to looking inside to find God there. Thus

Hinduism grew out of the Vedic tradition.

As part of this growth of ideas came the idea of renunciation, of giving up worldly things so as to better follow the internal quest. Within this context was born the **Jain** religion, founded towards the beginning of the fifth century BCE, although it created a prehistory for itself which reached further back in time.

Also out of this period of the growth of Hinduism from the Vedic religion and the development of an ethos of renunciation, sprang **Buddhism**. The Buddha was born in about 445 BCE.

You might think that **Judaism** goes back to Abraham, who came from Mesopotamia and settled in Canaan in about 1750 BCE. However, the abiding feature which marked Judaism is its belief that there is only one God, its own. Initially, the Israelites worshipped a number of gods. God's covenant with Moses is deemed to have taken place around 1200 BCE. Since an important part of the covenant was that the Israelites would only worship their Yahweh and no other Gods/gods, it is evident that they were not monotheistic at that stage. The first unequivocal assertion of monotheism in the Bible is not until the later part of the book of Isaiah, dating to the second half of the fifth century BCE: "For I alone am God! I am God and there is none like me" (Is. 46.9). Thus it could be argued that Israelite religion may date back to Abraham and that Judaism dates from the fifth century BCE.

Shintoism is the Japanese indigenous religion. Its roots are lost in an antiquity of nature worship.

The Chinese religions of Confucianism and Taoism first developed in a time when the ruler was considered to be a son of 'Heaven'. His authority came from this, together with his consequent powers to intermediate with the spirit world of the gods. Confucianism in particular had links, both in thought and practice, with the issue of political authority.

Confucius lived from 551 to 479 BCE, which fixes **Confucianism**'s starting point, though Confucius himself probably felt he was just transmitting a pre-existing set of ideas.

The beginnings of **Taoism** are uncertain. Probably somewhat after Confucianism, although there is a Taoist story that the writer of the Taoist *Daode Jing* instructed Confucius.

Christianity is easy to date at the beginning of the first century CE.

Islam is easy to date, since Muhammad is said to have lived from 570 to 632 CE.

The founder of **Sikhism**, Guru Nanak, was born in 1469 and died in 1539.

The **Baha'i Faith** was declaimed in 1863.

Generally, Judaism, Christianity and Islam have common roots and are often referred to as the Abrahamic religions, so called because they all see their prophet Abraham and his dealings with God as a significant element in their religion's history. So does the Baha'i Faith. Hinduism, Jainism, Buddhism and Sikhism have common roots – Sikhism also has some Islamic roots. The religions of Confucianism and Taoism, which both originated in China, share a common Chinese folk religious tradition.

This book is about current religious thought and so I refer to ancient religions only as necessary to explain present ideas.

Chapter 4

Basic Ideas

Before I start, may I tackle the issue of how I am to refer to God. Will I use 'He', 'She' or 'It'. 'It' must be more correct, for God is neither He nor She. But 'It' may sound a bit rude to some people. 'She' introduces issues of feminism that are inappropriate to the context. 'He' can be criticised as being both inaccurate and male dominated. None of the words are satisfactory and there is no right answer. My choice is to mostly use the word 'It' in this chapter and thereafter bow to tradition and use the word 'He'. If that is not to your taste please accept my apologies. And so we turn to spirit.

Spirit

If someone asks you what is the most basic concept of religion, you might say "God". But there are a number of religions that don't have a God, and there is another concept that underlies the idea of a God.

That is the concept of spirit. Spirit is an energy and consciousness which our senses cannot perceive. All current world religions believe in it. So the first question to ask yourself is not 'does God exist?' but whether spirit exists.

If you are convinced that spirit does not exist then the current world religions are not for you, but you may find satisfaction in some secular belief system like humanism, which derives a moral imperative, a reason to be good, from a study of what is beneficial for human beings.

Let us assume you are willing to believe that spirit may exist. If so, the next questions you must ask yourself are:

- is spirit connected to we humans?

- is it connected to other living beings or to non living things?
- does it exist on its own?

Why are these questions important? Well, if spirit can be connected to us, then that enables the idea of 'soul'. You can believe in soul without believing in a creator God. If spirit can be connected to other things, then that enables the idea that animals and perhaps things have souls. You could believe in the idea of a spirit of the earth. And if spirit can exist on its own, then you can believe that it takes the form of ghosts or other spirit beings. You can believe in 'gods', powerful spirit beings. And, most important, you can address the question of 'God', and whether It exists.

So you can see how important and fundamental the idea of spirit is.

Do Good and Evil really exist and what are they?

Good is a value which applies to human behavior. Religions say it is a value which is linked with and underwritten by some universal principle. Some religions say it derives from God. Others say it is simply part of the pathway to the ultimate, what gets you to your desired spiritual destination. It can be regarded as a universal truth or a universal path or both. Either way it is eternal and regarded by religions as linked in some way with the essence of the universe. Most religions use the word 'good'. Buddhists use the words 'wholesome' or 'skilful'. Use what words you wish. Everyone knows what we mean when we say 'good'. Secular humanists see good as being what benefits humankind – that leaves plenty of scope for argument .

People who do believe in good and evil are likely to have little trouble defining which is which. Societies have their cultural quirks. One may label a human act immoral, another may not: suicide, fornication, adultery, incest, underage sex, same-sex sex and human sacrifice come to mind. Nonetheless, there is an amazing degree of agreement throughout recorded history as to what is good and what is not.

Next, the nature of 'evil' must be considered. We must ask: is evil a positive force? If it is, then there will be problems down the line for those who believe in a creator God. For a later question will be whether this creator God is good. If you say 'Yes' and also believe that evil is a positive force then you have the problem of how something good creates something evil. In turn this can throw you back to the issue of whether there are one or more Gods and whether there is a good one and an evil one.

All is not lost if you find yourself in this position. You can join the Zoroastrians, a creed which flowered in Persia in the pre-common era, but which is nowadays found in India and to a lesser extent in Iran. The Zoroastrians believe in one creator God, but also in another uncreated spirit, the devil Angra Mainyu, from whom all evil derives.

Which brings us back to the nature of evil. Majority Christianity has a neat answer to the problem. It says that evil is the absence of good, that evil is what happens when good is not present. This is despite the fact that many lay Christians would regard evil as a positive force.

Islam accepts evil as part of God's creation, which we shouldn't question. Judaism, for the most part, doesn't see evil as some sort of force but as an inherent part of human nature, a tendency which our free will can follow or not. The Jewish Kabbalah tradition sees evil as arising from an imbalance between God's powers of judgment and compassion. For Sikhism, evil is a consequence of free will, a result of our ego taking over and separating us from God. Similarly, some God believers get round the problem by arguing that the creation of evil is not itself an evil act, being the necessary by-product of free will and moral value.

The non God religions see evil as being a characteristic of

actions which lead away from our spiritual objective. Confucianism and Taoism see such actions as destructive of 'the Way', Shintoism as destructive of 'Wa', Hinduism as a breach of dharma: all words for a deep natural harmony. Buddhists would refer to being 'unskillful' or 'unwholesome' rather than 'evil.' Some religions (Hinduism, Buddhism, Jainism and Sikhism), believe in karma, a process by which all our acts have a consequence. And for those, evil could be said to be a quality of those acts which produce a karma which stands between us and our spiritual liberation. More of that later.

Secular humanists, who don't believe in God or any religion, will refer to behavior that tends towards the meeting of human needs as good and to that which is hostile to that end as bad.

Now we can move on to God. Not just whether It exists, but what we mean by the word. Then we will return to the idea and issue of spirit, in the form of soul.

God

The very word 'God' is sadly unhelpful. It is an emotive word which comes with a lot of baggage. To many brought up in the Christian tradition it is irretrievably caught up with images of an old man with Caucasian features. In Western society the word calls up the Christian answer, and in Islamic cultures the Islamic answer. All these associations are barriers to clear thinking and choice. Nonetheless, we are stuck with the word.

So, let us ask the question: what do we mean by this spirit, 'God'? What is the one defining quality that makes It different from everything else? That must surely be that It has created our universe. If that is not the case, then 'God' is a mere spirit coinhabitant of our universe, a 'god'. Buddhism, Taoism and Shintoism believe in gods.

Debates about religion in the West often give the impression that you can't be religious if you don't believe in God. But there are a number of belief systems open to you if you don't believe in a creator God. Buddhists don't believe in a creator God. There is a corner of Hinduism, the Samkhya school, which doesn't. Nor do Jains, Confucians or Taoists believe in a creator God. You do not have to combine a rejection of the God idea with a rejection of matters spiritual. And, logically, you can be an atheist and still believe in an afterlife.

Really?

There is a variation of the idea of God the creator which can be found in Vaiseshika, one of the early schools of Hinduism. This is that God created the world but to do so used matter which had always existed. The gods of Shintoism did the same.

Hinduism has the idea that Brahma, a god aspect of God, created the world. And Plato and some early Christians known as Gnostic Christians believed that a demiurge, a demi-god created by God, did the work of creation.

If there is a creator God, is there just one or more than one? Judaism, Christianity, Sikhism, Islam, and the Baha'i Faith believe in just one. So does majority Hinduism, unlikely as that may seem bearing in mind the number and variety of Hindu gods. For most of Hinduism these gods are but different aspects of one God. It could be argued that it is not such a different idea from that of the Christian Trinity of God the Father, God the Son and God the Holy Spirit. Note that if you want your God to be all-powerful there can only be one of It.

Next, is this God eternal? The answer has to be Yes, unless you wish to face the problem of deciding how this God came into being.

So, on to the next question you need to consider. Is God good? Perhaps those who don't think so could set up a joint church with some Satanists. Or, this God could be both good and bad. Note that some religious groupings take the view that whatever God does must be good even if it seems bad to us and that it is not for us to question God's actions. Islam falls into that category. So do some Protestant groupings. Generally, Christianity takes the view that God will behave in accordance with our idea of what is just, fair and reasonable, the catastrophes of life notwithstanding. The idea of that sort of God, albeit sterner, is also found in Judaism and Sikhism.

What could be the next question? Perhaps: is God all-knowing? There is a variation on that idea, namely that God might be all-knowing but deliberately conceals Its knowledge from Itself, rather like closing your eyes when the match result comes up on the TV. That would be of relevance to the question of predestination, the idea that if God knows everything that is going to happen It must have willed it.

On the other hand, maybe It really isn't all-knowing. You may say that is a silly idea, unless we are suggesting that God may be suffering from some sort of ethereal Alzheimer's disease. Nonetheless the question needs to be asked.

Next, is this God something separate from us, which can be worshipped? Judaism, Christianity and Islam would say yes. Hindus might say either yes or no depending on which school of Hinduism they follow. Their Advaita school says that only God exists – you can't worship God if you're actually part of It. More of this when we talk about the soul.

An important question for you to ask is, is this God, as it were, a person? Has It a personality? The Abrahamic religions see God like that. The Hindu Yoga school has a God totally uninvolved with humankind – It is a non creator God which periodically dissolves the universe and starts the process of evolution again.

That blends into the next question. Does this God care for people individually? Believers would say, 'Do you believe in a personal God?' It is perfectly reasonable, if a little uncomfortable, to believe in a God who is not concerned about you.

This then leads to the question of whether God is interventionist. Does It intervene? For example, might It send a flood, or prophets, or a 'Son', or miracles and so on? If you offer sacrifice to It or pray to It, may It give good crops, or rain, or get you through your exams? Or might It survey the course of Its

22

creation, and the consequences of our free will, with concern and love, but make no interference, waiting only for our inevitable death before introducing Itself personally? People like the idea of a responsive intervening God and at grassroots level are likely to pray for things irrespective of their religion's theoretical beliefs.

Many people who believe in God like the idea of a personal God. It's reassuring to think that God will react to you in a way you understand and that It knows all about you. Such a God is easier to relate to and to pray to. However, bear in mind that this cozy arrangement has its own problems. If God knows all about you and has this close connection with you, then how will that fit in with pain, suffering and catastrophe? And consider how followers of religions with a personal God sometimes make their God behave rather too like us, with emotions like anger and vengeance.

At last, we come to the final question concerning God. Is It all-powerful, omnipotent? This is an interesting question. Most of the major God religions say yes. Traditional Zoroastrianism has a God which is not all-powerful. Some Jews question whether God is all-powerful. Some may think that having a God which was not all-powerful would explain a lot. *If would*.

Let us return to the issue of creation. Consider that God could have made the universe in a number of ways. Of these the top choices seem to be, intentionally, and caringly. But some may ask, was the universe made unintentionally? Or incidentally? Or unknowingly? Or mistakenly? Or as an experiment?

These choices are mixed up with another big issue, namely why did God bother to create the universe. If you belong to a God religion there are a number of ways of dealing with this issue. You can just ignore it. If you've already found faith you don't have to ask the question. Or you can say it is none of your business. Or that God's mind is unknowable. Or that it is so we can worship God. Perhaps you could say that it is to put goodness on a higher plane, by testing it, for does not goodness where there is choice have a different quality from goodness where there is no choice? Some Hindus say that God created the universe as 'lila', a spontaneous, joyful creative activity. Unsympathetic people might translate the word as 'sport' or 'play'.

Note that for all this talking about the characteristics of God, the major view within God religions is that God is unknowable and cannot be described. However, it is human nature to want more than the unknowable. Devotees seek a less sophisticated relationship with God than can be provided by some indescribable principle. Science has lured us into expecting certainty even in matters of religion. The Abrahamic religions distinguish between an unknowable God and the qualities It manifests in this world. It could be said that in their concentration on these qualities many followers have jumped to a description of God which is more like that of an all-powerful being of this world. Majority Hinduism solves the problem of the unknowable God by the manner in which It manifests itself in the form of a myriad of gods and their incarnations.

Soul

Remember, it is possible to believe in soul without believing in a personal God. An Opinion Research poll in 2000 found that nearly seventy percent believed in a soul, while only thirty percent believed in a personal God.

So let us assume that we have spirit attached to us in someway and give it this conventional name of soul.

What are the qualities of this soul? The word may mean different things to different people, and to different religions. Most use it to mean the bit of us that may live on after our death. But others may use the word to mean an essence connected to us, which gives us life: merely what makes the difference between a living thing and a corpse, simply vanishing on death as the corpse then decays away.

If, however, this soul does live on after death, then is it conscious and in what way? That's an interesting one. What of the Samkhya-Yoga school of Hinduism, which sees soul as pure consciousness without thought. Or the Hindu Nyaya-Vaisesika school which sees the liberated soul as absolutely free of thought.

And what of Jainism, which believes that everything has a spirit attached to it, even a stone or a subatomic particle? Is that a different kind of soul? Or is spirit/soul all the same, but limited in its expression by the capacity of the material it is connected to? An ancient Jain text says "... the soul assumes the size of the body it happens to occupy ..."

In these deliberations, much depends on what you think soul is attached to. It is much simpler if you take a conventional Christian/Judaic/Islamic view that only humans have spirit souls. But if you are a pet lover and think Fido has a soul, then what sort of soul is that? Is it the same as a human soul, but trapped in a body brain that lacks the capacity to abstract, or are there special dog souls?

These issues get more complicated if you believe in reincarnation and that souls can move between different life forms or even vegetable and non life forms.

Buddhism has a complex variation on the soul idea. This sidesteps the idea of a companion spirit element linked to living beings. Instead, Buddhism has a stream of consciousness whose true nature is beyond description. If you think that's complicated read the chapter on Buddhism!

Chinese religions believe we have two souls.

Perhaps we don't survive in any way. What then? The usual non believer package says: no God, no life after death. But just as it is logically possible for there to be no God, but for life after death to exist, so it is logically possible for there to be a God and for there to be no life after death. The Jewish Sadducees used to believe that. Some Jews still do.

If humans have a soul which continues to live after our death, the next question is, is that soul immortal, does it live forever?

Muslims and most Christians believe in an immortal soul. Several Christian Protestant groupings and some Jews believe that the souls of the wicked will at some point be destroyed. Some Zoroastrian scriptures suggest this too. Buddhists believe that their flow of consciousness can eventually disappear into the unknown and indefinable nothingness of Nirvana, yet without annihilation. Jains believe that soul has always existed and always will exist. Chinese religions believe that one soul goes with the dead body and dissipates with it. The other becomes an ancestor in the Heavens, an existence not unlike earthly existence, and dissipates into the cosmos after seven to nine generations. Japanese Shinto believes that the dead person is eventually incorporated in a collective spirit.

Those systems which believe in God believe that the soul is intimately connected with God in some way. Some say that it is part of God, some say that it is like God. The Catholic catechism says that 'God made me in his own image and likeness.'

If the soul is connected with God, further issues are: is the soul part of God and identical with God, or is it part of God and yet separate from God in some way, or is it just 'like' God. The last one is the choice of the Abrahamic religions and Zoroastrianism. A Hindu could have a choice between all three. Sikhs believe that on liberation our soul merges with God.

Another question to ask about the soul is where does soul come from and has it always existed? The God religion answer is that it has been made by or is part of God. If the soul is part of God, then the soul has always existed in that sense. Otherwise soul is presumably formed at conception, or birth, or sometime in between.

One school of Hinduism says that spirit has existed forever irrespective of whether there is a God or not. Jains, who don't believe in God, believe that soul has always existed. Far Eastern religions don't seem interested in the question.

To summarize. The idea of soul is that it is spirit that is somehow linked to the body (and, for some religions, to other things). This soul may exist for the life of the body only. Alternatively, after death it may exist for a while, or forever. It may, or may not, have existed forever before birth. It may be part of, or linked to, a creator God, or not.

A question worth asking is, does the body have a soul, or does the soul have a body? For example, the Christian idea is that the body is made and given a soul, whereas majority Hinduism believes that the soul acquires body after body.

Yet another question is whether this soul has our personality within it in some way. That would seem less likely if you believe in reincarnation, unless the soul contains a mass of personalities. Or does it have its own personality? Or what?

Most religions seem agreed on one thing, which is that the soul has a capacity to feel pain and pleasure, or some sort of spiritual equivalent. Most belief systems' ideas of what may happen after death wouldn't work without that.

The Material Universe

What is the nature of the material universe of these various religious belief systems? Well, if you believe in a creator God then It started it off. Religions which don't believe in a creator God usually believe that the material universe has always existed. Chinese religions are not concerned about the issue.

Another issue is whether the universe's progression is linear or cyclic. Linear history progresses in a straight line. A cyclic universe progresses in immense circles, forgetting as well as discovering truth. It is not unlike modern physics' theory of the big bang and big crunch. A number of religions have a cyclic view. Jainism and Buddhism, for example. So does the Yoga school of Hinduism. Abrahamic religions and Zoroastrianism and Sikhism believe in a universe which is linear, not cyclic.

There are different views of creation open to those who believe in a creator God. They may believe that God made the world out of pre-existing matter. That was a common view of creation in ancient religions. The Vaiseshika school of Hinduism believes it, and there are Shinto myths along similar lines but it is not a common belief now. Some early Christians and the Jewish Kabbalah tradition picked up the Greek idea that creation 'emanated' from God, providing a sort of ladder of connection between man and God. Christianity eventually settled for the idea of creation 'ex nihilo', out of nothing. Note that I deal with the issue of 'intelligent design' in the chapter on secularism.

God and the Universe

This section sets out a range of ideas as to how a creator God may be linked with the material universe which It has created.

Theism is the belief that God the creator is eternal, all-powerful, all-knowing, good, perfect, and separate from the universe It has created although It nonetheless is everywhere in that universe. Judaism, Christianity, Zoroastrianism, Sikhism, Islam and the Baha'i Faith fall into this category. The adjective of theism is theistic.

Some people believe that our soul is part of God, and that everything else is as well, so that God and the world are a unity and a whole. This idea is known as **pantheism**.

A variation on this idea is that **the material world is in fact an illusion** and that there is only God. The Advaita school of Hinduism takes this view.

Another variation is the idea that God is in everything in the world but is something more, and separate as well. The world is, as it were, in God. That idea is called **panentheism**. Panentheism is found in certain schools of Hinduism, and within the Hasidic tradition of Judaism. You could argue that it is to be found in Sikhism.

The Soul after Death

Let us return to the stage upon which the soul stands. That stage is set. We live. We die. What do religions say happens then, to this after-spirit, this soul?

When considering what happens to the soul after death the decision as to the nature of the soul kicks in. If your soul is part of God, then it will merge with God. An issue is then whether your life consciousness survives or whether it just disappears like a drop returning to a pool of water.

Sikhs believe our soul is united with God. If you are a Hindu you can follow a school which says your soul has an absolute identity with God but is yet still separate in some way, so your soul maintains some sort of individual identity. Jains, who don't believe in God, believe that souls are reincarnated until they can get free of material things, upon which they will revert to a natural state of energy, bliss and omniscience. Muslims and Christians believe our souls go to a Heaven state in the presence of God (or perhaps a Hell state). Zoroastrians believe that ultimately we will live in a world restored to its original physical perfection. Jews don't enquire much into an issue which is God's business.

The idea of Heaven and Hell is pretty unfashionable nowadays in much of Western society. Perhaps a summary of the mechanics will help. The basic idea is that the manner in which we live our life decides what sort of existence our soul has after our death. If you lead a good life you will have a nicer afterlife. If you lead a bad life, your afterlife will not be so pleasant. In fact it might be most unpleasant. I deal with how different religions approach the Heaven/Hell issue in more detail later.

The Heaven/Hell concept could be compared with the idea of Karma, found in Buddhism, Hinduism, Jainism and Sikhism. Karma means that every action has an inevitable and appropriate consequence for the perpetrator, possibly in a subsequent life. It gets round the problem that while we feel people should get what they deserve, that plainly does not happen within one lifetime. It also can go some way to solving the problem of how pain and catastrophe are often so unfair. It also links the idea of free will and fate in an interesting way. Remember, however, that Karma doesn't operate as a sort of judgment, it is simply how the universe works.

An issue for you to consider when thinking about life after death is that of reincarnation. This is the idea that after our death our soul is reborn. Many people seem to think that the idea of reincarnation solves the question of life after death. But after one life, or a thousand lives, you will still come to a point where there has to be an end, or alternatively eternity. Maybe you could believe that we are eternally reincarnated. Or you could believe that we can be reincarnated to a point where we cease to continue. Or you could believe that after an indeterminate number of reincarnations you reach some continuing eternal state. But you are still stuck with the issue of what that eternal state may be, just as you are if you have but one life.

An issue is: what exactly is passed on to the next life? All major established reincarnation systems agree that it does not involve the personality. Generally, reincarnation religions, including Hinduism, Jainism and Sikhism, believe that it is a soul divorced from a personality shed with the old body, that moves on to a new body.

Buddhism's alternative view is interesting. The Western layman probably associates reincarnation more with Buddhism than with any other belief system. Yet Buddhism does not believe in the soul in the same way as other religions. For Buddhism, reincarnation, or rather rebirth, is like using the stub of one burnt out candle to light another new candle, continuing a never-ending stream of consciousness, which ultimately translates itself into the no self yet no annihilation mystery of Nirvana.

People who are particularly attached to the idea that their 'self' or their soul involves their personality and would like that to survive into their afterlife, might be better not to choose a reincarnation belief system.

For those who do choose a reincarnation religion it is worth dwelling on the personality angle. It's easy to see your body as just the body you've got for the time being. But try considering that your personality may just be the one you've got for the time being. That may change how you look at things and how you look at yourself.

Note that all reincarnation religions believe in karma.

As we have already seen, another issue is whether reincarnation is just a human attribute? Are animals included? What about insects? Or stones? Or trees? Or potatoes? Or subatomic particles?

Within secularized Western society, reincarnation seems to have appeal to many seeking belief outside established religion. You may have encountered people who say they have been 'regressed' to a previous life. Many who have undergone this experience seem to have found their previous life to be that of someone in civilized society, often important, and usually materially well off. Few claim to have been peasants, or lavatory cleaners, or beggars, or used car salesmen. Those who are interested in reincarnation need to consider its more profound implications.

Worship – or daily relations with God/Spirit/the Principle of the Universe

If you are to adopt a belief system you need to decide what sort of practical life relationship you would like to have with its universal principle, which may or may not be God. Do you want to work things out for yourself or do you want to have someone tell you? Do you want an individual teacher? Do you want to be looked after by someone with a pastoral role? Do you want to be solitary? Do you want to go to a place with others and worship there?

'Worship' – there's a word! Books on religion talk about worship and worshipping, but the word 'worship' can mean quite different things. To understand a religion, you need to be aware of those differences. The most obvious, and superficial, form of worship involves *asking for something*. Another, overlapping, unsophisticated form of worship consists of *seeking to avoid something unpleasant*. In consequence, prayer may also involve *saying thank you*. It may also involve *penitence*, usually associated with *asking for forgiveness*. Worship may involve *veneration*, that is bowing down metaphorically, and perhaps physically, to acknowledge an inspiring example, usually a dead person or an object with special associations. Worship may include *submission*. Close to that is worship as *an act of acknowledgment, recognition, awe or praise*. Worship can be simply *an act of love of God*, particularly so in the religions where there is a clear separation of soul and God. It may involve *an attempt to get as close as possible to God or some universal principle*, of which more below. You could call it *a reaching for the infinite*. It may be *a means of seeking to behave in a certain way*.

Worship may take the form of prayer, saying something to its object, perhaps having a conversation. It may take the form of a sacrifice, actual or symbolic. The same act may mean different things. A Hindu may make an offering of food to Krishna and receive it back blessed, to consume himself – a sort of transaction with Krishna. A Jain may make an offering of food to a Tirthankara (who cannot be contacted since he has achieved enlightenment) and in doing so is emulating ascetic behavior – there is no transaction and the food is not given back. Worship is often incorporated in a ritual, a prescribed form of ceremony. Sometimes this will involve intention, sometimes it may have an almost magical significance. Worship may express itself in various methods of meditation. Worship may be together with others or alone, in a communal venue such as a church, synagogue, mosque or temple, or at home or anywhere.

Thus worship could involve someone saying or thinking:

- can I have something,
- can I avoid something,
- please forgive me,
- thank you for giving me what I asked for,
- I want to be like you,
- I will do what you want,
- you are awesome/wonderful, etc.,
- I love you,
- please love me,
- I want to be close to you,
- I want to be part of you,
- I want to be/behave like this.

And when they talk like that they may be talking to God or they may be talking to spirit beings, like angels or saints, or to the spirits of great people now dead, or to themselves.

These are all different ideas, embraced variously by different faiths in different combinations. Christianity is very strong on issues of forgiveness but there is no forgiveness as such in Zoroastrianism or Hinduism and perhaps Sikhism. Muslims pray that Allah will be merciful to them. Christians want to be close to God. Sikhs want to be part of God. Muslims' and Jews' first thought is to submit to God.

The structure of some religions does not theoretically permit praying for something but devotees seem to do so irrespective of this.

You may have met the term 'mysticism'. Mysticism is the pursuit of a direct connection with God or some universal principle: an immediate, conscious spiritual touching or joining or communication, to find understanding and wisdom. Those who follow this path are called mystics, and their principal method is meditation. Most established religions have a grouping which is mystical.

It is not necessary to have a God in order to engage in some forms of worship. It is still possible to venerate people and objects that inspire correct behavior. Jains don't believe in God but venerate their Tirthankaras, twenty-four illustrious Jains who are held to have achieved enlightenment.

More importantly, it can be argued that the essence of worship is a seeking for union or closeness between a person's spirit or soul or being, and something else. In very general terms, that seeking for union is at the center of most religions. That something we seek to get close to can be a creator God, but it can also be some universal principle, or it can be your soul's own true and free nature. As the Buddha says in the Dhammapada (218 trans. Muller revised by Maguire), "Those who aspire to oneness with the absolute ... they are called those who are heading upstream." A common method of that search, in non God religions and some God religions, is meditation, of which there are many techniques.

Some useful ideas

We've dealt with the ideas of spirit, God, soul and the universe. What next? I now set before you a number of ideas that are useful if you are to think and talk about spiritual systems, and I give you the word for each idea. Don't treat this as a list of definitions but as ideas which have labels.

Philosophy. There is sometimes discussion as to whether a particular belief system is a philosophy or a religion. The goal posts for that particular game are moveable for much depends on how you define religion. Philosophy is often defined as the rational investigation of the nature and structure of reality. Much depends there on the meaning of the word 'rational', which usually reverts to modern scientific method. This book sees philosophy as what would be left of an enquiry into reality if a belief in spirit were omitted.

The word **deism** is used to describe the belief that God created the universe and its laws but then let it go on its own way, having built into it for us reason and free will.

A **covenant** is a binding agreement. The Bible speaks of three covenants between God and man. One was God's promise to Noah that there wouldn't be another flood, one His promise to Abraham concerning his descendants' place in history and the third was the covenant with the Israelites, later the Jews, given to Moses at Mount Sinai. In biblical times a covenant was a formal treaty often used politically to bind two parties together. It had a set form. It would begin by introducing the most powerful partner, trace the relations to date between the parties and then set out the terms and conditions of the agreement and the penalties that would follow if the terms were neglected. Absolute loyalty was an essential element.

Some religions have the idea that God pervades the universe. The significance of this is that you can find God wherever you look. This idea is not the same as pantheism, which sees God and the universe as a unity. The word used to convey the idea is **immanent**. This derives from the Latin word to 'remain within'. So, if you want to say that God can be found and is accessible everywhere, you would say that God is immanent.

Another important idea is that something may be outside experience, outside the usual rules of the universe, and surpassing excellence. The word for this is **transcendent**. If you apply the word to God it means that God exists apart from and not subject to the limitations of the universe. If you apply the word to spirit/soul it means that it has attained a higher state.

When discussing the nature of religion, a model which constantly emerges is that the purpose of our life is to ensure that our soul/spirit achieves a certain state after our death. The adjective to describe this is **soteriological**. A majority of world religions have this view. Those which think that God gives us a hand in it use the word **'salvation'**.

A **revealed religion** is one in which God's word has been revealed, that revelation usually being set out wholly or perhaps just partly in some scripture. Revealed religions include Christianity – the Bible, Judaism – the Hebrew Bible or Old Testament, Sikhism – the Guru Granth Sahib, Islam – the Koran.

Another idea is that something can be incapable of description, that our language is incapable of saying what it is. Religions use this idea a lot. The adjective for the idea is **ineffable**.

Apophasis is the device of mentioning a subject by not mentioning it: 'I will not speak of his treachery'. It can also be applied to the device of describing God by saying what He is not. This device can be developed into a form of religious contemplation in which concentration on the unknown can cause the intellect to abdicate so that an awareness of God, as it were, fills the vacuum. Religions that believe in God accept that He is ineffable. Thus the **apophatic** approach is an attempt to find a way to know the unknowable. When pushed to the limit and faced with unanswerable questions, reason is reduced to silence and words no longer make sense, boundaries of thought and language break down. As a method it has much in common with the Zen Buddhist koan technique of meditating on, for example, the sound of one hand clapping. The apophatic approach is sometimes called negative theology or via negative.

A well aired issue is the problem of evil and how it could exist in a world made by a good God. A useful word for you is **theodicy**, which refers to the branch of theology which deals with this issue

A word most people haven't heard of, but a useful one, is **kerygmatic**. This describes a teaching designed to elicit faith rather than to convey knowledge. Thus, if you describe a part of the Hebrew Bible/Old Testament as kerygmatic, you would mean that it wasn't intended to be taken literally but to convey a spiritual truth.

You might run across the word **kenosis**. This means an

emptying of the self, the dismantling of egotism.

An idea which you find in most religions is the idea that you should not do to others what you would not want them to do to you. Shades of Mrs Doasyouwouldbedoneby in Charles Kingsley's 'The Water Babies'. A useful name for this idea is **The Golden Rule**.

An important idea is that of the priority given between what you believe and how you behave. It is a matter of balance and those who emphasize belief will say that belief governs, or should govern, behavior. That is **Orthodoxy**. Others say that it is how you behave that is most important. **Orthopraxy** is the word given to the emphasis on correct action and unfettered belief.

You are likely to meet the words dualistic and dualism. **Dualistic** means having two aspects. **Dualism** describes a system which has two aspects. Thus the idea that there are separate powers and sources of good and evil can be described as dualistic. So can the idea that reality consists of mind and matter. So can the Far Eastern idea that there are two souls. There is a tendency to refer to 'dualism' without explaining what sort of dualism. So if you see the word, note that it doesn't define a particular idea but merely categorizes it and make sure you know what sort of dualism it is referring to.

Esoteric is another word you will meet in connection with religion. It means a set of ideas available only to a minority, either by selection or because it is difficult to understand or both. Mystical religious traditions tend to be esoteric.

A **cult** is a specific system of religious worship but isn't a useful word because it is emotionally loaded, suggesting a quasi and exploitative religious belief system. Usually used about other people's beliefs.

Sect is another unhelpful word. It means a subdivision of a larger religious group, but has a disparaging inference suggesting exclusivity, extremism or heresy.

Millenarianism got its name from the belief that there will be a thousand-year rule by God's chosen either before or immediately after the return of Christ. Many Christians don't believe this. Among those who do are the Brethren, Seventh Day Adventists and Jehovah's Witnesses. The word has come to be applied to any religious group which looks forward to a sudden transformation of the world.

Messianism, sometimes associated with millenarianism, is the belief that a leader will arrive who brings in a new and perfected age. Judaism is the best-known example and many Christians believe that Christ will return in this way. The idea is found in Zoroastrianism and elsewhere.

The Word is an expression used by Christianity. It means the wisdom of God. Thus the gospel of St. John says of Jesus that 'The Word was made flesh and dwelt among us.'

Why be Good?

One of the most important and most practical aspects of religion is to provide an answer to the question why you should act in a particular way or not. What is the source of 'should' and 'ought', the moral imperative? In short, why be good?

For those who believe in a personal God which has revealed Its word to humankind, the reason is easy to find. God has said what the rules are and so you should follow them.

However, a religion may not have any 'revealed' writings dealing with behavior. For example, while Hindus have writings which many believe to be divinely inspired, much of their code of behavior rests upon a perception of eternal laws of behavior that are simply part of existence. In such a belief system the moral imperative derives from the need to live in harmony with what you might regard as the natural law of the universe, which in turn is God's creation.

Non God religions are in much the same situation. The rules of how we should behave are simply embedded in the universe, a natural law, how things are, part of the Dhamma, part of the

Way. Jainism, Confucianism and Taoism take this approach. Buddhism sees this Dhamma as arising from what aids us in our search for enlightenment.

If you are an atheist or an agnostic, you can still make certain assumptions about human nature: that man is essentially 'good' and that evil is a distortion and that if the distorting elements can be removed then the true nature is there to manifest itself. The thesis is that a thing should be what it is and that that gives reason for you to behave in a certain way.

This is not so unlike the Jain belief that the task of the jiva, or soul is to free itself from the material ties which hold it back from realizing its true nature and entering its rightful state of bliss and omniscience.

Another way is to take a secular humanist approach (do note that there are many Christian humanists and that it could be said that humanism is a characteristic of Christianity) and consider what behavior patterns would give the best life for most people. If you take this approach you are still importing your own value judgments as to what is beneficial for people.

Let us summarize the positions. I should not kill you: why? Because God says or indicates that it is wrong. Or because it violates the natural laws of God's universe. Or because it is against the natural law of a Godless universe. Or because it is against my own nature: that if I kill you I am violating my own existence. Or that if I could kill you, you could kill me, and goodness knows what the man next door will do: and then where will we all be?

How does religion explain pain, suffering and catastrophe?

Another issue which troubles many who seek a belief system involving God, is that of pain, suffering and catastrophe. If God is good, why are these things allowed? God religions try to deal with this problem in a variety of ways, of which examples are as follows.

- That God wants to punish people for a variety of reasons.
- That it'll be all right at the End.
- That it's all good really and we just can't see the big picture.
- That it purifies and disciplines us.

These are explanations sometimes given by followers of Abrahamic religions. Here are some more general examples.

- That God's ways are mysterious and unknowable and it is not for us to question them (Abrahamic religions, particularly Islam).
- That it doesn't matter, for getting to live with God is the important thing (Abrahamic religions, particularly Judaism).
- That it is to makes us humble (Abrahamic religions, particularly Judaism).
- That the Devil did it (Zoroastrians believe that pain and catastrophe are the fault of the uncreated Devil, who has spoilt God's creation with evil).
- That it's caused by something we did or failed to do in this or a previous life (Sikhism and Hinduism).
- That it's an illusion (some Hindus).
- That it is a test (Sikhism and Abrahamic religions).
- That it's Adam and Eve's fault (Christianity)
- That it's a product of the mass of sin that has accumulated over the course of history (some Jews have this sort of view).
- Other explanations are that God isn't all-powerful and that this is just the best He could do (some Jews incline to this view).
- Or that God isn't benevolent (very much a minority view among world religions that believe in God).

If you have a belief system that doesn't have a creator God things are much simpler. A belief in karma may satisfy your sense of fairness. Otherwise you are likely to think that pain, suffering and catastrophe are just how things are, and that there is no one to blame for it.

Is it selfish to save yourself?

It is worthwhile seeing how a religion deals with the problem of what might be called spiritual selfishness. This arises if the individual's prime task in life is to achieve a certain object for that individual's soul. A Christian's task is said by many to be to save his soul, to go to Heaven. So is a Muslim's. A Hindu's object is to end the cycle of reincarnation. A Jain's is to seek liberation for the soul. A Buddhist's is to be worthy of Nirvana. Taoists and Confucians seek self-cultivation and its results. Generally, religions try to solve the problem that all this might be a bit selfish by saying that the route to the desired end involves unselfish behavior. Thus Christianity says we should love our neighbors as ourselves. The Hindu Dharma requires selfless work and a principal characteristic of the Hindu who will not be reincarnated is selfless action. Buddhism puts selfless action at the heart of self-fulfillment. As for the monk, hermit, or religious mendicant, for the Christian system they contribute by prayer, for the Hindu system by their inspiring example. In the Buddhist system they contribute by nurturing the spiritual growth of the lay people. A Confucian would point out that the knowledge and virtue which comes with self-cultivation is to be used for the benefit of everyone else. For a Taoist, self-cultivation involves not just the person involved but the Tao which enfolds everyone and everything. And consider the mind-stretching Hindu comment: "Sacrifice the individual for the sake of the family; the family for the sake of the region: and sacrifice the world for the sake of the soul." (Udyoga-parva 37.17). And also the Buddha's words (Dhammapada 166) "Do not forget your duty to yourself for the sake of someone else's need ..." As the Buddha said elsewhere, how can someone stuck in the mud help someone else stuck in the mud.

Moral Relativism

Moral relativism is opposed to moral absolutism, which holds that a moral principle applies whatever the circumstances. Strictly speaking, the idea of moral relativism is that there are no absolute or universal values, no universal standard by which an ethical proposition can be assessed.

However, the words can be used in a more general way to suggest that an apparent moral truth may alter according to circumstances and other moral issues.

Take for example the proposition that you should not kill. Jains say that this is an absolute proposition and that it includes the killing of any living thing. Pacifists say that it is an absolute proposition which includes all human beings. Most religions accept the idea of killing in what is seen as a just war. Most accept killing by judicial process. Some accept 'mercy' killing, or the killing of unborn children. Such variation tends be something of an ad hoc process.

Hinduism has the idea of 'sila' or inner coherence, the center of the interelatedness of human attributes. The Hindu scripture, the Mahabharata says, "In case of conflict between one dharma and another, one should reflect on their relative weight, and then act accordingly; what does not denigrate and obstruct the others is dharma". It is a concept of moral balance.

Your choice

Next, there is the question as to what sort of life these choices may lead you to. Will you make your choices and see what they will require of your personal life? Or will you simply choose a system which suits your personal inclinations? Which will be your cart and which your horse? That's up to you. Just be sure that you don't deceive yourself. Will your belief system depend on how you want to behave or the other way round?

You will be aware that many if not most members of religions cheerfully ignore the rules for much of their lives. Some religions call that 'sin'. However, it is not a good idea to choose your religion on the presumption that you can sin when it suits you. Common sense says that in so far as you have a choice it is sensible to have a religious life which is compatible with your preferred way of life. For example, if you are gay and are attracted by Christianity you might be happier if you joined a liberal Protestant Church rather than an Evangelical denomination. You note the words, 'in so far as you have a choice'. For, for all this choice put under your nose, you may at any time get Faith, and then you have no choice.

Among the choices set out above are some well-worn combinations. For example, you will see, as you read on, that Judaism, Christianity and Islam, the Abrahamic religions, have many of the same underlying beliefs. Hinduism, Jainism, Buddhism and Sikhism also have some common roots. So do the religions of Confucianism and Taoism which both originated in China.

So, there you are. You must decide whether you will consider taking some of these ideas on board or not, and if so which ones. And then, at long last, you will be in a position to see where this chain has led you, to what belief system, and what other beliefs you may now choose or accept to be a signed up member.

Chapter 5

The Influence of Greek Ideas

This is a book on current world religions and this is a chapter on the religious ideas of the Greeks. What is that doing here? Well, it may assist your appreciation of some religions, mainly Christianity, if you know how their ideas were influenced by Greek thought.

Some useful things to know about **traditional Greek religion** are:

- That it had a religious establishment of spirit beings. These were gods, who were not all-powerful, who like humans were subject to vices and frailties, and some of whom were involved in the creation of the world. This setup has long gone and has had no lasting influence on living religions.
- That on the cultural side, the Greeks created the literary idea of allegory, that a story might have deeper meanings than at first appeared, and that idea has had considerable lasting effect.
- That the ideas of a number of Greek philosophers, particularly Plato and Aristotle, have particularly influenced Western thought.

Plato (428/7-348/7 BCE), a pupil of Socrates, proposed that every earthly object was modeled on a perfect form which existed on a higher plane. He saw virtue as an objective and higher level of reality. Plato's allegory of the cave has men chained in a cave with their backs to the sunlight, seeing only the shadows cast by objects in the outside world, assuming that those shadows are the true reality. Plato believed that each person had an immortal divine spark in them, a soul, eternal, imprisoned in the body. It was intellect which was the way to perception, to the connection with the forms in their higher reality, enabling us to find our way back to them. Intelligence was divine and immortal, linking us to the gods, enabling us to grasp ultimate truth. Thus we could discover these forms within ourselves. In later life, Plato saw creation as being that of a divine being, an essentially good demiurge, which created the world, including the gods, out of preexisting matter, and behind which was an unknowable higher deity encompassing oneness and goodness.

Aristotle (384-322 BCE) Plato's pupil, believed in a God who was completely impersonal. Aristotle saw creation as emanating from God in a hierarchy. Man, with his intellect was in a privileged position in that hierarchy. The intellect made him kin to God. His duty was to purify his intellect and so become immortal and divine.

Aristotle saw sense perception as the way to conduct the examination of reality and founded what we see as modern scientific method. By the exercise of reason we could share in God's life, we could become aware of a superior level of existence. Unlike Plato, Aristotle didn't see the forms as having a separate existence – they only existed in the material objects of our world.

Aristotle distinguished between 'being', what existed of itself, and reality or existence.

He also developed an idea that Plato had worked up, the idea of 'telos' or goal (from which the word 'teleological' derives). Everything was directed to a final end, a final purpose. Nature did nothing in vain. Change was a striving for fulfillment.

You need to appreciate how the Greek philosophers regarded **ideas**. An idea wasn't just something we 'knew' but something which happened to us. So Aristotle saw his thoughts not as belonging to him but happening to him, that his intellect was activated by the object of his thought. Thus in contemplating God he was participating to some extent in the divine life.

"thought thinks on itself because it shares the nature of the object of thought, for ... thought and object are the same."

You also need to appreciate how **Greek philosophers** saw their calling. For them, their task was to become fully aware of the superior level of existence by cultivating their power of reason. They saw this as awakening self-knowledge. This required both intellectual striving and a dedicated lifestyle. They weren't interested so much in ideas as in living a virtuous life, with practical meditative exercises and a disciplined lifestyle. When asked for a definition of justice, Plato's teacher Socrates said, "I make it understood in my acts." So theory was secondary to and dependent on practice and a way of life, and science was seen as a spiritual discipline. The philosophers sought transcendent wisdom in a universe which they assumed to be rational. And they had a duty not just to bask in this, but to enlighten others. We should all seek 'virtue' which for them meant what made a human being a good human being. Philosophy wasn't just theory but a way of life which could transform you.

The **Stoics** had some ideas that had later influence. This school was founded by one Zeno in the third century BCE. The Stoics believed that divine reason controls everything. Reason is always good, however things may appear. We ourselves don't have free will but we do have the choice to accept our fate willingly. Doing this, we can be in a rational unperturbed agreement with nature. That will bring freedom from emotion and desire, virtuous behavior and happiness.

If you choose to read up Geek philosophy you will quickly come across the word **'ethics'**. This is a translation of the Greek word 'ethiks'. Do note that for the Greeks the meaning of the word was 'matters to do with character' rather than the sense we give the word ethics today.

Philo of Alexandria (30 BCE-45 CE) was a Jewish Platonist. At the time Alexandria in Egypt had perhaps a million Jews, who spoke Greek rather than Hebrew, even translating their sacred books into Greek. Philo applied allegorical method to the Bible – as a Platonist he saw the timeless dimension of reality as more real than its physical and historical dimension. He looked for the higher or deeper meanings of Bible stories. For example, he argued that the story of Cain and Abel was really about the battle between love of self and love of God. As a Platonist he saw this study as a remembrance of something already known to him at a deep level.

Philo drew a distinction between God's essential nature and his powers. We could not know the One but God could communicate with us through the Other, through his activities in the world. Philo believed that when we glimpsed the Word, God's presence in this world, which was one of God's powers, we were taken beyond reason to a recognition of God.

Neoplatonism emphasised the religious dimension of Plato's thought. Plotinus (205-270 CE) was an Egyptian Neo-Platonist who influenced all three Abrahamic religions. His universe emanated from the impersonal God, rather like the rays of the sun. The material world was a sort of overflowing of God. Mind and then soul were the first two emanations and had an inherent desire to return to the center, the One. So there was an ultimate One of absolute perfection, then Intelligence or Mind which was an image of the One which our inferior senses could know and then spirit or soul. God, the One, was like the center of a circle which contained the potential of all future circles that could derive from It, like the ripples from a stone dropped into a pool. So if you meditated on the universe you meditated on God and Plotinus believed that understanding of the truth of reality could be found by exploring the self. This involved purification and contemplation. Plotinus talked of "there being no part of us which does not cling to God". Indeed God was our best self and experience of it was ecstatic.

The purpose of this briefest of overviews is for you to note that the Abrahamic religions, and Christianity in particular, have been greatly influenced by **the following ideas found (but not all exclusively) in Greek thought**:

- that there are absolutes which exist on a higher plane;
- that we should look beyond the immediate to the universal;
- that a spark of God is in us and that this might be eternal;
- that the truth of reality can be found by exploring the self;
- that creation might have been by emanation from God;
- that things are directed to a final purpose;
- predestination;
- that texts are to be interpreted allegorically;
- that God's unknowable being is to be distinguished from his knowable and manifested powers, that a distinction can be made between His essence and His powers;
- that 'being' and existence/reality are thus to be distinguished – this idea is at the root of the questions early Christianity had to grapple with as to the nature of the Trinity and exactly how God the Son related to God the Father;
- that the way to examine reality is by an examination of the evidence of the senses – this idea, deriving from Aristotle, has had a profound effect on the Latin tradition of Christianity and on Protestantism.

Chapter 6

Proof and Belief

Thomas Aquinas, the thirteenth-century theologian, famously set out a number of 'proofs' of God's existence (in the First Part of his Summa Theologica, ST,1a,2-1, which you can find at sacred-texts.com). Proof in this context is an unfortunate word. Nowadays we see the word as leading to scientific certainty. However, both believers and non believers in God agree that it is impossible to scientifically prove whether God does or does not exist. The so-called proofs are arguments that render the idea of God intelligible and, the proponents would say, intelligent. The proofs seek to reconcile belief and reason. All religions that believe in God accept that His nature is incomprehensible to us.

The meaning of words changes and when you hear the phrase 'proofs of the existence of God' you are likely to interpret them in the same way as scientific proof. But the so-called proofs are philosophical arguments, likely to be a bit of a disappointment to someone expecting proof.

Most believers in God aren't too fussed about the so-called proofs. The seventeenth-century philosopher Descartes said that the one thing he was sure about was the existence of his own self. Arguments that we don't really exist have little meaning when they come up against the undoubted feeling of our own existence. Many believers in God have a belief in that way, a conviction like a direct connection with an absolute truth. It is sometimes termed faith.

Generally, proponents of God's existence say that the universe seems unable to explain its own existence. Why and how is it here? Science may explain the process of its big bang and growth but what happened before? And before that? What is the beginning and the end of everything? Opponents may say that if eternity is good enough for the world of spirit it is good enough for the material world.

The Five Ways put forward by Aquinas respectively each start with one of five propositions: that things change, are dependent, are perishable, are limited and are directed. That which is unchanging, independent, non perishable, unlimited and not directed by another, is what people call God.

The first argument is that everything changes, that to change something requires a mover and that there must be a 'first mover'.

Second, Aquinas argues that everything must have a cause. We never observe anything causing itself, so the universe must have a cause, which we call God. That's known as the cosmological argument. Atheists say that if God can exist without a cause why can't the universe. Believers in God would say that God has qualities that the universe doesn't have, which explain why God can exist without a cause.

Third, everything in nature can be or not be. If it's possible for every thing not to be, then at one time there could have been nothing in existence. But if at one time there was nothing in existence it would have been impossible for anything to have begun to exist. So we must consider the existence of some being 'causing in others their necessity'. This is sometimes called the argument for a necessary being.

Some say that the first three arguments are essentially one argument.

Fourth, there is a graduation in nature, from less to more – to hottest, noblest, and so on, the maximum state being the cause, as fire is the cause of all hot things. It follows that there must be such a maximum state of being, goodness and all perfection, and this we call God.

The fifth argument considers the complexity of the universe and concludes that everything 'moves to an end' and this must involve the direction of some intelligent being. The arrow is aimed by the archer. Everything has its purpose within it. This is termed the teleological argument.

This has developed into the argument that the complexity of our world is such that it could not have come about by chance but must have done so by design, the designer being God.

Incidentally, these ideas had been floating round for some time before Aquinas wrote his stuff. The 'necessary being' proof was based on an argument by the tenth/eleventh-century Islamic scholar Ibn Sina or Avicenna. The prime mover, the perfection argument and the teleological argument derive from Aristotle.

With reference to the argument from design, secularists talk of the 'God of the gaps', meaning that some religions use the idea of God to explain what cannot be explained. They point to how this approach is coming under pressure as more and more unexplained phenomena find scientific explanation.

Another argument is known as the ontological argument. This is a logical argument which aims to show that there is a logical contradiction if we say God does not exist. We conceive of God as a perfect entity. But a perfect entity which did not exist would not be perfect. Therefore, upon pain of contradiction, God must exist. Aquinas didn't think a lot of this argument.

On a common sense level today there seem to be two principal arguments: what started everything off? – and the design argument. The key questions for philosophers, lay people and children to consider is: why anything rather than nothing, why does anything exist at all? Ask yourself. And: can something come from nothing? When you've thought about those enough you will better understand what the dry proofs are about.

Both secularists and non God religions can argue for an eternal universe. Aquinas himself said, "there is no proving that men and rocks and sky did not always exist." He also said, "it is well to remember this so that one does not try to prove what cannot be proved and give non-believers ground for mockery, and for thinking the reasons we give are our reasons for believing." (ST,8.46.2)

That brings us to the meaning of belief. Nowadays the word means intellectual assent to a proposition. But the word Aquinas uses, 'credens', derives from 'cor d'o', 'I give my heart'. And the word translated as belief from the Greek Testament means loyalty and commitment. In other words, faith.

Finally, you need to appreciate that the proofs weren't intended to convince an unbeliever, since in the thirteenth century there weren't any atheists – atheist was a word you sometimes applied to those who had a different conception of God from your own, but virtually everyone believed in God. The proofs were an accompaniment to religious experience. They weren't set out to prove anything in the modern sense but to explain the grounds for belief.

Chapter 7

A Slice of Ideas

Knowing the Unknowable

A principal object of most world religions seems to be to get as close as possible to a universal principle, which may be God, or natural law, the nature of things, the nature of ourselves, the Way or whatever. The way to this is usually some sort of ritualized behavior, often involving effort and discipline. Methods of meditation may be involved. All this involves a lifestyle dedicated to the end object, in which the doing is usually more important than the believing. The reward for many is a feeling of connection with the universal principle of choice and, for some, an experience of transcendence and loss of ego.

God religions agree that He is beyond our understanding. So how can we communicate with what we can't understand or conceive or properly know? In order to get closer to God, many religions adopt a mystical approach and one which involves very hard work. The object is to step outside our capacity to conceive or describe. Effectively it is to step to some transcendental dimension. The means is spiritual exercises of a meditative kind usually accompanied by a dedicated lifestyle. Such approaches are found in the Islamic Sufi tradition and within parts of Orthodox Judaism, notably Hasidic Judaism. The approach has to a great extent been lost by Christianity though less so in the Orthodox tradition.

An easier way of getting us closer to God is to bring him closer to us, and a number of religions do that by personalizing Him. Some religions believe that God can manifest Himself in what may appear to be a number of forms. Most Christians believe in the Holy Trinity: God the Father, God the Son and God the Holy Spirit. They are Three in One, together yet separate, a mystery, a truth revealed by God. God the Father is unknowable, but God the Holy Spirit is His presence in the world and God the Son is truly human as well as truly God. A number of Protestant groupings offer an immediate contact with Jesus or with the Holy Spirit, which many find attractive. You could, however, ask whether Western Christianity has underplayed God's incomprehensibility, has made Him almost human and has attributed human feeling to Him.

Most Hindus believe that Brahman, the one universal God who is beyond comprehension, presents Himself in many faces, in the forms of the many Hindu gods. They are all various aspects of Brahman. In turn, some of these gods take human or even animal or fish form, some of them a number of such forms. So, Vishnu is an aspect of Brahman, and himself has taken human form as Rama, Krishna and others. Such a god in a living form is called an avatar.

The Jewish Kabbalah describes ten different aspects (sefiroth) emanating from the single impersonal and unknowable God (En Sof) and the tenth of these, the Shekinah, envisaged in female form, is God's presence in the world.

The effect of such ideas in these different faiths is to enable an impersonal unknowable God to become more accessible.

Some non God religions have the same sort of problem. The beginning of Taoism's famous text, the *Tao te Ching*, talks of the Way, a universal force, that is nameless yet named. Buddhism takes the view that we can only understand Nirvana and what it means to be realized, when we have got there. It solves this problem by distinguishing between mundane and super-mundane knowledge. Mundane knowledge we can understand. It will do for now while we strive for a state where we will truly understand how things are and where we will have super-mundane knowledge. As for achieving this state, the koan method of meditation of Zen Buddhism seeks to burst beyond the boundaries of the mind. Both Abrahamic religions (the Jewish

Kabbalah tradition) and Buddhism (Tibetan) have used the expression 'untying the knots' to explain the idea of unlocking our minds to universal meaning.

It is interesting that the fastest growing religious groupings may be those which offer the devotee the prospect of a direct and immediate connection with the universal principle, tapping into the hunger for spirituality that flowers in the same garden as secularism. The adherents.com database is cautious about whether judgments can be made about which religions seem to be growing fastest. Nonetheless it cites (in alphabetical order) Evangelicals, Hinduism, Islam, Jehovah's Witnesses, Hasidic Judaism, Pentecostalism, Seventh Day Adventists, Unitarians, Zen Buddhists and some other minor groupings. There is a clear majority here of groups that offer the hope and prospect of a direct spiritual experience of a universal something or other.

Orthodoxy and orthopraxy

As I explained in the Basic Beliefs chapter, orthopraxy emphasizes correct action and unfettered belief. Judaism is a good example, so are Buddhism, Hinduism and Chinese religions. Once you accept that there is no God but God and that Muhammad is His prophet, Islam is about what you do rather than what you believe. Orthodoxy emphasizes belief and Christianity is foremost in this. However, the Greek Orthodox theologian, Maximus the Confessor, observed in a letter long ago, "Theology without action is the theology of demons".

Heaven and Hell and life after death

The nub of the Heaven idea is that there is a very nice state that we can attain after death. Whether we achieve this depends on how we behave in our life. The idea seems centered on our getting as close as we can to whatever is the universal principle of our belief system.

The next question which arises is what happens to you if you

don't behave in a way which qualifies you for Heaven. Welcome
to the idea of Hell. Christianity and Islam have Hell, and it is for
eternity, although some modern Christians think this idea is a bit
unkind and even unchristian. Not all religions which believe in
Hell believe in an eternal life in Hell. Seventh Day Adventists and
Jehovah's Witnesses, some Zoroastrians and some Jews believe
that after Judgment Day the unrighteous, in and out of Hell, will
all be destroyed, so there will be no need for Hell which will
cease to exist. Some Jews, a few, don't believe in life after death.
Other Jews believe that a stay in Hell is limited to one year.
Catholicism believes in the temporary Hell of Purgatory as well
as the permanent Hell and some Muslims have a similar idea. A
variation on the Hell idea does away with Hell altogether,
replacing it with a Heaven in which you will find yourself nearer
to or further away from God, depending on how well you
behaved in life. Those Universalists who believe in Heaven
believe that. So do Christian Unitarians. So do adherents of the
Baha'i Faith. Orthodox Christians, who don't believe in
purgatory, believe that Hell is a torment of being in an impure
condition in the presence of God.

In the reincarnation religions the Hell idea doesn't exist at the
end of the line, when you are no longer reborn; for you don't get
to the end of the line unless and until you have satisfied all the
requirements. However, the situation is different when it comes
to rebirth. Some reincarnation religions believe that there are Hell
realms into which you can be reborn. That doesn't apply to
Sikhism. However, many Hindus believe that you can be reborn
into a variety of temporary Heavens or Hells as a result of good
or bad karma. Buddhism believes that you can be reborn as a
Hell-being, or as a 'hungry ghost' obsessed with insatiable
desires or, more desirably, into a Heaven realm, or even as a god.
And Jains believe you can be reborn as a Hell-being (or a
subatomic particle, take your choice), or as a god, a deva, a
shining one. These all involve the Heaven/Hell idea on a

temporary basis.

As to the permanent basis, in the God religions the Heaven idea varies according to the relationship between God and the soul. Some religions believe that the soul is part of God. In that case the successful soul merges with God. Sikhism believes that the soul merges with God. So do some Hindus. This is one sort of Heaven.

Christianity and Islam are dualistic systems where the soul and God are quite separate. You can see that that is another, quite different, sort of Heaven. Christianity seems to have a Heaven in which we worship God and find that a blissful experience. Islamic descriptions of Heaven seem rather more practical in their material pleasure, though some argue that these are figures of speech. Jews pay little attention to the issue of Heaven although a Kabbalah tradition postulates a structure of a Heaven with seven levels.

Generally, the Chinese religions are more interested in this life than the next. The Chinese word 'tian' is often translated as 'Heaven,' but that is misleading. However, Confucians have the idea of becoming a sage, such a person being in harmony with the universe. And many Taoists have the idea of transcending into a transfigured celestial being. These ideas have some correspondence with the Heaven idea.

Chinese religions also have the idea of a realm to which our dead ancestors go. The traditional Chinese view is that we have two souls. One is buried with the body and finds its way to the underworld. The other ascends to 'Heaven' and is venerated in a tablet in the family shrine. After seven to nine generations it dissipates. Shintoism believes that after death you become a kami or spirit, and your descendants should and will venerate you as such. However, after thirty-three years you will lose your individual identity and merge with the family's collective spirit. It is difficult to relate this set of ideas to the Heaven idea.

The non God reincarnation end of the line Heaven idea varies.

For Jains it consists of the soul, spirit, jiva, being freed from the toils of matter and finding its true nature of bliss, energy and omniscience. For Buddhism the goal is Nirvana. We know little of this except that it exists, it's permanent, it's very nice, and that it isn't a place or a state and cannot be described.

In some religions there is an issue about the reuniting of your soul with your physical body. This idea seems to have originated with the Zoroastrians, and is found within the Abrahamic religions. So that sort of Heaven will be different once it has to accommodate itself to the physical presence of the just. Many Jews and Christians do not believe in the resurrection of the body.

Another, associated, issue if we are going to Heaven, is when do we go there? Is it on death, or is it at the end of the world? If it's at the end of the world is there a temporary Heaven that we go to in the meantime? Thus some religions, such as Zoroastrianism, Christianity and part of Judaism have a structure of a judgment on death and then going to Heaven, and then a second judgment of everyone, living and dead, with the righteous going to a Heaven which somehow embraces physical existence.

Although the general principle seems to be that it is our behavior which will enable us to achieve the Heaven state, some religions, or groupings within religions, muddy the waters on this point. The issue of forgiveness weakens the idea. And within Protestantism there are a number of ideas which do more, as follows. The idea that good works are not enough, that God's grace is essential and that it is only available to certain people. Even that His grace, if given, cannot be resisted. An extension of these ideas is that God chooses who to select for Heaven and that this is not to do with good works (though doing good works is a characteristic of those who have been selected). The tendency to limit Heaven to a select number either of a religion or within a religion, is largely confined to parts of Christianity and to Islam.

Reincarnation religions

Hinduism is a (mostly) God religion which believes that all living things have a soul/atman which on death is reincarnated in another living thing. It has a range of ideas about what happens when we are no longer reborn.

Sikhism is a God religion which believes that all living things have souls, and that following death such a soul is reincarnated, probably in another living form. When no longer reborn, the soul merges with God.

Jainism is a non God religion which believes that all things, living and inanimate, even subatomic particles, have a spirit/jiva attached to them and that this jiva is reincarnated/attached elsewhere when the material being or thing it is attached to ceases to be. Jiva may even exist on its own, attached only to a burden of karma, to await the reincarnation of attachment to living or inanimate matter. When no longer attached to matter or karma (which is for Jains a form of matter), the jiva attains a state of bliss, energy and omniscience.

Buddhism is a non God religion which believes that all conscious forms consist of a ceaseless flow of energies and appearances, mind and matter, and that on the death of such a form that flow then continues in another such form, into which it is, as it were, reborn. Such a form can be any living being, or a spirit being such as a god, Hell-being or ghost. When no longer reborn, this consciousness enters the unknown but blissful and permanent state/non state of Nirvana.

Judaism: Some, not many, Jews believe in reincarnation, which is strictly for humans.

Taoism: Some Taoists believe in reincarnation.

All reincarnation religions believe in karma.

Where do new souls come from, as the world's population increases? Are souls created or are they always there? There has to be an explanation. Do they come from other worlds/realms? That's a Buddhist answer. From animals and other living beings?

Most reincarnation systems allow that. Perhaps everything has and always has had a soul (matter being neither created nor destroyed). That's a Jain answer.

Will we meet again? I was talking to my wife about the future of robotics and whether politics would require its control to ameliorate unemployment. Eventually I said, "Well, it won't affect me unless reincarnation is true." Upon which she said, ever romantic, "I wonder if we will meet again?" That's a nice idea but try as I might I couldn't make it work for me, though I wanted to. Firstly, how does it make sense of the whole idea? All reincarnation systems agree that the personality does not continue to the next life, so what is the value, significance or reason for there to be a long-term connection between souls? And wouldn't the idea tend to confine souls to rebirth patterns that would enable such connection, particularly being born in the same country? A Buddhist would say the idea is a grasping and an attachment (although a realized Buddha would have knowledge of all its previous lives).

Interplay between this world and the world of spirit

This idea crops up in a number of religions. The Jewish Kabbalah suggests that a flow of spirituality from God links everything and that this flow is weakened or strengthened by whether we keep God's commandments to us. Other parts of Kabbalah see creation as being flawed, and that we can help put that right by our obedience to God's laws. Some Taoists believe that sin blocks the communication between earth and 'Heaven' and can cause blockages which can, for example, cause natural disasters.

Forgiveness

This is an interesting one. Most people consider that to show forgiveness and mercy to others is a good and moral act for humans. But is it a good idea for a religious belief system to have a function which forgives people and frees them from the spiritual consequences of their acts?

Most Christians see forgiveness by God as being at the center of Christianity. It is why Christ came to Earth. And we can be forgiven not just at final judgment, but during our life. The popularity of the idea is not surprising, and you might conclude that it has had much to do with Christianity's success. It accords with modern humanist values and the modern secular and psychological way of looking at things. However, the idea that we may be forgiven our sins is absent from many belief systems. On reflection it is not difficult to see why. This get-out-of-jail card can make nonsense of a system which operates on the basis that if you behave in a certain way certain spiritual consequences will follow.

The Islamic God, Allah, is forgiving and merciful at final judgment, as long as you truly believe in Him. If you don't you may be in for a tough time.

Jews believe that God will forgive them if their repentance is sincere and provided they don't repeat previous sins and failings. As a Jew you will observe the penitential season ending on Yom Kippur and during which you will review your deeds. Note that if you sin against another you should seek that person's forgiveness before atoning to God.

If you are a Zoroastrian, however, you will not expect forgiveness, but justice.

Sikhs don't emphasize the idea of forgiveness, but do believe that meditating on the name of God can dissipate the bad effect of karma.

The Jain lay people venerate the most illustrious of their enlightened ones, the Tirthankas, but appreciate that they aren't going to stir from their omniscient bliss to respond (not that you would think that if you see Jains praying in their temples). Technically the mechanism of the Jain idea of karma doesn't allow for the interference of forgiveness.

There is no God to do the forgiving in Buddhism. Yet

Buddhism does have a few spiritual shortcuts to thwart the discipline of karma and spiritual cause and result. Buddhism has the idea of what is sometimes (wrongly) referred to as the transfer of merit between people. Other parts of Buddhism have the idea that you can solicit enlightened beings for the privilege of being reborn in a Pure Land, where the hurdles of spiritual development are lower and easier. And some Buddhists believe that you can pray to bodhisattvas, enlightened beings who have stayed here or in other realms rather than enter Nirvana, to transfer some of their merit to you. It could be argued that these things can in some way be compared to forgiveness in its function, namely in mitigating the normal process of spiritual cause and effect so far as our actions are concerned.

Hinduism doesn't have a God in the forgiving business but does have loopholes which might enable karma to be avoided, notably self-realization, Bhakti devotion and the rites for the dead.

In Confucianism, Taoism and Shintoism there is little idea of forgiveness. However, the idea of transactions between this world and the spirit world is prevalent, together with the idea that these transactions can be used for advantage in this life and in the next. It's not the same as forgiveness but can be so in its result.

Praying for the dead

Maybe everyone prays for their dead loved ones, perhaps even atheists. Here, I'm not talking about that or about what may be said at funeral rituals. I'm looking at religions that have a belief structure that provides a mechanism which puts prayer in at one end and delivers a possible tangible result for the deceased at the other.

The idea is to help the dead person's spirit to attain a desirable state. The idea will vary according to whether a reincarnation religion is involved or not and whether the religion is a God religion or not.

For a reincarnation religion the object is to achieve a good next life, rebirth, for the dead person, or self-realization/unity with God. For non reincarnation God religions the object is to improve the state of the dead person's spirit after death.

There's not so much of this sort of thing in non God religions, which is understandable, for how are prayers going to work if there's nobody to pray to? Not that that always matters in practice. Jains will pray away despite the fact that they only have their Tirthankaras to pray to, realized dead humans, who won't be responding. As I have said, I deal with what the religion says rather than what some of its devotees may get up to.

One non God reincarnation religion which does pay a lot of attention to this issue is Tibetan Buddhism. Tibetan Buddhists believe that there is a period of between seven and forty-nine days between death and rebirth when various rituals may help a good rebirth to be more likely.

But, by and large, Buddhists, Hindus, Jains and Sikhs don't pray for the dead outside funeral rituals, although human nature may cut across this.

Chinese customary religion, within which Confucianism and particularly Taoism sit, is very concerned with the fate of deceased ancestors. There are various ways in which the living members of a family may seek to help their predecessors in their afterlife. Taoism in particular has many ways in which the living members of a family may seek to look after the interests of their dead ancestors.

Believing in God does not necessarily mean that a religion has a mechanism for improving the lot of the dead. For Zoroastrians, the dead will be judged by a strict calculation of their good and bad deeds. But their funeral service includes prayers for the dead and the funerary rituals are important.

Jews pray that God may have mercy on the dead person. Perhaps it helps that most Jews believe that Hell is a temporary state which may last no more than a year.

It is in Islam and Christianity that the practice of praying for the dead is most established and can hope for a real result.

Islam has a structure whereby we are judged at the end of the world. That gives the living plenty of time to pray for the dead. These prayers may be directed to God, but mostly to the spirits of dead people who may have the influence to intercede with God. The Prophet Muhammad is, understandably and obviously, preeminent here. Furthermore, Muslims may recite parts of the Koran and send the reward for this on to the deceased. And Muslims pray collectively for the forgiveness of the dead.

Christians of the Orthodox and Catholic Churches pray for the dead. The prayers may be for individuals or for groups, even the dead as a whole. But Catholics believe in the temporary, pre-Heaven punishment state of Purgatory, and that adds another dimension. Catholics believe that the suffering of Purgatory's inmates may be lessened or shortened by our prayers. Protestants have a variety of views. They don't believe in Purgatory. And some disapprove of praying for the dead.

Is everything an illusion?

A number of religions have subgroups which believe this. The Advaita school of Hinduism believes it. The Buddhist Mahayana Yogacara Mind Only School believes that the external world is merely an illusion. Jewish Habad Hasidism believes that only God exists, although it accepts that the world is real enough from the point of view of its creatures.

Time and the present

Can morality exist without time? Without time you can't have consequence. If one thing cannot lead to another, can you have morality, a standard which measures behavior?

God religions see God as being outside time, which is part of his creation. Philo of Alexandria liked that idea and so did St

Augustine. Later on, Stephen Hawking saw time as contained within the universe.

There is now an almost magical obsession with the present. It is seen as the goal of the past. Yet soon it will itself be a sad old thing on the shelf of history. We are only too willing to condescend to the past, to relativize it, but to treat our temporary present-soon-to-be-past as somehow superior. It may be so in some things, science for example, but not necessarily so for others. Ideas don't improve or get worse with age. It could be argued that an old idea, despite its lack of novelty, is essentially as new as a new idea. However, the present does have one all important characteristic. It is the needle on the gramophone which plays the only tune in town: it is the only point at which things can change.

People often see time like a series of picture frames. But there isn't any indivisible unit of time, so there isn't anything to link a particular frame to (although Jainism does believe that there is an indivisible unit of time). Theravadan Buddhism had this problem when it conceived the idea of a series of dhammas following one another in time. For without an indivisible unit of time this leads to an infinite regression. The difficult Buddhist concept of 'emptiness' sought to resolve this. *The Tibetan Book of Living and Dying* by Sogyal Rinpoche (Rider Books 2002) puts the issue simply at chapter 3 page 37: "If everything is impermanent then everything is what we call 'empty' which means lacking any lasting, stable and coherent existence ..." (for emptiness isn't actually empty). It continues, "Think of a wave in the sea. Seen in one way it seems to have a distinct entity, an end and a beginning, a birth and a death. Seen in another way, the wave itself doesn't really exist but is just the behavior of water, 'empty' of any separate identity but 'full' of water. So when you really think about the wave you come to realize that it is something made temporarily possible by wind and water, and that it is dependent on a set of constantly changing circumstances. You also realize that every wave is related to every other wave." Whether you are Buddhist or not, time can be seen as a wave.

Perhaps each day lives forever and we create in them our own Heaven or Hell. The Jewish Kabbalah's *Zohar*, in its account *'Jacob's Garment of Days'* says "... all the days of his life are arranged above..." ... "If he succeeds, that day returns to its place, if not, that day comes down ... moving into his house to torment him." "... if the person leaving the world is pure he ascends and enters into those days and they become a radiant garment for his soul." Figures of speech, but could they be a more literal truth? I quote from Daniel Matt's translation starting at page 45 in Skylight Paths' 2002 *Zohar Annotated and Explained*.

Teleology

Teleology is the idea that things may have a special purpose inherent in them, that such a purpose may guide and dictate the development of a thing. The idea is sometimes used to explain how the universe may have developed according to the plan of some creator entity. Aristotle, the founder of scientific method, believed in teleology. The idea is also found within the Samkhya school of Hindu philosophy, which holds that the effect is present in the cause and that development is inherent in pakriti/matter. Christianity likes the idea. Advocates of Scientism attack it. Does modern physics' demonstration that it is possible for a future event to influence the course of a past event echo this idea of future purpose? Is the view that the present is the purpose of the past, the object of the exercise, the high point, a form of teleology?

Exclusivity

Hinduism is an undogmatic religion with a wide range of beliefs. Lord Krishna says (Baghavad Gita 4.11), "However men approach me, even so do I welcome them, for the path men take from every side is mine." Jains are tolerant and would not wish to impose their view on you although they have a firm idea as to how the universe works in spiritual terms. Sikhs believe that truth can be reached through other religions, but lies beyond them: they see God as transcending all other concepts of God. Zoroastrians believe that all will be judged for their actions by God in due course. Judaism has a wide range of beliefs and concentrates on the Jewish people. There is no exclusivity in Buddhism and a wide range of belief within it – it's how you live your life that matters. Catholics and the Orthodox believe that followers of other religions can achieve salvation, that salvation being by the grace of the Christian God. Many Protestants believe that people of other and no faith can achieve salvation, but some believe that that is open only to certain people. Islam takes the view that only Muslims can go to Heaven.

Liability to fundamentalism

We all know what fundamentalism is but it's more difficult to put it precisely in words. Strictly speaking it is a belief in the exact truth of a sacred text. I would round that out to say: adherence to a sacred text or some equivalent, which is read in a literal and narrow way, combined with a belief that your interpretation is right, plus an intolerance of other views and a punitive attitude to non believers.

In modern day belief systems where is this combination found? I would say: in parts of Islam, in parts of Protestantism and in those devotees of Scientism who are aggressive secularists. If you look at the development of fundamentalism in Islam and Protestantism, it is usually linked to a literal interpretation of a sacred text. Scientism's equivalent to this is current 'scientific knowledge' including working hypotheses, to the exclusion of all else.

No doubt some of you will produce examples in other belief systems, but I challenge you to find such major present threads in them.

People tend to think of fundamentalism as a reversion back to an old and discarded view. But, for the most part that is not so, and fundamentalism is largely a modern phenomenon, particularly in Islam. Which brings us to another element, which is the discarding of more than a millennia of teaching and interpretation.

Thus Protestantism embraced the idea that each person could read the Bible and find its truth on his or her own rather than be guided by a Church which often placed an allegorical interpretation on the text. In parts of Protestantism this led to a literal interpretation of the text.

Islamic fundamentalism, for the most part a modern phenomenon, flowered in the preaching of clerics willing to ignore many centuries of Islamic teaching and interpretation, and to teach their own, selective and literal view of the text without regard to centuries of Islamic law.

As for Scientism, it disregards millennia of culture, instinct, tradition; to reign supreme, oblivious to the way modern physics is nudging into areas that might be common ground with spiritual believers. Aggressive secularists almost embrace religious fundamentalists, easy targets, and seek to present those views as generally representative of religious belief.

Identity, 'I' and our perception of ourself

The word 'identity' has a ring of certainty about it. It suggests we can know who we are and objectively verify that. Fine for our personal appearance and a court of law. Less so for our inner self. Many identify this inner self as our personality. Psychologists and psychiatrists will be pleased to assess it.

But when we move on to the issue of how we identify ourselves to ourselves, matters get more complex. "I think, therefore I am", says Descartes. Thinking is only part of it. Descartes defines our own identity in terms of our own perceptions. Coming from the other direction, most God religions think we have a little bit of God in us. In the case of Christianity our bit of God is something of a reflection – he made us in his own image and likeness.

The Western obsession with 'I' grows in the soil of non reincarnation God religions, particularly Christianity. We look forward to our individuality continuing, hopefully for an eternity of happy 'I'ness in Heaven.

The East is less concerned about 'I'. From a religious point of view that is understandable. The merging of the soul with God, as in Sikhism and some parts of Hinduism, weakens the strength of 'I'. Reincarnation disposes of the Western clinging to the personality which is seen as 'I'. The whole disposition of Buddhism tends against 'I'ness. We are but a continuous stream of phenomena, in a series of lives, leading hopefully to the non state yet non annihilation of the indefinable Nirvana. The Dalai Lama in *My Spiritual Autobiography* at page 100 says. "The self is the root of mental poisons." "Things we perceive as separate are actually connected, but our 'I' separates them." Jainism elevates 'I' as the essence of everything, even subatomic particles, and then dissolves it in the omniscience of the realized spirit. There is plenty of 'I' with Chinese religions, which are more concerned with this life than the next, but within a context that puts the group above the individual: our task lies in playing our part within the group.

Sacred texts as spiritual events

Some religions see scripture as not just something to be read, but an activity to do. This used to be a predominant view within Christianity. Taoists regard the ritual chanting of texts as an activity which unlocks a potential within the sounds. The writing encodes the interaction of Heaven and Earth, they are part of the celestial fabric. The texts are traces of originals in Heaven and deities echo their recitation here. Muslims regard the act of reading the Koran as itself an act of devotion. A Jewish

Hasidic view is that "a man should attach himself to the words [of the prayer book] and later he can put his soul into the words." (Sefer Baal Shem Tov).

The interpretation of texts, and translation issues (with particular reference to the Abrahamic religions)

Where does the meaning of scripture lie? One approach is that scripture directs us to a hidden level of reality. Karen Armstrong refers to "the Word that lay hidden in the earthly body of the sacred page". The path to this understanding was to first master the literal meaning of the text, then the moral sense and finally the spiritual allegorical sense.

The early Christian scholar Origen (185-254 CE) said of some texts, "impossibilities and incongruities ... present a barrier to the reader and lead him to refuse to proceed along the pathway of the ordinary meaning."

The Hebrew in which the Jewish Bible/Old Testament was written had no vowels. The text was vowelized later. Arguing against vowelization, the thirteenth-century Jewish kabbalist Bahya ben Asher of Saragossa wrote, "without vowels, the consonants bear many meanings and splinter into sparks. Once vowelized, a word means just one thing. Without vowels, you can understand it in countless, wondrous ways." (*Commentary on the Torah, Numbers11:15*). This changes ambiguity into a rich source of meaning which itself can be an alternative to the allegorical approach.

Another approach is to take the literal meaning of the words of scripture. That sounds straightforward, but a number of problems can arise.

One is that of ambiguity, unless you take the view of Bahya ben Asha, above.

And ambiguity may be found where it is not apparent. For example, the Jewish Kabbalah's Zohar gives a literal analysis of the opening words of Genesis to support a view of creation which is quite different from that of the apparent words. The opening words of the Hebrew Bible are usually read as, "In the beginning God created ...". But the Hebrew word for 'in' also means 'with'. And the Zohar reads the Hebrew words in the exact order in which they appear, which has the word 'God' at the end. This produces, "With the beginning, it/Ein Sof/the ineffable source created God.", God being one of the higher serifot. (*Zohar 1:15a*)

A literal approach may also face considerable problems linked to alterations to the original text. The vowelization of ancient Hebrew is one example, for the vowelizer has interpreted the original text.

The tendency to a literal interpretation makes issues of translation all the more important. Does it make sense, for example, to take the narrow literal meaning of words in English when they are a translator's own interpretation of the meaning of the original words in another language?

Both Hebrew and Greek have no punctuation. The punctuation in translations, which so affects the meaning of the text, rests on judgments made by the translators.

The Babylonian Talmud has the Rabbi Yehudah say, "One who translates a verse literally is a liar; one who adds to it is blasphemous." (*Qiddushin 49a*). You don't have to look far to see what he's getting at. Let's have some illustrative examples.

In Mark's gospel 3:31 there is a reference to Jesus' 'brothers', but the Greek word in the original can mean cousins or other close relatives. More controversially, when Matthew's gospel at 1:23 quotes Isaiah at 7:14 as referring to Mary as a virgin having conceived he is relying on a Greek translation of Isaiah in which a Hebrew word meaning a young woman old enough to be married was translated as 'virgin'.

Translations of Confucian texts usually translate the word 'tian' as 'Heaven'. But 'tian' can mean the source of morality, the universal principle, natural law, ultimate reality, or where our ancestors may go. Such translation is misleading to Western readers who have their own understanding of the word 'Heaven'.

As I point out in the chapter on Islam, different translations of the Koran at 16.93 have it say on the one hand that God 'leads astray who he will' and on the other that He 'confounds who he will'. That's a bit of a difference isn't it? At 113 of the Koran one translation speaks of the 'evil' God had created whereas another uses 'mischief' rather than 'evil'. Again, a significant difference.

I'm not seeking to argue particular points of translation here, but to select a few examples out of many in order to illustrate the dangers of adopting a literal interpretation of sacred texts.

The Hebrew/Old Testament was written in Hebrew. But the Orthodox Church relies on an ancient Greek translation known as the Septuagint. This differs from the Hebrew version in a number of places. The Orthodox Church gets round that by considering the translation to have been made under the inspiration of the Holy Spirit. The idea that the translator is guided by God is one answer to the translation problems to which I have referred but it won't solve the problem of competing translations.

The literal interpretation of sacred texts is a modern phenomenon for Christianity. Until printing was widespread it wasn't possible for most individuals to have a copy of the Bible. And a printed copy of the Bible wasn't much use to laymen until it had been translated from the Latin or Greek in the fifteenth and sixteenth centuries. In any event, for the majority of the last two thousand years most people were illiterate, so they only experienced religious texts when they were read out to them, usually by priests who would give their own often allegorical explanation.

Finally, at the beginning of the chapter on Taoism I set out two alternative translations of the first chapter of the *Tao te Ching*, Taoism's famous and much translated text. Fast forward and read those. Then consider the following translation by Derek Lin (Skylight Paths 2006).

The Tao that can be spoken is not the eternal Tao
The name that can be named is not the eternal name
The nameless is the origin of Heaven and Earth
The named is the mother of myriad things
Thus, constantly without desire, one observes its essence
Constantly with desire, one observes its manifestations
These two emerge together but differ in name
The unity is said to be the mystery
Mystery of mysteries, the door to all wonders.

I think this is a lovely translation but by comparing it with the others you can see it is itself an interpretation. I got this translation from the internet, where the search description described it as 'an accurate translation'.

Finding good in apparent ungood

Elements within Judaism, Hinduism and Buddhism seek to explore desire to see the transcendental quality within the ungood. For example, a Jewish Hasidic technique is to deal with inappropriate desire by identifying its divine quality, tracing it back to the archetype of love. In this way you can let go of the inappropriate desire and desire the source instead.

Tantric Buddhism sees everything as sharing in the Buddha nature. So when faced with what Buddhism sees as defilements we need to see how those defilements share in the Buddha nature. The idea is that in that way the defilements can be transformed into their true nature. For example, if you consider greed it can be followed back to a source of longing for ultimate bliss.

Antinomianism

Antinomianism is the idea that if you are in the right belief club you can to some extent do what you like. This is more sophisticated than mere self-indulgence or corruption. In some cases it has taken the form of a mystical belief that you have attained a perfection so absolute that you are incapable of sin whatever you do. Fortunately, examples lie in past times, but should you come up against such a tendency you now have a name to put to it. Note that this is one of those words which are only applied to someone else. Principally, such ideas have emerged in Christianity, but there have been past and occasional tendencies within the Islamic Sufi tradition and in Judaism, notably the so-called Frankists in the eighteenth and nineteenth centuries. The word is sometimes applied to religious practices that seem to some to be evil/bad/unwholesome. Such criticisms are sometimes made of Hindu or Buddhist Tantric practices which seek to explore or ritualize how evil/bad/unwholesome acts fit into the interdependence of things or relate to the universal principle.

Missionary religions

A missionary religion is one which seeks to convert people to its view. Christianity and Islam are missionary religions. Judaism is not, nor is Zoroastrianiasm nor Sikhism nor, generally, Hinduism. Chinese religions have had their periods of seeking dominance within their geographical area. Buddhism started out as a missionary religion and has that tradition to a limited extent. Shinto is the indigenous religion of Japan. The Baha'i Faith has a plan of expansion. Some individual secularists and secularist organizations have a missionary approach.

National/folk identity

Judaism is identified with people of Jewish inheritance. Zoroastrianism tends to be confined to Parsees or people of Iranian descent. Sikhs usually derive from the Punjab in India. Hindus are usually from the Indian subcontinent. Chinese religions are largely confined to people of Chinese origin. Christianity, Islam and Buddhism are spread more widely. These are generalizations and they ignore the issue of conversion.

Politics and power

Religion is less mixed up with power and politics than it used to be, but such problems still emerge. The big one is the issue of political Islam. A good illustration of the way in which issues with an overtly religious connotation may really have little such connection is that of Northern Ireland where a sort of tribal political conflict has gone on with each side waving the flag of its claimed religious affiliation. In recent decades Hindu nationalism has found a voice in the Indian BJP party. In Sri Lanka the Sinhalese majority is Buddhist and Buddhism and its institutions have been drawn into politics. Buddhism has had an unfortunate experience in Myanmar (formerly Burma) although it could be argued that has been the product of an immigrant issue. Although many of the early Zionists were intensely secular Zionism has now developed a religious dimension. Generally, Chinese religions have paid a heavy price for their past involvement in failed political structures.

Chapter 8

Secularism and Non Believers

This chapter is about aspects of **secularism**. The word 'secularism' means having nothing to do with religion. I have used the provocative alternative 'non believers' deliberately because it raises a question I wish to highlight. That is, is non belief a belief?

Whatever the case, I propose to treat secular views involving moral value in the same way as I treat religious views. That seems fair when describing a secularism which presents itself as a default position in relation to any religion.

One view which denies that secularism is a belief is termed **Scientism** by its opponents. Scientism's supporters say that the only propositions which should be accepted are those which can be proved by scientific method. They regard this as a self-evident and self-justifying truth, the way things are. Some people criticise Scientism by saying that just as some Christians take the Bible as its own authority, so Scientism adopts scientific method. And that Scientism is just yet another belief system. It is common ground between atheists and believers in God that you cannot prove God's existence by scientific method. Like some religions, Scientism sometimes displays the characteristic of intolerance.

Secularists tend to home in on the question of God's existence as the main issue. We have already seen how a prior question which is as, perhaps more, important, is whether spirit exists. Secularists deny that too.

Some secularists take a gentler approach and say that whether God or spirit exists is a matter to be decided on the balance of **probabilities**, but again based on what can be proved scientifically. That seems a tempting and reasonable proposition within our Western culture and so I suggest a brief diversion into the probable.

To open the argument up, let's have a look at a number of ideas. How probable do you think they are?

1. That a thing can be in different places at the same time.
2. That a thing can be a particle and a wave of radiation at the same time.
3. That objects may follow different physical laws according to whether they are observed or not.
4. That there may be as many as eleven dimensions.
5. That there are an infinite number of universes.
6. That our universe may be a fake.
7. That a future event can influence a past event.
8. That the past takes no definite form.

These are all respectable scientific views of some physicists. They are respectively referred to in the following pages of *The Grand Design* (Des.), by Stephen Hawking and Leonard Mlodinow and of *The Goldilocks Dilemma* (Dil,) by Paul Davies. 1 – Des. p83, 2 – Des. p68, the 'double-split' experiment, 3 – Des. p83, 4 – Des. p140, 5 – Des. p118 suggests 10 to the power of 500 universes, 6 – Dil. P208-10, 7 – Des. P82 the 'delayed-choice' experiment, 8 – Des. P82.

Compare these ideas with the probability of the idea that spirit exists.

Secularists will say that the possibility of their scientific ideas can be supported mathematically.

Those who believe in spirit may then ask whether it is in effect an act of faith for a scientist to insert infinity into an equation.

Here are some more points to consider. Scientists cannot obtain any objective result because the act of observation affects their understanding of the object of their investigation (the Heisenberg Principle of Uncertainty). And Kurt Godel's theorem shows that any formal or logical mathematical system must contain propositions that were not verifiable within that system.

There will always be propositions which are only verifiable from outside.

The point is that the common assumption that it is possible to achieve objective certainty can be challenged.

Consider also the humbling fact that scientists don't know what ninety-six percent of the universe is made of (Dil p136).

The reasonable probability argument based solely on scientific method perhaps has another angle, that of the working hypothesis. If there is no afterlife, how can it matter if you believe in one? But if there is an afterlife it could be a disadvantageous mistake if you choose to believe that there is no such thing. Science expands its knowledge by the use of the working hypothesis. Many of its propositions are used for years, even decades, before they can be demonstrated to be correct. A 'scientific' analysis might argue that it would be sensible to assume there is an afterlife until such time as we can prove that none exists. That angle would then move the argument on to whether believing in an afterlife had a benign effect on the individual and society.

Here's another direction, beyond the detailed ambit of this book, which you might care to follow up. The Dalai Lama suggests that the "Buddhist analysis of reality concurs with the conclusions of quantum physics, according to which particles of matter are real while still being devoid of ultimate solidity." (*My Spiritual Autobiography*, page 93 with more on pages 123-125).

Arguments between atheists and believers in God often concentrate on the issue of **creation**. When considering this, remember that not all religions believe in creation. Some, including Buddhism and Jainism and some traditions of Hinduism, believe that a universe has always existed. Atheists also tend to concentrate on the literal words of the Biblical account of creation in the book of Genesis. Remember that while a significant number of Christians believe this account, many see it as an allegorical story. Many advocates of Scientism set up a false alternative between atheism and a belief in the most literal interpretation of the Biblical account of creation.

Indeed, Western secularists have a tendency to see religion through Christian blinkers and to concentrate on particular parts of the Abrahamic religions as if that disposes of religion as a whole.

For those who take an allegorical approach to the biblical account of creation, that can lead to the idea known as **'Intelligent Design'**. This is the idea that there is some sort of intelligent creator which designed the laws of nature which led to the present day state of the universe and in particular to our evolution. Thus many Christians take the view that evolution is a fact but that it is an instrument of God's devising.

However, Intelligent Design can cover a wide spectrum of belief, not just with a Christian interpretation. You may think that God in effect wrote the program, started the universe off and left it to it to play itself out. That God got life started and then left it to evolution. You may think God intervenes every so often. You may see this Intelligence as having the conventional qualities that the Abrahamic religions attribute to their God: all-powerful and all-knowing. But you may see this God/ Intelligence as not all-powerful and the universe as simply the best it can manage. You may believe this God/Intelligence has a purpose, or no purpose, or this and that specific purpose. You can think it is some sort of super computer. Perhaps whatever it is came from a previous universe. Of course, you always have the problem of who created the creator, unless you say It always existed, outside time, that's the usual answer.

Generally, those who believe neither in God nor in spirit take the view that:

- we do not continue in some way after death;
- our existence does not have any meaning or reason;
- goodness is not based on any universal value but exists only in the context of human beings – no thinking beings = no good.

The principal question to be dealt with in the discussion between secularists and people of religion is, **why anything?** Why is there something, anything, rather than nothing?

Another issue is **the manner in which people choose to define religion**. In the chapter 'What is Religion?' I have explained that there is no one correct definition of religion but many, and that these definitions are functional, depending on what you want to use them for. Secularists have a tendency to see the definitions they use as defining truth, burying secularist assumptions within their exclusive definition. They seek to explain away as well as to explain. Thus an anthropological analysis of religious behavior may assume that the spiritual aspect is of little significance. And a psychological or political analysis may assume or conclude that religion is intrinsically meaningless and may be harmful.

If you think religion is rubbish, what alternatives are open to you? I suppose **atheism** is a first stop, certainly if you like the idea of Scientism. That's the atheism which says, "I know that God does not exist." But there is another atheism which says, "I believe that God does not exist." We have seen how big a difference there is between these two positions.

Or you could be an **agnostic**, someone who does not know whether God exists or not. But there are two choices here as well. Some agnostics believe that the existence or non existence of God is unknowable. Others take the view that they do not know whether God exists or not, but that the question is not necessarily unknowable. These are very different positions, are they not, the second leaving the door open should unexpected evidence turn up.

So, if you take your position as some sort of atheist or agnostic, does that sort you out as a secularist? Yes, if you are an atheist who 'knows', but not necessarily otherwise. For you could follow a non God religion. You could be a Buddhist or a Jain or follow certain traditions of Chinese religion or follow the

Samkhya school of Hinduism or be a certain sort of Quaker. Bear in mind that poll which found that almost seventy percent of those polled believed in a soul while fewer than thirty percent believed in a personal God. However, none of that would be open to you if you also believed that spirit did not exist.

Perhaps you might stretch a point and take what could be termed the '**Gaia**' approach. This does not involve an organised church, movement or creed. In its broadest terms, the idea is that there is some sort of earth spirit in a non material dimension, which relates to all material things, and through which they are connected in some way. There's plenty of scope for believing what you wish within this framework and plenty on the internet for you to explore.

Let us explore more conventional secular ideas. A principal view is that of **humanism**. The central principle of humanism is the meeting of, the satisfying of, human needs. That is the basis of desired human behavior, of how you ought to behave. Behavior that tends to the meeting of human needs is likely to be referred to as good. Behavior that is hostile to that end may find itself called bad.

Many followers of religion would regard themselves as humanists in general terms. And some self-defined humanists regard themselves as 'religious humanists'. Some such religious humanists define religion in a 'functional' way. Frederick Edwords, Executive Director of the American Humanist Association defines religion for humanists as 'that which serves the personal and social needs of a group of people sharing the same philosophical world view.' That is to say, it gives a basis for moral values, an inspiring set of ideals, a method for dealing with the harsh realities of life, a rationale for living life joyously and an overall sense of purpose. Some humanists may believe in a spiritual life of some sort.

However, humanism per se would seem to largely fall outside our working definition of religion. And the majority of self-styled humanists are secular humanists, and don't want to have anything to do with the word 'religion' which they see as superstition.

So, how do such humanists work out their moral values based on what satisfies human needs? They do it by reason, experience, and by observing what human beings share as values. It could be said that humanists import universal values into their system, but they will reply that they are merely drawing conclusions from the evidence as to what seems best for humanity. Nonetheless they have a system of values underpinned by observations as to the nature of humanity.

It is to be expected that humanism sets its sights on human rights, democracy, equality, mutual respect, freedom of belief, non discrimination, education free of any religious teaching. It is hostile to faith, revelation and perceptions arising from altered states of consciousness. It will accept imagination as a source of ideas which must then be tested by reason. It is heavily into compassion. It is tuned into science, technology and, as Frederick Edwords puts it, 'enlightened social thought'.

As to numbers, the British Humanist Association says that at least 15.5 percent of the UK population is non religious according to the 2001 UK census, and points out that an Ipsos poll of November 2006 'revealed that 36% of the population shared humanist beliefs on morality and the nature of the universe.' In 2008 the American Humanist society reached a peak of 10,000 members.

I deal with Christian **Unitarianism** at the end of the chapter on Christianity. But Unitarians have a wide range of views and some could be secular, so I give Unitarians, most of whom would describe themselves as humanists, another mention here.

The largest grouping of Unitarians is the **Unitarian Universalists** (UUs) who have a number of organisations, the largest of which is the Unitarian Universalist Association of Congregations, which operates mainly in the USA and has more

than one thousand member congregations. Individual congregations run themselves and decide matters of worship and
management. UU is a creedless approach to spirituality,
although some UU congregations may regard themselves as
Christian. But a majority don't.

The 'Universalism' bit of UU relates to the belief that all living
things are related in some way to some higher element, which
can be found in all people and faiths, and that there is some sort
of spiritual oneness. Each person seeks the meaning in this. All
sacred writing is to be treated with respect. Truth may be found
there or elsewhere. As to principles of life, these are set out nicely
in the children's version prepared by the Unitarian Universalist
Association, as follows. 'Each person is important, Be kind in all
you do, We're free to learn together, And search for what is true,
All people need a vote, Build a fair and peaceful world, We care
for Earth's lifeboat, That will bring us back to UU.' Services tend
to be in the Protestant style.

Some people with secular views seek to convert others to the
same point of view, just as some religions are **missionary**
religions. In the UK their National Secular Society and the British
Humanist Association both helped organise a campaign of
atheist adverts in 2009.

As a diversion, you may consider something that lies in a mist
between secularism and religion, namely the mysteries of
postmodernism. This is a difficult subject and it is not within
this book's ambit to go into it in detail. But you might be tempted
to explore further elsewhere.

Broadly, postmodernism says that no definite terms, boundaries or absolute truths exist. That makes it a bit difficult to
define postmodernism itself. The idea that truth is an illusion
may seem a bit terminal for religion. But could such an idea open
the way to a new theology? What lies between what exists and
what does not exist, between what we know and what we do not
know? Could that be termed God? This is close to some religions'

tradition of unknowing, of reaching to something otherwise unreachable by considering what it is not. Could this be a religious trapdoor in an area often considered the province of secularism? Over to you, and off to the internet.

Can the interface between the secular and the spiritual become more than a mere frontier?

It has been suggested that a secular society could create structures that mimic religious structures in order to encourage what is perceived as good behavior. Alain de Botton's *Religion for Atheists* examines this idea. But such top down micromanagement may be seen as lacking the bottom up dynamic of the individual conscience, driven by the petrol of a universal moral imperative.

Perhaps the idea is capable of expansion. Let us return to humanism's system of values based on what is best for humans. A person of religion might say that this is not so unlike the Buddhist view that behavior should depend upon what leads to the desirable result. Or it could be argued that the moral dynamic of humanism is that a thing should conform to its own nature, should be what it truly is. If so, that would be not so different from the idea of natural law, the Dhamma, the Way. Some could argue that such an interpretation of humanism is nearer to the idea of the Jain inner nature of soul realising itself. A Christian interpretation would be that moral theology starts from human experience. All these views start from a search for a moral imperative, something to put the 'ought' into life.

So maybe the gap between religion and secular humanism is not as wide as the secularists suggest. The Dalai Lama in his *My Spiritual Autobiography* has some good ideas on this and I quote. 'I don't believe in the creation of mass movements and ideologies.' 'It is perfectly possible to practice the essence of a faith or culture without associating it with a religion.' 'So ethics is the basis for a secular spirituality for everyone, one that is not limited to a group of believers in one religion or another.' 'Of course one can cultivate human qualities without having a religion. But as a general rule, religion allows us to increase the qualities more effectively.' (pages 117, 136, 106 and 89 respectively).

Granted other religions may lack the flexibility of view of the Dalai Lama. But in most there is scope. The Catholic Church is far from its earlier position regarding other faiths. Consider the document *Nostro Aetate*, which says, 'The Catholic Church rejects nothing which is true and whole in these (other) religions. It regards those ways of acting and living and those precepts and teachings which, though often at variance with what it holds and expounds, frequently reflect a ray of truth which enlightens everyone.' Sikhism's Guru Nanak says, 'God's light pervades every creature.' The Hindu Lord Krishna says, 'Whoever worships me, in whatever way, I entertain them in that way.' Judaism does not deny Heaven to gentiles.

Does aggressive secularism choose to muddy these particular waters with quarrels to avoid a possible logic of the principles which may underlie moral behavior?

Indeed, is the acceptance of a need for a moral imperative something that could unify the non spiritual and the spiritual, leaving out only the fundamentalists on either side. That way religious and secular moral systems could be seen to rest on a common basis, giving rise to something beyond mere toleration of one another.

A note on the numbers of atheists and agnostics

adherents.com suggests that atheists and agnostics number about twelve percent of the world's population. That may surprise some of those of you who may live in Europe, since that continent has more atheists/agnostics than elsewhere. As to atheists alone, adherents.com gives various figures, the highest being 4.4 percent.

You may find interesting the following two extracts from Phil Zuckerman's chapter on "Atheism: Contemporary Rates and Patterns ", in *The Cambridge Companion to Atheism*, edited by Michael Martin, Cambridge University Press: Cambridge, UK (2005) which I found on adherents.com.

> Between 500,000,000 and 750,000,000 humans currently do not believe in God ... The nations with the highest degrees of organic atheism (atheism which is not state-enforced through totalitarian regimes but emerges naturally among free societies) include most of the nations of Europe, as well as Canada, Australia, New Zealand and Israel. There also exist high degrees of atheism in Japan, Vietnam, and Taiwan. Many former Soviet nations, such as Estonia, Ukraine, Kazakhstan, and Belarus also contain significant levels of atheism. However, atheism is virtually non-existent in much of the world, especially among the most populous nations of Africa, South America, the Middle East, and much of Asia ... In many societies, particularly those in Europe, atheism is growing. However, throughout much of the rest of the world – particularly among the poorest nations with highest birth rates – atheism is barely discernible.

Is worldwide atheism growing or in decline? This is a difficult question to answer simply. On the one hand, there are more atheists in the world today than ever before. Additionally, the nations with some of the highest degrees of organic atheism (such as Great Britain, France, and Scandinavia) have been experiencing a steady increase of atheism over the past century, an increase which shows no indication of abating (Bruce, 2001). On the other hand, worldwide atheism overall may be in decline. This is due to the demographic fact that highly religious nations have the highest birth rates in the world, and highly irreligious nations have the lowest birth rates in the world. As Norris and

Inglehart [Norris, Pippa and Ronald Inglehart. 2004. *Sacred and Secular: Religion and Politics Worldwide.* Cambridge U. Press] observe, 'the world as a whole now has more people with traditional religious views than ever before – and they constitute a growing proportion of the world's population.'

Part II

Non God Religions

Chapter 9

Jainism

To consider joining this religion, you will have decided that you believe:

- that spirit exists,
- that it is connected to us, and to animals and things,
- in reincarnation,
- and in karma,
- that goodness is a universal principle
- and that there is no creator God.

As a Jain you will believe that matter and spirit can neither be created nor destroyed and has always existed. **Time** is endless, a series of cycles, like a wheel turning, going upwards and then downwards. It's not so unlike science's idea of the big bang creating the universe, and the big crunch ending it, and then starting all over again. In the ascending six ages of this circle, humans progress in knowledge and happiness, in the descending arc of six ages they deteriorate. This is very different from the Western view of history as a linear march of progress.

For Jains, reality consists of spirit and non spirit. Spirit is called **jiva**. It is soul. It has no beginning. It is eternal. In its pure form it has consciousness, bliss and energy. Anything else is called ajiva, and that includes even our innermost thoughts. So, a jiva is a unit of pure consciousness. Jains believe that everything has a soul: humans, animals and things. Unfortunately, this is not a good situation for the jiva. What the jiva really needs is to be on its own so it can experience its true nature and get on with the bliss bit. While it is tied up with ajiva, this isn't going to happen, and the jiva is not fully alive and is only semi-conscious.

The problem is **karma**. It is karma that binds the jiva to the material world. Jains have their own, unique, view of karma. As a Jain, you will believe that karma exists physically on a subatomic level. Karma traps the jiva. Hinduism and Buddhism see karma as a process. For Jainism, it is a substance.

Jainism won't give you an explanation of how this state began, of how the jiva first came up against karmic particles. There's no Garden of Eden idea in this religion. Jains don't believe in any First Cause or Beginning. This is just how things are.

Jains believe in **reincarnation**. We die and our jiva goes on to a new existence. This may be as a human, but could be as an animal, or as an insect, or even as a bit of rock. The jiva, or soul, can even not be attached to anything at all, other than its burden of karma, its karmic body. The *Tattvartha Sutra* (TS), an ancient Jain text, says "Like the light of a lamp, the soul assumes the size of the body it happens to occupy ..." (TS 5.16 trans. Nathmal Tatia). "The soul is never bereft of sentience, however feeble and indistinct as this may be in undeveloped organisms." (TS 2.8 commentary). The jiva may exist in this world or in other parallel or overlapping worlds perhaps, like the realms of Hell-beings or the various Heavens.

To find bliss, our jiva needs to work itself out of this cycle of death and rebirth. To do that it has to get itself free of karma, and so free of ajiva or non spirit. This achievement by the jiva is known as moksha.

What awaits the jiva that achieves moksha? A state of infinite bliss, of infinite knowledge, of infinite perception, of infinite energy. The liberated jiva understands and knows everything in the universe. It has reasserted its true nature. It is a state beyond both good and evil.

All things are connected in that they have souls. For a liberated soul this connection is complete by virtue of omniscience.

And karma unites the pursuit of your own salvation with the

benefit of others. As the Tirthankara Mahavira says, "Non-violence and kindness to living beings is kindness to oneself. For thereby one's own self is saved from various kinds of sins and resultant sufferings and is able to secure one's own welfare."

So, how far have we got? We have established that this religion is centered on the primacy of the individual, in the form of the jiva. Unlike Buddhism it does not see this as an ever changing flow of consciousness. Unlike some branches of Hinduism it does not seek the merger of the individual with a universal consciousness. Unlike the Abrahamic religions it does not place the individual, after but one life, in a permanent relationship with a creator God, for there is no creator God in this religion. However, the Jain self is not the self of Western thought, but a self without any attributes that we would associate with individual identity: no character, personality or temperament. At the same time the Jain self is more inclusive for, as omniscient spirits, jivas which have achieved moksha or liberation are part of an interconnected web, including everything and, in their case, aware of everything.

Souls are separate, but they cannot live independently of one another. They have to share their pleasure and pain with others and they influence each other. And they create a common environment. (TS 5.21 and commentary).

Back to **karma**. Karmic particles are subatomic life forms of subtle matter, a scientific-sounding way of saying that they can't be scientifically identified. These particles attach to the soul or jiva, weighing it down and clouding its perception, standing between the soul and enlightenment. The pure life energy is corrupted and imprisoned.

It is the soul's karmic body which produces the soul's physical bodies and the vicissitudes of its many lives. Every human action or thought, even if trivial, creates karma, which attaches to the soul. For Jainism, the word attachment has a literal sense added to it. There are different sorts of karma, each in different shades.

All karma drags the soul downwards spiritually. Some karma attaches to the jiva but does not stand in the way of spiritual development which could end in the releasing of the jiva.

Fortunately, the soul has an inherent knowledge and intuition which may enable it to destroy the deluded world view that imprisons it. But some souls won't succeed in that and will see no end to reincarnation. Jainism is not a religion which believes every soul will attain liberation.

For Jainism, your intention is the important thing. A doctor may cut flesh and inflict pain but that does not cause an inflow of pain-producing karma. "It is the evil motive behind the infliction of pain that attracts evil inflow" (TS 6.12 commentary). It is the intention that makes the difference. Jains regard thinking as doing.

What are the practicalities of traveling this path to bliss and omniscience? Getting born as a human is a good start, to say the least. Jains believe that only when attached to human form can the jiva achieve liberation.

If you are so lucky as to be a human, how can you improve your karmic situation? Well, you can just wait, for eventually karma will exhaust itself and drop off, after having caused suffering. That will help, but won't be enough. New karma constantly arises. However, as a human there are other ways open to you. One way is to stop karma accumulating. Another is to avoid the karma which drags you down spiritually and seek just to acquire the karma which does not do that. This is why being a human is so important, for it gives you opportunities to deal with your karma that other lives cannot. For example, as an animal you have less or no ability to make moral judgments and so your karmic possibilities are limited. It is possible, though difficult, to actually get rid of karma by a process of wearing it away by such activities as restricting diet, subjecting the body to physical rigors, service to others, study, meditation and by renouncing the ego. Jains believe that only those who follow the ascetic path can actually destroy karma.

Getting reborn as, or embodied in, a human, will depend on the karma your jiva has built up. If it's too negative you won't get a human next time. Much also depends upon your state of mind at death: being calm and contented and focused on spiritual matters works best. If you don't get a human, perhaps you'll get a dog, maybe a worm, maybe a plant, or even an atomic particle. You may even not be connected with anything at all. If you have generated a lot of negative karma you may be reborn as a Hell-being. That is particularly bad, because you have no chance of building any good karma at all, and just have to wait and wait in most unpleasant circumstances until you have through time shed enough karmic particles. Jains also believe that you can be reborn as 'gods' in another world. Pleasant as that may be it is still a rung below a human being since, again, there is no opportunity to improve your karmic position and progress on the road to moksha: the jiva just has to wait, albeit pleasantly, until rebirth in a human.

You will observe that this traffic is not just a oneway route. You don't necessarily work your way up and up. If you mess your karma up your spiritual state can go backwards. However, the process has a compounding aspect. If you accumulate a lot of bad karma, you are that more likely to have more bad thoughts, deeds and emotions, which in turn attract more bad karma.

There are one hundred and forty-eight kinds of karma. Of their categories there are four types that are considered destructive karma and that particularly hamper any spiritual progress, as follows.

Knowledge obstructing karma is produced when you close your mind, deal in one-sided information or denigrate open-minded people. It is produced by prejudice, fanaticism, indifference. It prevents you from understanding the truth.

Intuition obstructing karma is produced when the capacity for spiritual insight is denied and when it is held up for ridicule.

It interferes with perception.

Energy obstructing karma is produced by actions which obstruct the positive flow of energy from the soul. Examples are meanness of spirit, lack of generosity, unkindness, lack of kindness, causing suffering, indifference to suffering, laziness, contempt for social justice, contempt for spirituality. One of its characteristics is that it delivers a bit of its punishment sooner than later, for such people often find themselves dissatisfied and unhappy despite any success.

The fourth destructive type of karma is **deluding karma**. This dangerous form attaches to the conviction of absolute truth. Any closed system of values which excludes other possibilities can give rise to it. It is the karma of intolerance, fanaticism, race or caste prejudice, social engineering, authoritarianism. It is more subtle than just having strong views. It is where the delusion of rightness gives anger and hatred to the person, so they view individuals or groups in a way that is destructive to the idea that we should be generous and positive to our fellow beings. Jains also see moral relativism as an extreme of opinion in just the same way as fanaticism: both as sets of convictions which brook no alternative and which inflame violence of the mind, if no more.

Another type of karma is **pleasure and pain-causing karma**. This applies where your actions or thoughts cause gain or pleasure, disadvantage or pain, to other humans or animals. If pain, then bad karma is produced: if pleasure, then the karma will not impede spiritual progress. There are other types of karma which are not destructive but which may affect birth, physique, lifespan and status.

That deals with the mechanics of karma and from it you can see something of the behavior Jainism will expect from you. To give you a better idea of that let us move on to Jainism's **Five Vows**. These are abstinence from:

- violence,
- falsehood,
- stealing,
- carnality,
- and possessiveness.

Each of these needs some explanation, for they are broad brush-strokes. For Jains, violence means more than physical violence. It includes psychological violence, the assumption of absolute truth, the forcing of one-sided arguments on others. Remember that the intention is as important as the outcome. If you attack another on the basis of their falsehood, then even if your accusation is true, if your intention is hurtful the value of that truth is undermined and bad karma is attracted. Even if the thoughts all stay in your head, they will still generate the wrong sort of karma. Falsehood includes self-delusion. If you abuse truth or use it as a weapon it becomes a falsehood. Stealing is taking anything that is not given. If you acquire possessions in a way which generates harm or contaminates your mind, then you are stealing. As for carnality, this covers respect for others and the reduction of others to the level of objects to be used. Possessiveness can be a form of mental violence. You will see that the vows overlap and are interlinked. It has been said that the last four vows all protect the first and most important one, of non violence. So they are all interdependent.

The so-called **Three Jewels** of Jainism are **Right Faith, Right Knowledge and Right Action**. These three things have to be in balance. On their own they don't, can't, work properly, in a Jain's view. Right faith doesn't work without right practice, and you can't act rightly without right knowledge. Right practice is something that has to be developed gradually. Jains don't see any conflict between reason and faith.

All this adds up to Jainism's **dharma**. Dharma is a way of life, a code of behavior, a natural law and underlying truth of the universe which just is.

Where have we got to now? We can see how the Jain system works, how the individual soul is the center, how karma attaches it to non soul or ajiva and prevents the soul from realising itself, how behavior generates karma and how we need to behave if we are to struggle free from the bonds of karma.

To someone raised in an Abrahamic religious culture, this may look like a pyramid structure of souls, with the jivas of particles at the bottom and those of humans towards the top. However, Jains see all life forms as of equal importance in terms of the universe. It is just that some are more spiritually bound down than others, and some have gained more spiritual opportunities than others.

Having explained all that, we need to go right back to the beginning and look at three interlinking ideas of Jainism. These are **aparigraha** or non possessiveness, **ahimsa** or the principle of non injury to life, and **anekantavada** or non one-sidedness.

Before we do that, we should tackle a few practical points. One is that Jains take a very long view. They accept that it may take many, many lives for a soul to achieve liberation. They believe that the universe is on the downward path of the wheel of time, which makes it even more difficult, if not impossible, for any soul to complete the task until the next phase of the universal wheel of time comes round. They believe that only when in human form can the soul succeed in this task. They also believe that the final stages of the journey require great discipline and a far from normal life, in fact the life of the ascetic.

Most Jains accept that they have not reached that stage. Thus there are two standards of behavior, two interpretations of the Five Vows for Jains: one for **ascetics** and one for non ascetic, **lay Jains**, who lead an ordinary life. For the ascetics, the vows involve a strict interpretation. For lay Jains, the vows are practical rules of conduct for living in society and protecting themselves from bad karma.

So, **aparigraha**, or **non possessiveness**, means the renunciation of possessions for the ascetic. For lay Jains, what is relevant is what is done with their possessions, and why they are owned. Providing for family and others is one thing, having possessions for self-centered reasons is another. However, just the physical act of renouncing possessions in whole or in part isn't enough, whoever you are. Furthermore, non possessiveness doesn't just apply in relation to material objects, but to people and animals. Also, remember that the inside of your head is as important as your visible actions. If you act just to appear virtuous that doesn't work. In this religion there is no God keeping an eye on your secret sins: just the inexorable and unavoidable working of a karma that asks no questions and can be told no lies.

As a Jain you will seek to develop this indifference to material things, and meditate upon it. You will reduce your dependence on material things. Perhaps you will own less, or perhaps you will use your wealth to help others or to promote Jain values in an indirect way. Inside your head you will seek to stand aside from desire, craving, attachment to possessions or feelings. The Jain text, The *Tattvartha Sutra*, says, "Clinging is possessiveness." (TS 7.12) "Possessiveness is clinging to the animate and the inanimate. It may refer to clinging to something in the external world or to feelings within the self. It is desire, coveting, craving, longing, yearning, greed, clinging ... Nourishing the passions of the mind is also a form of emotional clinging." (TS 7.12 commentary).

The next idea is that of ahimsa. **Ahimsa is the principle of non injury to life, non violence.** Non violence is an essential part of Jainism, and to the outsider the most obvious aspect. Ahimsa doesn't just apply to humans and animals, but can be extended to include harm to the environment. It sits at the center of Jain thought in that it lives within all the principal Jain ideas. You can see how non possessiveness relates to it, and withdrawal from the world and getting rid of attachment. For the ascetic the principle is taken to extremes, with a mask over the mouth to prevent the accidental swallowing of an insect and the ground scrupulously swept for insects before sitting down or walking. For the layman it will among other things involve vegetarianism and the avoidance of food the production of which may risk the lives of living things. Both the ascetic and the layman will seek to train thoughts so that destructive thoughts don't flourish. You can see how an environmentalism, which in Western society might appear as a single issue obsession, here is the outward manifestation of an inner journey.

It is easy for people to emphasise Jainism as a religion of renunciation. However, Jains would say that the idea of renunciation is part of an overall idea which, if followed by everyone, would enhance the richness of life and transform the quality of the environment, as well as leading, eventually, to bliss

The third idea is **anekantavada,** or **non one-sidedness**, sometimes translated as non absolutism This is an interesting idea, but one which may be quite difficult to take in for those raised within a Western culture. It also goes some way to explaining why Jainism is not a missionary religion and does not have as many adherents as might be expected.

For Jains, dogmatic certainty is a form of attachment, a source of bad karma, something that holds back spiritual progress for the soul. Jains sees truth as something which can be approached from many directions. All knowledge, apart from omniscience, is only partial truth from a particular viewpoint.

Anekantavada is not the same as moral relativism. Nor the same as tolerance, or diversity, or even pluralism. It is something beyond all of those. Jainism has its own belief as to the way the universe works. It does not see this as rivaling other competing truths. Other truths may lead to the ultimate goal of truth and release of the soul, depending on how people behave. Jainism sees dogmatism as a delusion, an attraction to destructive karma. Aidan Rankin, at page 189 of *The Jain Path*, published by O books in 2006 and to which this chapter owes a considerable debt, says, "Truth is more than the sum of many parts." "We view the summit from whichever path we take, but the path itself is not the same as the summit." Truth "has 'many folds' or layers, as well as a multiplicity of entry points. It is hidden, it is elusive, but it exists in its own right and is grasped fully at the point of spiritual liberation ...". He quotes the tale of the blindfolded men who examined an elephant. One examined and then described the leg, one the trunk, one an ear and one the tail. Based on their experience each gave a wrong description of the animal. What is right from an individual viewpoint may be one thing, and the truth may be something quite different. The interconnectedness of the Jain universe is reflected in this view. The Jain idea of multiple viewpoints is called **syadvada**, which can be usefully translated as 'maybe'. The religion is not concerned to win any argument. That would be a source of bad karma, and in any event pointless, since Jains see all belief systems as being a journey towards truth and are concerned more with seeing what can be found in common. Jainism looks for the words 'both/and' rather than 'either/or'.

To follow the path of Jainism you don't have to believe the jiva/karma/moshka structure. Jains believe that that is how the universe works, but they also believe in non one-sidedness. If you treat all life as sacred, and that everything has life, and act accordingly, minimise your consumption, and use any wealth you have positively, then your feet are on the path.

It may seem surprising that a faith which to you might seem tailor made for those with environmental concerns, and so modern in its ancient way, does not have more followers. Perhaps people are put off, as you may be, by the sternness of its lack of any easy way, and by its long, long view. Perhaps you have never even heard of it, since it does not propagate its beliefs.

Furthermore, if you are attracted by some of Jainism's ideas note that Jainism warns of the arbitrary interpretation of scriptural teaching. That includes Jain teaching. If you convert for spiritual gain that will attract bad karma, if you see Jainism as 'right' and other views as 'wrong', that will attract bad karma. Jainism teaches humility in all respects, and seeks to influence rather than convert.

Jains are likely to be detached enough not to demur when Hindus describe it as a development of **Hinduism** dating back to between 700 and 500 BCE. The religion has been greatly admired by both Ghandi and Einstein. The **name of the religion** comes from the Sanskrit for 'to conquer'. Needless to say this conquest is one involving an internal battle of the soul. It has nothing to do with conquering opponents

There is one main division within Jainism, dating back to early days. The **Digambaras** (Sky Clad) take the view that only souls with male bodies can attain liberation and that male ascetics should be naked. Their ascetics follow the strictest forms of vows. Their scripture varies in parts from that of the other principal group, the **Svetambaras** (White or Cotton Clad). Digambaras are more common towards South India and Svetambaras in West India.

An **ascetic** may be a wandering monk, or may live in a monastery for specified parts of the year. An ascetic will have a cover for his mouth, a long duster to sweep the ground ahead free of insects as he walks, a drinking gourd, a bowl and, if he is not a Digambara, a loin cloth. There are also Jain nuns.

As a **lay Jain** you will know that ultimately you will have to pass through lives of asceticism if you are to free your soul, and you will aspire to that one day. You will be aware that the universe is in a long, long stage where it is difficult for anyone to complete the liberation of their soul. This will not worry you, for you will have a long view of things. As to your daily way of life, you will be a vegetarian. You may be vegan. You will probably avoid eating at night, that being a time when there is a greater chance of attracting insects which could be inadvertently harmed. You will probably avoid wine, honey and other foods which might harbor life forms. You will probably avoid potatoes, garlic and onions. You will take a number of vows arising from the Five Vows. These may also include vows to avoid unnecessary travel and to give to ascetics and charities. You will perform certain rituals, meditate, and fast from time to time. You will be true and faithful to your chosen partner and avoid sex before marriage, pornography and sexual thoughts. As a Jain you will take your work seriously and conduct your calling in a disciplined way. Many lay Jains are business people or professionals and have high reputations. Lay Jain communities tend to be prosperous. As to life events, birth and marriage for example, until recently the religion had no longstanding celebratory rituals for these and there is a tendency to follow local custom. Above all you will know that you cannot hide from the consequences of your action and thoughts, nor find some easy forgiveness somewhere. You will see your inner thoughts as important, sometimes more important, than your actual actions.

Jain teachers recommend as 'respectable' the **jobs** of government, writing, farming, the arts, commerce and various crafts. Understandably, military service is not recommended and agriculture has come to be regarded as likely to involve injuring living things. A business career is the most popular. Jains have an association with financial success that may seem to contrast with the religion's ascetic ethic.

It may seem strange that a religion which has no God is involved with images, but Jainism is. If you join, you may find yourself venerating the **Tirthankaras**. There are twenty-four of these according to Jain tradition, and the last one, Mahavira, died in about 527 BCE. The Tirthankaras are the most illustrious of those who have achieved enlightenment, whose jivas have become free of karma and achieved bliss, energy and omniscience. The word means fordmaker: they make the passage across the river for us to cross. Jains believe that the Tirthankaras appear in each ascending and descending half of the time cycle. The Tirthankaras are not worshipped but they are venerated and they represent an ideal state that is achievable. Yet reverence can approach adoration and Jains are usually raised to regard the Tirthankaras as superhumans whose lives are marked by super-natural occurrences.

The Jain Sthanakavasis grouping doesn't venerate such images, and monks and nuns don't either. But images may be found in temples or in household shrines. And much Jain religious activity is centered on the building, consecration and veneration of these images. The idea is that lay Jains, in vener-ating the Tirthnakaras' images, meditate with the images in their mind as a source of inspiration. This is not worship as submitting before a superior force or in the hope that prayers will be answered. Theoretically, Jains appreciate that the Tirthankaras, in their omniscient bliss, are not going to respond in any way. Not that you would think that if you were to go to a Jain temple in India and see people praying there.

Meditation may also be by the ancient and highly regarded samayika method, seeking equanimity by a process of mentally forgiving and begging forgiveness of the entire world of human beings. **Fasting** is another important Jain practice, one which distinguishes their practice from that of Hindus. As a Jain you will regard pilgrimage as something that is good for your karma and you are likely to go on pilgrimage.

Worship, or **puja** may involve hymns, prayers, bathing the images and making offerings of flowers or food to them. Puja may take place at home or in a Jain temple. Jainism's many festivals are generally linked to a Tirthankara's life events, namely: their conception, birth, renunciation, attainment of omniscience (the lot of most liberated souls), and final emanci-pation (a state just for Tirthankaras, which requires a certain sort of karmic destiny). Festivals may involve fasting, recitation of scripture, preaching, parading of images, communal confession.

For the most part there is no special priestly caste in Jainism and lay people are encouraged to carry out ritual services on their own, individually or in groups. Ascetic teachers should be revered and visited and given alms. A visit to an ascetic may include a confession of transgressions of the vows. Such confession to an ascetic teacher is also part of the major Jain rite of Samvatsari, accompanied by pleas for forgiveness to family and friends – by letter to those not present. The rite also includes an eight- to ten-day selective fast. At its end participants extend their own forgiveness to all beings and ask that they do likewise: "I ask pardon of all living creatures. May all of them pardon me. May I have a friendly relationship with all beings and unfriendly with none."

You will also believe that religious merit is gained from hearing and reading **Jain texts**. Two of the best known are the *Acaranga Sutra* and the *Tattvartha Sutra*. The full title of the *Tattvartha Sutra* translates as A Manual for Understanding All That Is. It was written in Sanskrit by a philosopher monk in the second century CE and was based on Jain scriptures said to record the sermons of the last Tirthankara of the present cycle, Lord Mahavira. It incorporates various commentaries. In this chapter I refer to the translation by Nathmal Tatia published by the Institute of Jainology in 1994. Jain texts are regarded as guides rather than blueprints. Jain teachers give advice and warning, they don't lay down dogma: they are sources of wisdom not of indoctrination. There is not much in the way of philosophical disagreement in the history and development of Jainism, which is not surprising given the nature of the religion.

Jainism has incorporated some popular figures of Hinduism, such as Krishna and Rama into its own mythology, but not as divine figures. For example some Jain texts describe Krishna as being destined to be reborn a Tirthankara.

The principal Jain symbol is the **Pratika**. It has a drawing of a hand, upon which is the word 'Ahimsa', the principle of non injury to life. Above the hand is a swastika, whose four arms represent male and female ascetics and male and female lay persons. Above that, three dots represent right faith, right knowledge and right action. Above the swastika, a crescent symbolises the place of liberated souls, with a dot within representing such liberated jivas. Underneath the symbol are the words, 'All life is interdependent'.

An interesting aspect of Jainism is the number of apparent paradoxes in its belief system. It is centered on the individual, the individual jiva or soul, but the jiva is devoid of all the things we see as involving individuality. It has a rigor in its thinking and yet great freedom. The soul is individual and yet in its liberated state united with everything in its omniscience. It is a religion of both abstract reasoning and intuition. It is in many ways suited to modern times, with no God, an anti-ideological stance and a dedication to non violence and the environment. Nonetheless, its followers are not that numerous. However, they would probably be content if you just read this account and took the principles set out in it to heart.

A word of warning. A Jain scholar has warned me not to "make overinterpretations from New Age perspectives" of Jainism. And perhaps I have done that here and there, particularly as regards environmentalism. After all, Jainism is not concerned about the environment per se. As a cause it has nothing to do with the Jain path to liberation. It's just that the day to day activity of a well led Jain life dovetails with the behavior that environmentalists urge on us. And it is fair to say that some young Jains see an association between Jain thinking and New Age objectives.

As to numbers, there are probably between four and five million Jains, perhaps as many as seven million, nearly all in India. A modern introduction to the *Tattvartha Sutra* suggests there may currently be about 2,500 Jain monks and more than 5,000 nuns.

A note on the Jain universe.

The Jain universe is one of infinite time and space and one of submicroscopic living organisms and infinitesimal units of matter, including things that we would not consider to be matter. An atom is the single unit of matter and occupies one unit of space. But it is possible for an infinite number of atoms to occupy one space unit (TS 5.11 and 5.14 commentary). A time unit, the smallest unit of time, is the time it takes for an atom to move from one space unit to another. An innumerable number of time units make the smallest countable unit of time. The largest unit of time is 'unmeasurable'. (TS 4.15 commentary). An object is referred to as a 'real' and a real has "existence, non-existence and inexpressibility" (TS 5.31 commentary). That is what constitutes existence – a real has a constant beginning and ending and so persists: it flows through constantly changing modes. It is neither being nor non-being, neither real nor unreal. As to under-standing a phenomenon, there is no perfect viewpoint, only partial truths which contain grains of everlasting truth (TS 531 commentary).

Within this universe, our speech, thoughts and actions are manifestations of vibrations of the soul in association with its mind and body. These vibrations are caused by the karmic particles which adhere to the soul and which are in turn attracted by our speech, thoughts and actions.

You may feel that these ancient ideas strangely echo ideas of modern physics. The cycle of the universe's life. The alliance of the eternity of space and time. The infinitesimal building blocks of matter. The way in which objects at an atomic level are contin-ually beginning and ending. The bewildering and unexpected ways of the quantum subatomic world which sometimes defy logical possibility. The way string theory postulates the most basic unit of matter as a one-dimensional vibrating loop. Might a modern physicist be driven to say, "It is, it is not and it is inexpressible" (TS 5.31 commentary)?

Chapter 10

Buddhism

To get to consider this religion, you will have chosen to believe:

- that spirit exists (but not soul as other religions understand it),
- in what other religions would refer to as universal values,
- in reincarnation/rebirth,
- in karma.

If you are a Buddhist, you will see your faith as a working hypothesis. Suck it and see. Try it and see if it works. If you find something that works better, do that. What is the authority for this? The Buddha, no less. The Buddha compared the faith to a raft. You need a raft to get across a river, but once you've got across you don't carry the raft with you, you leave it behind (*Majjhima Nikaya* Ch31 134-5). When pressed as to whether God existed, the Buddha refused to comment. The question was simply an irrelevance, like the attitude of a man shot by an arrow who refuses treatment until he knows who shot the arrow.

So, as a Buddhist you won't just not believe in a creator God, you will consider the question to be of little relevance. You will accept the ideas of reincarnation and karma. You will believe in spirit, but won't believe in the idea of soul as understood by other religions. If you think that sounds simple, it isn't. If you think it sounds complicated, you're right. This is a complex and subtle religion with some central ideas that are difficult to understand. However, it's not complicated to practice and you don't have to understand the complexities to follow the teachings. Nonetheless, remember that the Buddha also said, "… a fool will perceive the truth as little as a spoon perceives the taste of soup."

(*Dammapada* 64). As usual, you are warned that a short introduction such as this cannot cover all the many variations of belief
in Buddhism.

You will believe that Buddhism can lead you to a knowledge
that can be attained but which is incapable of being described by
the words and grammar available to us. You will call this
knowledge '**supermundane wisdom**'. It is a knowledge of how
things really are. To attempt to define it in words, to reduce it to
doctrine and dogma is False View. It lies on the other side of the
river, where the raft can be abandoned. In this journey you can
be helped by '**mundane wisdom**' if you can attain that. This can
be reduced to words, and relates to how things seem, to relative
rather than ultimate and indescribable truth. Mundane wisdom
will show us the way, but we need to be aware that it is empty in
relation to supermundane wisdom. There is a difference between
the teaching and the truth.

A journey implies travel from one place to another. What is
the origin of the Buddhist journey? The origin is Dukkha, the
destination is Nirvana. Essentially, Nirvana is complete freedom
from Dukkha, so we should look at Dukkha first.

Dukkha is often translated as 'suffering'. Hence you often
hear that the Buddha said that life is suffering. However the
word, although technically a correct translation, calls up a
narrow meaning to the Western ear. For Buddhism there are a
number of kinds of suffering. One is physical and mental pain.
That is the meaning that the West would seize on. However, for
Buddhism the idea of suffering is much wider. Above all, dukkha
is a product of the impermanence of everything. You are healthy,
you will get old and decrepit. You are in love, it will fade and
you or your partner will die. You have a good meal, it will end
up as faeces and you will be hungry again. There is no lasting
satisfaction and that is another form of suffering. Essentially,
whatever is impermanent is dukkha, and everything is impermanent. And that really means everything. Even the self to

which you are so attached is impermanent, a mere flow of consciousness. To a Westerner, the word 'suffering' simply fails to convey this complex of ideas. Because of this, some scholars translate the word 'dukkha' as 'unsatisfactory' and I would go along with that.

So, as a Buddhist, you will see that nothing is permanent and nothing is satisfactory. And it is desire, craving, and attachment that are the problem, for it is they that bind us to dukkha. The Buddha said that satisfying desire by possessing its object is like a thirsty person drinking salt water to satisfy thirst.

Nirvana is freedom from Dukkha. Its nature is hidden within supermundane wisdom and ultimate knowledge. We know it exists because some people have experienced it and said so. We know it is very, very nice. It is not a Heaven idea. Buddhism doesn't do Heaven in the sense that other religions do, nor soul, nor God. Nirvana is not a place, it is outside space-time. It is what 'is', whatever that might be. There is no 'self' in Nirvana, and if you ever have ultimate knowledge of it there won't be any 'you' to know it. You will have achieved your full potential, so that your stream of consciousness ceases to exist and is yet not annihilated: our language cannot describe or define what happens. To pass to Nirvana you have to achieve enlightenment. And, as you will see, if your journey to Nirvana is one of desire for it, you won't achieve it.

In short and as the Buddha said (*Dammapada* 277), "All conditioned things are impermanent. The one who knows this will cease to be miserable."

A bit of scene setting might be helpful at this stage. Buddhism thinks big. It deals with the universe(s). There are other worlds in the universe, and you may be reborn there. Yes, one day you may be an alien. There are other 'realms', not so fanciful an idea in this age of possible parallel universes. There are Buddhist **realms** of Heaven, places where gods live, quite different from the Heaven idea of Abrahamic religions. These gods may be spirit beings

Hospiscare

Caring in the heart of Devon

Fore Street
90-92 Fore Street
Exeter
Devon
EX4 3HX
Telephone: 01392 253298
VAT Regn No: 991239004
Registered Charity No. 297798

You Were Served By Pauline F
On Till 2 at 14:23:35 on 15/05/2023

Product Details	Quantity	Total £
Clearance	1	0.50
Sub Total	1	0.50
CASH Tendered		0.50
Change		

Receipt No:104847

"Thank you for your purchase today. Helping local
people and their families in your community.

Hospiscare your local hospice charity
www.hospiscare.co.uk"

8 1 2 2 2 0 0 8 0 0 2 0 1 0 4 8 4 7

who have a happy and immensely long life but who die eventually. Or they may be lesser gods with physical form. There is also a realm of quarrelsome and sensual gods. In this way Buddhism absorbs many of the Hindu gods. There is a realm populated by Hell-Beings, most unpleasant. The realm of Hungry Ghosts is full of beings with insatiable appetites. You can be reborn into any of these realms and states, as a human or as some other living being. These realms are interpenetrating, and coexist, but we can only perceive the realms of animals and humans. You will note that this view of the cosmos provides the answer as to where the new 'souls', as non-Buddhists would term them, for an ever increasing human population come from.

Richard F. Gombrich, in his book *Theravada Buddhism* recalls how a monk once said to him, "gods are nothing to do with religion." The point is that the gods, and much else, in Buddhist tradition, are essentially a part of the universe's furniture, and a part which is not essential to the purpose of Buddhism. They are simply other inhabitants of the universe, with their own problems, and are irrelevant to the object of Buddhism, which is the quest for the goal of Nirvana.

This scheme of universes has no beginning and no end. If a universe or part of it disappears another appears or evolves. So, these universes progress in cycles. They are **cyclic**, an idea compatible with the big bang/big crunch idea of modern science. This is different from a linear view of history, which sees everything building on the past, and ideas being discovered. A cyclic view sees all ideas and truths as having been already discovered, but forgotten. We have to preserve what we can and rediscover what we can.

So, you can see the wide variety of existences that your **reincarnation** could involve. The best thing to get is a human. That is better even than a formless god, which is a pleasant, long, but temporary dead end. Only humans have the chance to achieve enlightenment and Nirvana. It has been said be said that

Buddhism's attitude is that everlasting life is everlasting death. It's a very different religion.

Karma is a key. For Buddhism, karma is a process whereby all actions performed with intention have a result for the perpetrator, in that or a later life. The intention is the vital thing. An important aspect of karma is the effect it may have on the manner of your reincarnation. It is possible for you to go down as well as up in reincarnation, although there is a natural tendency for the best to get better and the worst worse. The more advanced you are morally, the nearer you are to Nirvana. A Buddhist saying is, "If you want to know the past (cause), look at your present (effect). If you want to know the future (effect), look at your present (cause)."

We now get to another difficult bit, possibly the most difficult bit for those brought up within a non Buddhist tradition. This is **the nature of self**. Buddhism doesn't believe in the soul. The Buddha said that asking where someone went to when they had died was as meaningful as asking where a fire had gone to when it went out. Buddhism simply defines human personality in a way which excludes the idea of soul. You will believe that we consist of what are called the **Five Aggregates**: namely, body or form, feeling, memory or recognition or imagination, volitions and consciousness. These components exist in a pattern which continuously changes. One moment leads to the next, each is different, each is part of a process. To give an analogy with a modern gloss, all the cells of our body are replaced over a period of two years: we are the same in a way, but different. Equally, we were a baby, we become an old person: we are the same, but different. It is rather like Trigger's broom, in the TV comedy "Only Fools and Horses", which he had had fourteen years and which had had nine handles and twelve heads. It was the same broom, but it wasn't. In the case of Buddhism, the handle and the head are changing constantly. In effect, we are a stream of consciousness, the mere temporary union of our components.

The Dalai Lama has said, "Selflessness is not a case of something that existed in the past becoming nonexistent. Rather this sort of 'self' is something that never did exist. What is needed is to identify as nonexistent something that always was nonexistent."

You may see how all this gives rise to the Buddhist view of reincarnation, which is different to that of the other reincarnation religions. Indeed, it is better to use the word **rebirth** in Buddhism than the word reincarnation. An entity dies. It is reborn. One moment gives way to another, the moment of death may give way to the moment of rebirth. The moment between death and rebirth may be as the passing of one moment to another in life. For you, as a Buddhist, rebirth is like the lighting of one candle from the stub of another, and with the passing light goes the karmic burden and inclinations. This cycle of death and rebirth is called **Samsara**.

Returning to the issue of self, a Buddhist principle, known as the principle of **dependent origination**, gives rise to the following analysis. We suffer because we are born, we are born because we are caught up in the cycle of reincarnation, we are caught in this cycle because we are addicted to attachment, we are addicted to attachment because of craving. Craving arises as a result of feeling, which is a product of the senses and their contact with things, these contacts and feelings belong to an individual, who has a consciousness, which is conditioned by the karmic burden from previous existences and this existence, which influences are in turn a product of ignorance and delusion.

Buddhism likes causal chains and describes our very existence as a causal chain. The idea is that that **nothing exists without a cause and that things only exist in relation to other things**.

In this way the Buddha teaches that nothing exists independently or forever. Not just us, but everything. Any idea which separates one phenomenon from another is an illusion, arising from our own perceptions. If we hang onto that illusion it will result in dukkha for us. Everything is just a temporary collection of processes. If you want to understand Buddhism, you must get your head round this idea. And do note that it is quite different from the idea that everything is an illusion. That isn't what Buddhism is generally saying, although there is one Buddhist school, Yogacara, which has that view.

Thus, we are a stream of combinations of our constituents, and have no unchanging self-nature. As for things, they only exist in relation to one another and also have no unchanging self-nature. The universe is the combination, existence, disappearance and recombination of mind and matter. Everything is a ceaseless flow of energies and appearances, in which nothing exists without a cause.

These are really difficult ideas to take in, and express themselves more fully in an idea later developed by a form of Buddhism known as Mahayana (of which more later) This idea was termed 'sunyata', a word translated as 'void' or, more usually, as '**emptiness**'. This is yet another translation problem since the word conjures up to Western ears connotations that don't apply, since 'emptiness isn't empty. I would stick to the word 'sunyata' but everyone seems to use the word 'emptiness', so I suppose we are stuck with that. Early Buddhism looked at the flow of energies and appearances as based on building blocks that couldn't be broken down further – physical things like earth water, fire, air, elasticity and so on, mental things like compassion and greed, and consciousness. The idea was that these constituents of everything arise and cease continuously. They were referred to as dhammas. However, some Buddhists didn't agree with this analysis. They pointed out that since there was no indivisible unit of time there was no point on which to hang the existence of a dhamma. This view was adopted by Mahayana Buddhism as it developed. And it led to the idea of emptiness, that the dhammas weren't real. Within emptiness the word for the apparent brief flowering of existence in the flow of being is 'tathata' which can be translated as 'is-ness' or 'thus-ness' or, more usually, '**suchness**'. It is the nature of all things. For emptiness, as I have said, isn't nothing, it is just empty of separate, independent permanent existence. This is what the Heart Sutra, an ancient Buddhist text means when it says, 'Form is the Void and the Void is the Form'. Note that emptiness isn't a definition, but a sort of anti-definition which explains how we cannot adequately define reality.

If we can understand all this we will abandon our Western attempt to conquer the universe, and will acquire Right View, and use our energy to conquer our mind and our illusion of self.

You may well ask whether these complex ideas, which might to you seem so far from the Buddha's try-it-and-see common sense approach, are of practical value. Buddhists see this view of existence as enabling and being a vital part of the change and flow of things. An understanding of the ideas of impermanence and emptiness is a cure for the spiritual sickness of grasping, which is a primary cause of dukkha. What's the point of attachment if there isn't actually anything to be attached to or anything to be attached? The Buddhist scholar Edward Conze in his *Buddhist Thoughts* at page 243 said that emptiness was a ladder that reached out into the infinite rather than a theory; and that that ladder was not there to be discussed, but to be climbed. A proper understanding of impermanence, emptiness and suchness can endow the now with great richness and purpose. A saying of Mahayana Buddhism is, 'True Emptiness, Wonderful Existence'. This will be the philosophical basis of the daily practices of your Buddhist life. But it will be the practices that are important, not the ideas.

Within Mahayana Buddhism there are variations on the idea of emptiness. Traditions vary as to whether emptiness has an ultimate reality or not. Some emphasise the doctrine of dependent origination and say we live in a relative rather than an inherent existence, a bit like the difference between mundane and supermundane wisdom. Others say that emptiness has ultimate reality within it, and that when the mind is empty of conceptual accretions it is revealed as a pure radiant mind.

If you're tempted to Buddhism you can go into these matters more deeply. For the moment, the important thing is to get some feel for the Buddhist take on self and soul and existence, which is so different from that of other religions.

Let's move from the idea of self and soul to **the body**. Initially the Buddha lived the life of an ascetic but he abandoned that way of life, adopted a normal diet, and devoted himself to a form of meditation which led to his enlightenment. The Buddha saw that the body, though transient, is the means of our release from delusion. A Buddhist scripture has the Buddha say, "Within this very body, mortal as it is and only six feet in length, I do declare to you are the world and the origin of the world, and likewise the path that leads to the cessation thereof." Our body is our means of salvation and we must not deny it the care it needs.

Buddhism is said to have **Three Jewels**: the Buddha, the dhamma and the sangha. **The sangha** is the community of monks and nuns who nurture and teach the Buddhist code of conduct and way of life, and is sometimes used to also include the lay men and women who follow it. The dhamma is the truth within us, in our heart and mind, the universal value and truth, the principle of righteousness, that which really is. 'Dhamma' is the word in the ancient Pali language. You may also find it referred to as 'dharma' which is the word in the Sanskrit language. You need to appreciate that the word is also used in two other ways. One is to describe the nature of a thing as in the paragraph above on 'emptiness' and the other means righteousness.

As for **the Buddha** (which means the enlightened one), he is thought to have been born in about 485 BCE. It is said he was a prince who renounced everything, became a mendicant, and then found a Middle Way between attachment to the pleasures of the senses and attachment to the mortifications of renunciation: a way which led to enlightenment. He chose to stay in this realm and live out his life teaching others how to achieve enlightenment. Enlightenment is seeing things how they really are. The path to it is not that of faith nor of reason, but of personal effort.

That is a broad picture. Let us now consider how The Buddha suggested we should seek to live our lives. An entry point is **the Four Noble Truths** (Buddhists seem to like counting things). These are: the fact of dukkha, as described above, how dukkha arises, how it ceases and the path leading to its cessation. Together with the karmic teaching of moral causation these are called 'right view'.

In short, everything is transitory and ultimately unsatisfactory and unsatisfying. We are attached to this situation by our craving and desire. We can solve the problem by getting rid of our desire. Buddhism provides us with a method for doing this. Other religions would say this is a question of good and evil. Buddhism prefers to define behavior in terms of its spiritual result. 'Skilful' behavior is what leads to freedom from dukkha. 'Unskilful' behavior binds us more closely to it. Skilful behavior is virtuous and 'wholesome', unskilful behavior may be 'unwholesome'. It's a slightly different way of looking at good and bad.

Let us next look at the bad bit. Unwholesome states come from three things: **greed** and or **aversion** and or **delusion**. Greed doesn't work, and it is addictive; if you get what you want, any pleasure is transitory. Aversion or hatred or resentment produces suffering, whether you have such feelings for yourself or others. Delusion prevents you from seeing what you should be doing. If you are a Buddhist you may see these things as mental aberrations.

Obstacles to dealing with all this properly are **the Five Hindrances**. These are: attachment to things of the senses, ill will, torpor of mind or body, worry and doubt, especially self-doubt.

So, how do we get away from unwholesome states and onto the road to Nirvana? By following **the Noble Eightfold Path**. This constitutes: right view, right intention, right speech, right action, right livelihood, right effort, right mindfulness, and right concentration.

This works as follows. We need to see life correctly, then we have to act, and we need tools to enable us to do this. To see life correctly requires our view and intention. Those are two elements of the path, and require and increase insight and wisdom. Next, to act requires words, action and livelihood. These are another three elements of the path, and involve morality. Finally, the tools we have are effort, mindfulness and concentration. Those are the other three elements of the path. These elements are all interlinked, and depend on one another. Our spiritual development on this path can be in one life but for nearly everyone it is going to be over what may be a long series of existences.

The Noble Eightfold Path will be at the center of your life as a Buddhist, so it is worth going through it again, this time as summarised by Gerald Heard, an Anglo-Irish historian and philosopher (quoted in Nancy Wilson Ross's *Buddhism A Way of Life and Thought* at pages 24-5, published by Collins in 1981). First you must see clearly what is wrong. Next you must decide that you want to be cured. You must act and speak so as to aim at being cured. Your livelihood must not conflict with your therapy. That therapy must go forward at the best speed that can be sustained. You must think about it incessantly and learn how to contemplate with the 'deep mind'.

Although these steps are set out consecutively, they are inter-dependent. They need to operate simultaneously in your life. They are your chance to interrupt the chain of cause and effect that imprisons you in your life.

Let us consider them again. Right understanding deals with the content and direction of your thought. Right motive relates to the drive behind that thought, to the elimination of emotional and self-attachments which affect it. Right speech involves an exchange notably lost in the self-centered monologues of modern communication. Right action is more than just rule following. When achieved it becomes part of a state of serenity surrounded by wholesome action. Right livelihood was simpler in the Buddha's day, when it involved not butchering cattle, selling fish, hunting or going to war, but the point is clear enough. Daily work should be able to be a means of self-purification. Right effort involves a combination of intuition and will. It is will that enables us to change. Later, I will deal further with right mindfulness and right concentration.

It is what you do that matters rather than what you believe. An ancient Buddhist text, the *Dammapada* (at 19) says, "A man who talks much of his teaching but does not practice it himself is like a cattleman counting another man's cattle".

The big **five rules, or precepts,** of behavior for lay Buddhists are to avoid: destroying living beings, taking what is not given, behaving wrongly because of sexual desire, speaking falsely and taking intoxicants or drugs. These are interpreted widely. For example, speaking falsely includes backbiting and so on. Indeed it extends to being careful about anything you say. Remember, it is your intention that is the most important thing, not just the mere act.

This behavior is underpinned by a number of things. One is shame, which Buddhists have compared to a corpse round the neck of a person fond of adornment. Another is awareness of consequence: who wants to end up as a Hell-Being or Hungry Ghost? Another is wisdom, the understanding of what actually benefits you and what harms you. A fourth is compassion, feeling for others. Other vital qualities are patience, contentment and humility. Giving is important, but it has to be giving without the expectation of return

If you are a newcomer to Buddhism, you will learn a lot about the religion by considering **the Divine Abidings**. The object of these is to condition yourself to treat others as you would wish to be treated. They are subjects for meditation, of which more later. The Abidings are: loving kindness, compassion, gladness, and equanimity. As interesting, are the enemies of the Abidings. Each Abiding has both a 'near' and a 'far' enemy. If you have a good think about the near enemies that will tell you quite a bit about Buddhism.

Loving kindness is unselfish love, which is capable of being extended to everyone else. It is aimed at hatred and dislike. Its far enemy is aversion, which is straightforward. Its near enemy is attachment to the senses, which is a more subtle idea. Loving kindness succeeds when it gets rid of ill will and fails when it just produces affection. **Compassion** is aimed at cruelty, its far enemy. Its near one is mere grief or sadness, another more subtle idea. **Gladness** is gladness for others over their happiness and is perhaps better called sympathetic joy. It is aimed at envy. Its far enemy is dislike of or boredom with gladness for the happiness of others. Its near enemy is dwelling on your own personal happiness. **Equanimity** involves facing situations with tranquillity, accepting they may be beyond your power to deal with, or that they are not really your concern. This is aimed at distraction and worry. The far enemy is greed and hatred. The near one is indifference. So, these **near enemies** are: attachment to the senses, grief, dwelling on your own happiness, indifference. You can see that this is all to do with the idea of self. Self is the obstacle, with its attachment and craving: the bonds that bind us to dukkha.

Craving can be **for the pleasure of the senses**, but there are other, more subtle cravings. There can be cravings **for existence, for being**. An example would be those religions which offer an eternal soul with identity. Buddhism would see both the craving for sensual pleasure and that for being, as rooted in greed. Craving can also be **for non being or non existence**. An example would be any quasi religious materialistic system. Buddhism would see craving of non being or non existence as rooted in aversion or hatred. You can see how profoundly different this religion is from conventional Western belief systems.

What are you to do as a result of all these ideas? Well, if you want to get further on you have to get to grips with the **Perfecting Qualities**, or **Perfections**. One group of these is: giving, renunciation and aspiration. I have already talked about **giving**. **Renunciation** is at the core of Buddhism. For what does the elimination of dukkha involve if not renunciation? As the Buddha said, "Do you renounce what is not yours? And what is not yours? Mind is not yours. Body is not yours." **Aspiration** is of great practical importance, and reduces this demanding system to one more easily managed. The idea is that you should only attempt what you can realistically do given the stage that you are at. The next Perfection is **virtue**. Next come a group of three: **patience, energy** and **collectedness**. These are the ones required for successful meditation. Finally there are **wisdom, wholesome means** and **truth**: which further along the line will be vital to the search for supermundane wisdom and the attainment of actual reality.

The major tools to enable us to follow the Buddhist path are the seventh and the eighth aspect of the Noble Eightfold Path, mindfulness and concentration, which are to be pursued within the practice of meditation.

The object and effect of **mindfulness** is to, as it were, break the continuity of the mind which manifests itself in a multitude of intrusive thoughts, so that a state of total alert awareness is achieved. This is 'right **concentration**'. It is a state in which subject and object become one.

You could equally call 'right mindfulness' 'right meditation'. In her book Nancy Wilson Ross describes the stages of meditation as observation, then non observation, then participation and finally absorption. She compares absorption to the metaphor of the ocean entering a drop of water.

So, mindfulness is a state in which you are completely absorbed in the moment, in whatever you are doing, being oblivious to anything else. What you are doing could be anything, putting your foot on the ground for example. It could be awareness of an action, of a physical sensation, of a feeling. It could be awareness of a thought: not thinking the thought but being aware of it. You can be mindful when meditating or when you are not meditating. It is noticing and knowing what you are feeling, thinking or doing.

Meditation is a method and state of mental concentration. It involves dealing with the random thoughts that so occupy the mind, to gently let these float away on their own and to stay in the present moment, so that your innate wisdom can manifest itself. There are a number of methods. One is to concentrate on a mantra, a word or phrase. Another is to concentrate on your own breathing without letting that concentration affect it. Another is to follow your thoughts but to stand aside from them as if they were someone else's, so you have complete awareness and yet separateness from them. Meditation can also involve visualisation techniques. Remember that meditation is a means not a goal.

You can't be successful with effort unless you are mindful. And you can't be mindful without concentration. In turn, the mind can't concentrate without loving kindness, generosity and moral conduct. Effort, concentration and mindfulness come together in meditative absorption.

You may, or may not, consider a subject while you are meditating. There are a number of such exercises that are recommended, particularly in the Theravada tradition. For example, you could perform an exercise in dealing with aversion by thinking of those you love most and applying the feeling of loving kindness to them. You could then include in this circle others who are less dear to you, and so on until you include those who you really dislike and then include everyone indiscriminately. So you put yourself in a practical way in the mindset to feel loving kindness for everyone and to pursue your own liberation in a way which does not separate you from the rest of humanity. Or in a meditation on the issue of greed you might consider the decay of a dead body and how that puts the beauty of the body in context, or the passage of tasty food in the gut and its turning into faeces. Another meditation might be to consider the attributes of the Buddha. Another might be a meditation in which you consider your own body, from skin to flesh to bones, considering how transitory it all is. And you may meditate on death. These exercises are but one style of meditation. You might call this type of meditation a medicine for the mind.

Another type of meditation exercise is known as samatha. This involves using an aid on which to concentrate. This might be a colored disc, or the repetition of a word or phrase, or a dwelling on an aspect of your breath. The object is to still your mind and develop calm and concentration.

A higher and most strenuous form of exercise is that of vipassana meditation. This aims to develop insight as well as calm and concentration. Here the idea is that after becoming calm and focused your mind is led on to look at and behind the appearance of things. Whereas in samatha distractions are ignored, here they are objects of a total but detached awareness.

For Buddhists, meditation can lead to an insight into truth. It is in meditation that you can experience an inner and proper understanding of what your head believes. Meditation can, as it were, put flesh on the dry bones of ideas.

At a higher level, meditation can bring an experience of happiness, peace and bliss. Other religions can experience meditation in this way.

At a yet higher level, meditation, for Buddhists, reaches beyond this bliss, through the gateway to ultimate truth and supermundane wisdom.

You can read these paragraphs on meditation again, or perhaps a hundred times. They are a few words, but they describe the most distinctively Buddhist technique. If you become a Buddhist, meditation will be an important part of your daily life.

Buddhism is very conscious of the argument that it is selfish to concentrate on one's own spiritual development and meets it head on. As the Buddha said, how can a person stuck in the mud help pull out another person stuck in the mud? It is also in the nature of Buddhist morality that if you follow it you reduce the sufferings of others. Giving is a good example. The giver benefits by way of good karma and the person given to benefits from the gift and the example. As Buddhist scripture says, "Protecting oneself, one protects others; protecting others, one protects oneself." (*Satispatthana Samyutta No.19 – Discourse on the Foundations of Mindfulness*). Discussions on religion sometimes refer to the Golden Rule. This is the principle of do as you would be done by. Or, in the words of Buddhist scripture, "What is displeasing and disagreeable to me is displeasing and disagreeable to the other too. How can I inflict on another what is displeasing and disagreeable to me?" (*Veludvareyya Sutta, Discourse to the People of Bamboo Gate*).

There is, of course, the problem that this analysis depends on the very idea of **self** that Buddhism wants to eradicate. However, you have to start somewhere, and the elimination of the self belongs to the end of the journey rather than the beginning. Loving kindness is a good example to explain this. Loving kindness can build up to the point where it does not distinguish between one person and another, so that it is not involved with attachment. Eventually it can become not just selfless, but without discrimination.

You should be clear that although there is a great emphasis on what you should not do, **this is not a negative morality**, for Buddhists believe that the best counter to behavior which is to be avoided is to practice the opposite. So, loving kindness is the antidote to acts of harm. Generosity is the counter to taking what is not given. Contentment is the counter to sexual conduct which harms someone else or yourself. Truthfulness is the counter to false speech. And mindfulness or awareness is the counter to the attractions of intoxication.

Buddhism believes that **intention is paramount**, that the motivation behind an act is more important than the act itself. It is possible to have situations where a morally good intention requires a normally repugnant act. Punishing an evildoer might be an example, although the Buddha is said to have refused to become king because kings deal out capital punishment. Anyway, don't get the idea that this means that Buddhism isn't that interested in good deeds, far from it. Buddhism just thinks that we should start with the mind because that is where the deeds flow from.

In fact, the whole of Buddhist morality, Precepts, Abidings, Perfections, and all, is aimed at developing a morally good mind, which then just naturally thinks and acts in a skilful/wholesome/beneficial/good way.

As a lay Buddhist you will have respect and reverence for **teachers**. Buddhism emphasises that the path to spiritual improvement almost invariably requires a teacher who has more experience than yourself.

You will venerate the Buddha, and perhaps other Buddhas, often in the form of the Buddha images found in Buddhist temples and homes. You may venerate relics. These may be relics in the sense of 'relics of reminder' such as images of the Buddha. This is not image worship but an acknowledgment of the Buddha's qualities and works. You will bow, and perhaps prostrate yourself before them, an act of humility, to be performed with precision, grace and mindfulness, honoring the Buddha and his way to enlightenment. You may light candles as you express your desire to be enlightened and help others. You may light incense, thinking how virtue might pervade you like the smell of incense. You may offer flowers, thinking how their short life is ended and how they will wither, as your body will one day. You may offer food and water, with the desire that the Buddha be honored before you have some. Your worship may be at home or in a temple. The Buddha had an infinite number of previous lives, and you may dwell on the details of some of these. **The Buddhist form of worship is called Puja**. It often involves chanting. The chants are reminders of different aspects of Buddhist teaching. You should remember the purpose behind all these acts of worship, and that one of the Three Fetters tying us to continued existence is infatuation with ritual. For many religions the essence of ritual lies in the doing of it. For Buddhists it lies in the intention behind it.

Remember, as a Buddhist you will not be subject to some authority which takes particular issues and tells you what is right and what is wrong. You have the framework of the Precepts. Within that, you have to make **moral decisions** for yourself. The Buddha said you must find out for yourself. As a Buddhist you will have compassion for all living beings, even cockroaches, all the more so since you will have been non human in past lives. You may be a vegetarian, particularly if you are a Western Buddhist, but not necessarily. Indeed, in a Tibetan tradition there is the view that the animal being eaten, and prayed for by those eating it, may by its fate secure a better birth next time. You will believe in the protection of the environment. There might be circumstances of judicial punishment and defensive war in which you might come to the conclusion that overall compassion overrides the prohibition on the taking of life. Generally, Buddhists have not resorted to force to defend themselves. Abortion should in principle be avoided, but is not absolutely prohibited. Your view would depend upon applying compassion to the particular circumstances. For Buddhists, morality is concerned with what you do to others, so suicide is not a moral issue. In practice it is a foolish act, which will attract bad karma and be a bit pointless. Encouraging someone to commit suicide is a moral question, and breaks the precepts.

Like all religions, Buddhism has its **festivals and celebrations of life events**. Traditionally not weddings. Those are considered a purely civil matter although some 'modern' Buddhists have Buddhist style wedding ceremonies.

Death is a much more serious matter. You will believe that your state of mind at death will influence how you are reborn. You will be pleased to have someone, perhaps a monk, recite scriptures to you in your last hours. Monks will conduct your funeral service, chanting scripture about how life is imper-manent, and giving a talk. Your relatives will arrange a memorial service. You will be cremated. If you are a great teacher, your body will be reduced to relics and distributed to various centers.

It's now time to talk about the groupings within Buddhism, and the ideas they may involve. It may be helpful to lead into this by considering the monks and nuns and their rules and life, and then how Buddhism spread, and where it is most practiced now.

The Buddhist community of men and women comprises monks, nuns and lay people. The word **sangha** (group) applies to the whole community, but is often used to mean just the monks and nuns. Nuns are far less numerous than monks, except in Taiwan, and their lives differ in certain respects. So for the sake of simplicity I will limit this paragraph to **monks**. The job of the monks is to preserve and preach the dharma for the benefit of the lay people. In turn, the lay people have the job of supporting the monks. The monks have few possessions: robe, bowl, razor, needle, belt, water strainer, and medicine if required. This is not to say that monasteries as institutions cannot be wealthy, directly or indirectly, which has at times been a problem.

In the Theravada tradition the monks go out daily with their bowls, not so much begging as giving the laity the opportunity to make a gift of food, which is then taken back to the monastery. If it's meat, so be it, though sensitive laypeople may avoid such an offering

As you would expect, monks have a more detailed and demanding list of precepts or rules. Chucking out rules are: no sex, no killing humans (no surprise there!), no taking of anything not given to you, no falsely claiming spiritual attainment (unless you are mad, or just conceited or ignorant). Those are just the chucking out rules. Monks are subject to many other rules. One strain of Buddhism had no less than 227 rules for its monks.

It is important to appreciate that schools of thought within Buddhism have formed on quite a different basis from those in, say, Christianity. For Buddhist monks, formal differences centered on the particular set of rules followed in the monastery, not on differences of doctrine. It was what you did that mattered most, not your views. There might have been a strong tendency for monks of a particular order to have the same doctrinal views. But such views were seldom the cause of any original splitting off. Monks in the same monastery could have different doctrinal tendencies but they would interpret them in a way which avoided schism. And splitting off because of differences about rules and liturgies was not considered schism. That is not to say that at different times and places there was not hostility between different schools of thought, something the Buddha would have disapproved of.

Buddhism is **a missionary religion**, less so than some others, but nonetheless one which seeks converts, something deep within its history. Remember, the Buddha initially had but a few followers, who he sent out to take the message to others. On a one-to-one daily basis, someone further along the path to enlightenment than another has a duty to give moral guidance, but by example.

Let's have a brief **geographical survey of Buddhism**. It flourishes in Sri Lanka, Thailand, Laos and Cambodia, (where the sangha was greatly damaged by communist rule) and Burma. Also in China, Taiwan, Korea and Vietnam. Also in Tibet, Mongolia, Bhutan and in Ladakh and Sikkim in India. Also in Nepal. Also in Japan. Otherwise, not very much in its historical home, India. Islam and Hinduism put paid to that, although a revival began in India in 1956 and there may now be ten million converts there. It is an increasingly popular religion in the West. Estimates of **numbers** vary. A mean figure of about 500 million is suggested by adherents.com

As to Buddhist **scriptures**, it is said that the Buddha was born in about 485 BCE and he reputedly lived for about eighty years. It is thought that the first records of what he said were written down in 29 BCE in a Sri Lanka monastery. In the scriptures are accounts of what the Buddha said, together with stories of his previous lives, and various philosophical teachings. Mahayana Buddhism relies partly on other scriptures which are attributed to the Buddha but which, it is said, were initially hidden, and produced later.

The **two main schools of Buddhism** are Theravada and Mahayana. Everything which is not Theravada, is Mahayana. Indeed, Mahayana could be better described as a movement rather than a school and itself covers a number of schools including the Lotus School, Pure Land School, the school known as Zen in Japan and Ch'an in China and Soen in Korea, and Tibetan Buddhism.

Theravada Buddhism is dominant in Sri Lanka, Thailand, Laos, Cambodia and Burma. This is the most conservative grouping of Buddhism, in that compared with any other group it has had less change since ancient times. The word 'Theravada' means Doctrine of the Elders. It is a monastic tradition. Its implication was that you weren't going to get to Nirvana unless you had reached the stage where you were a monk or nun, and that they had all the authority when it came to religious matters. However, in the last century lay people have taken more important positions in many Theravada dominated communities, the authority of the monks is thereby diminished and deciding for yourself is more of a reality.

Within both the Theravada and the Mahayana tradition a lot of emphasis is put on '**merit making**'. This involves acting in a way which produces good karma. Yet another Buddhist list is the Ten Ways of Making Merit, some of which are old friends. They are: giving, virtue, meditation, reverence, helpfulness, dedication of merits to others, rejoicing in others' merits, listening to dhamma, teaching the dhamma, and straightening out one's views in accordance with the dhamma. The reason you will want to make merit is so you will be happy now and in the future. It may get you reborn again as a human, or as a god. However, if you wish to advance towards Nirvana you will have to eventually perform merit making without having the idea of self in your head, an idea much more profound than mere selflessness. Within Theravada it is common for young men to become monks for short periods as a merit making activity.

One aspect of merit making is often (wrongly) described as the **transfer of merit**. Humans cannot transfer merit, but Buddhism has a sleight of hand which almost amounts to the same thing. This is founded on the idea that intention is all. So, I do a good act and get merit, I then wish that others could share in this, and as a result I get more merit. You see my act and empathise with it, wish you had done it, and so you get merit from that. I do one act, I get two lots of merit, and you get one. For Buddhists who are not into the more intellectual aspect of their religion, regarding Nirvana as many, many lives hence, and more concerned with an advantageous rebirth, perhaps even in a Heaven, this is a useful and important way of accumulating spiritual cash. Even those too poor to give can in this way gain the merit of giving.

If you go to Thailand you may see popular merit making: groups of people, even a whole village perhaps, with bells and drums and shouting, to let you know you may join in or just empathise and be happy that they are happy.

Mahayana Buddhism, in its various forms, is dominant in China, Taiwan, Korea and Vietnam, Tibet, Mongolia, Bhutan, Ladakh and Sikkim in India, and in Nepal and Japan.

As I have said, Mahayana Buddhism is that which is not Theravada Buddhism. Mahayana Buddhism is complex and varied, and to reduce it to simplicity is difficult. Christopher Humphries, writing for Penguin in the 1950s, compared Theravada to the hub of a wheel from which the spokes of Mahayana projected. So the best approach may be to survey a number of Mahayana ideas which occur in one or other of its various schools.

Theravada's enlightened being is an Arhat, who enters Nirvana on enlightenment. Mahayana has another, major, idea – that of **the bodhisattva**. The bodhisattva chooses another path to Nirvana, that which leads eventually to becoming a Buddha, albeit after an uncountable number of lives. Mahayana sees this as a superior path. Following it, the bodhisattva remains here when, had he taken the Arhat route, he could be in Nirvana. While he so remains here he devotes himself to helping others attain enlightenment. Some suggest that that is the bodhisattva's prime motivation. The bodhisattva is able to appear in all realms, of humans, animals, ghosts, gods, and Hell-beings, and can assume the forms of animals or human beings. To some Buddhists the world may be full of bodhisattvas in disguise.

Another Mahayana idea, which may appeal to you, and certainly has appealed to a lot of people, is that **bodhisattvas can use their own merit for the benefit of those who haven't enough**. Furthermore, these beings can be contacted through prayer and meditation, to solicit this help.

Linked in with these ideas is a variation on the idea of the Buddha. The **Three Body Doctrine** sees the Buddha as having three forms. One is his historical body. One is the Dhamma, the principle of eternal truth. The third is known as the bliss body, reflecting the situation of the Buddha in having reached that goal.

Moving on from this, the **Lotus School** of Mahayana developed the idea that **everyone can and will become a Buddha**. Some may be a lot further back on the track than others, but they can begin their journey from wherever they are, although they will need the skill and guidance of a teacher. This cuts across the standard Mahayana view that there can only be one Buddha per world at a time and makes Buddhahood easy.

Another idea of the Lotus School is that the Buddha is everlasting; he has always existed and always will. His birth, death and enlightenment were just a means to educate the deluded. In other words **they see the Buddha as a sort of super-human reality**, outside Samsara, like Nirvana.

Another very popular Mahayana idea is that **we all have an inner Buddha nature**, and that the way we can all become Buddhas is by uncovering this nature and becoming what we truly are.

So the Theravada tradition emphasises one's own liberation while Mahayana can be seen as less elitist, leading all people to enlightenment, offering accessibility to all, religious and lay people alike. Mahayana calls itself the 'Greater Vehicle', being like a huge wagon carrying many to a release from rebirth. One line of thought is that we can all become bodhisattvas and that those who have achieved this condition can help others on their way and that perhaps we can all become Buddhas. Another line sees the bodhisattva and buddha path, and the arhat path as alternatives. Mahayanists have criticised the Theravada approach as hindering spiritual growth for the many. Mahayana emphasises the fact that different people are at different stages of spiritual development and that each needs the method best suited to his or her stage. It has also been said that Theravada emphasizes the humanity of Buddha, while Mahayana emphasises the Buddha-nature of humanity.

Tibetan Buddhism was for centuries hidden from the West but this was changed by the Chinese invasion in 1959 and the flight of the Dalai Lama and his entourage to India. Some Tibetan teachers have accepted a new role as the carriers of their religion to the West. Tibetan Buddhism has a wide range of practice and teaching, both Theravada and Mahayana, and even fragments of Tibet's shamanistic folk religion known as Bon.

Tibetan Buddhism has four main traditions or lineages. These are the Yellow Hats, headed by the Dalai Lama, The Red Hats, the Ancients and the Sankyapa. The Yellow Hats provide the formal governing body of Tibetan Buddhism, but the schools aren't regarded as more or less important but just as different. The Yellow Hats have a reputation for greater erudition. The famous Tibetan Book of the Dead is particularly associated with the Ancients.

Tibetan Buddhism tends to be preoccupied with the relationship between life and death. There is a non Theravada idea that there are intervening states in our life which are called **bardos** (bardo means a transition or gap). These bardos are opportunities for us to be liberated. The trick is to recognise them and use them. Tibetan Buddhism has teachings which are keys or tools for this. The most significant bardo is that between death and rebirth. After all, there's no difficulty in recognising this one. How you deal with this gap will affect whether and how you are reborn or whether you are liberated. Our whole life is a preparation for this great opportunity. The idea is that the qualities of buddhahood which lie within each of us are veiled by our body and that when the body is discarded these qualities are fully displayed. If we recognise them and surrender to them we will be liberated. The problem is that most of us will be unprepared for this and won't recognise the situation for what it is. Instead of surrendering, we will withdraw, and hold onto, grasp, the familiar, lose the chance of liberation, and have to be reborn. The process to rebirth is on average forty-nine days and not less than a week. The bardo teachings give us methods to try to ensure that in this period after death we seize the chance of liberation or at least secure a good rebirth. There is also a set of practices for the living to perform for the dead during this period, to help the dead to make the most of the opportunity. These practices are set out in The Tibetan Book of the Dead. It is said that reading from this book to a dying person will put them in the best frame of mind to achieve either liberation or a good rebirth. Much may depend upon your last thoughts. Methods are also used to seek and recognise liberation opportunities in life.

Tibetan Buddhism has its own emphasis on meditation. It uses the mantra, spoken aloud, believing that certain sacred sounds can establish inner vibrations which open your mind to higher experiences. This involves the ear, heart and mind, and its power is only released to the initiated. Nancy Wilson Ross quotes the metaphor of the magnifying glass concentrating forces which already exist. Another method is concentration on sacred diagrams or mandalas. Another is visualisation. These methods are used in conjunction with one another.

Tibetan Buddhism is entwined with **Tantric Buddhism**. This is a form of Mahayana which originated in India comparatively late, in the second half of the first millennium CE and which always coexists with other, older, forms of Mahayana. While it also exists in the Far East, it is mainly prominent in Tibet and Nepal.

Tibetan Tantrism focuses on the view of the universe as a continuous fabric. Matter and spirit, things that are conscious and which are not conscious, individual humans and the forces of space and time: all are interwoven, interdependent, part of a great continuity. These forces work in the human being just as they work in the universe at large. And so they can be transformed by the power of your mind, through the practices of meditation. For Tibetan Buddhism, Samsara and Nirvana aren't different realms, they are the same. It's our misperception that makes them appear different.

Tibetan Tantrism adopts the Mahayana idea of the universal Buddha nature in us all. And its effect is to offer a quick route to buddhahood.

Tantra, in its various forms, has a particular attitude to what Buddhism regards as evil or defilements. Everything shares in the Buddha nature, so what needs to be done is to find how defilements share in the Buddha nature so they can be transformed into their own true nature. For example, greed can be seen as being ultimately founded on a longing for ultimate bliss. Followers seek to understand the interdependence of all things, and discover their Buddha nature.

Tibetan Buddhism sees Tantra as the pinnacle of the Buddha's teaching. Unlike other forms of Buddhism, Tantra is esoteric, and taught only to initiates, so a teacher or Lama is essential. This is because there are dangers of misinterpretation. Tibetan Buddhism is sometimes referred to as Lamaism.

That Tantra has come in for criticism, demonstrates the dangers of interpretation. At times and places it has aimed at supernatural powers, albeit as a step to spiritual progress. In particular it is sometimes associated with the practice of acts, sexual and otherwise, which would usually be regarded by Buddhists as unwholesome.

Another major school of Buddhism is known as **Cha'n** in China and **Zen** in Japan. Cha'n came first historically, but I will refer to and concentrate on the school here as Zen.

This school, which developed one thousand years after Buddha's death, was founded on the view that Buddhism had become too attached to its scriptures and that the best way of understanding Buddha's message was to look inwards, in meditation, to one's own heart and mind. The authority of the Buddha is used to justify this intuitive approach. Zen saw itself as going back to Buddhism's roots. "Look within, thou art the Buddha", the Buddha had said. Zen's object is to get rid of the thoughts which attach you to the world, and see into your own Buddha nature. This way to enlightenment can take a long time, or it can happen suddenly. It emphasises the need for a teacher. Different techniques have been used, ranging from the teacher interrogating the pupil to the teacher beating the pupil.

Let's go back to the idea that everything is an endless flow of energies and appearances, and that everything is interwoven in a great continuity. Zen says we can connect directly to that through our own nature. But how to do it? Zen has a dim view of the powers of the rational mind, which divides 'this' from 'that'. Instead, we have to tap our deepest intuitional faculties.

It's worth recalling the conversation between the ancient Buddhist master, Bodhidharma, and the Chinese Emperor Wu-ti (set out in the *Anthology of the Patriarchal Hall*). Recounting everything he has himself done for Buddhism the Emperor asks what merit he has earned thereby. "No merit whatsoever" is the reply (a denial of works, forms and rituals). What is the most important principle of Buddhism? "Vast emptiness and nothing holy" says Bodhidharma, (referring to the void, the emptiness that has a positive quality, within which lies life's true meaning). "Who are you who thus replies to me", says the Emperor, as well he might. "I do not know": end of conversation, leaving the Emperor with a typical Zen (Cha'n in this case) riddle.

Since all people inherently have Buddha nature, we only have to break through the barriers of delusion that embrace us. This requires a properly directed and executed effort. Zen has two methods of achieving this object: Rinzai and Soto. **Rinzai** uses the famous **koan** method. This is designed to make the mind break out of its reliance on intellectual understanding, into an intuitive understanding. A well-known illustration is the pupil who was told to show the sound of one hand clapping. Eventually he was able to say to his master, "I was able to collect no more, so I reached the soundless sound." **Soto** concentrates on silent sitting. These methods can be intermixed, the choice of method being largely a matter of personal character and preference.

Attachment to this attainment should be avoided. If enlightenment comes it comes, if it doesn't it doesn't. If you think you're going to get something out of it, you're already heading in the wrong direction, and won't find your true place in the universe: the ego is truly tenacious. There is no goal. Only a process like that which leads to a ripe fruit dropping from the tree.

The **Pure Land School** has been very popular for understandable reasons. This idea is that an individual Buddha, by virtue of his enormous karmic merit, can produce a separate world which is a sort of paradise. Furthermore, individuals can seek to be reborn into such a world which, being pure, offers an easy road to enlightenment. Methods involve reciting a Buddha's name and sometimes visualising the Buddha. In these ways the individual, by association, absorbs some of the merit of the Buddha. This evasion of the usual rules of karma is explained by the infinite compassion of the Buddha. Understandably, those who believe this devote themselves to the veneration of and meditation upon the respective Buddha. This is a Buddhism of faith. On death the Buddha's name is invoked, and hopefully that is followed by the desired rebirth. Daily chanting reinforces the faith. A popular Buddha for this purpose is the Buddha Amitabha, one of the many Buddhas of the Mahayana tradition. Some forms of Japanese Pure Land Buddhism don't involve meditation at all. The Pure Land School accepted the Zen approach – both depended on seeking your own Buddha nature – but saw it as too rigorous to be practicable. Many would not be helped by it. Something simpler was needed for average people. Pure Land is a simple system of faith and salvation. The Zen school adopted some Pure Land methods, notably the recitation of Buddha names.

You may well come across schools of Buddhism influenced by the thirteenth-century Japanese monk, **Nichiren**. These devote themselves to the Buddhist text known as the Lotus Sutra, the very title of which is venerated, often by chanting the name. They believe that the Buddhahood is beginningless and that all Buddhas are emanations of the one Buddha. Also that the Buddha is present in everything, including us. As for Nirvana, nirvanic existance *is* the Buddha. Thus we can open our innate Buddha nature in this world, and such enlightenment can be instantaneous. Nichiren claimed his views to be the truth and condemned other schools as false, an unusual view within Buddhism. Nichiren devotees often have a missionary attitude

There is a school of Buddhism that has a different idea altogether. This is the **Yogakara** school which believes that only the mind is real. Only mind exists and this consciousness is self-subsisting and doesn't depend on external objects. The division between subject and object is just a product of ignorance, and the school seeks to use methods of yoga to achieve an insight and realization which will lead to Nirvana. Some Yogacara ideas have influenced other Buddhist thought. Google the word and you will bring up Western yoga sites.

This is not a historical survey of Buddhism. Nor is it a geographic survey of which Buddhists believe what where. It necessarily skates over the great and detailed subtleties of Buddhist philosophical debate. However, an introduction is an introduction and it is in the Buddhist tradition to distinguish the way to understanding from understanding itself. Do you like the ideas or don't you? That's the question. Answer that: and if you do, you can then direct yourself to the appropriate corner of Buddhism.

So, **do any of these ideas attract you?** Some of them offer the chance of a quicker result than working your way to Nirvana through thousands of lives. Some offer something close to the idea of forgiveness, a dismantling of the iron laws of karma. Some introduce the idea of faith rather than doing and seeing the result. Some introduce the idea of praying for salvation. Some offer a multitude of figures to pray to. Some almost flirt with the idea of soul.

If you live in the West you are likely in practice to have a wider range of Buddhist institutions available to you than if you live in a country where Buddhism is a traditional religion. For example, in the UK there are Theravada communities in London, Hertfordshire, Northumberland and Sussex; there are communities of all four Tibetan traditions; there are Japanese Soto centers in Northumberland and Berkshire.

As a Western Buddhist, if that is your choice, you may be some distance in your daily spiritual life from the Tibetan exiles reciting invocations to various bodhisattvas or Buddhas over prayer beads, giving offerings to those qualified to recite scriptures on their behalf, or turning prayer wheels.

You will be unlikely to associate Buddhism with nationalism, as has happened in Sri Lanka.

You may become a member of the Friends of Western Buddhist Order, founded in 1968, which not only is active in the West, but also has endeavored to help a Buddhist revival among the Dalits, the so-called Untouchables of India.

You may struggle with the tendency of Western culture to ideology. You may be engaged with social and ecological issues and how you wrap all that up with Buddhism. Some Buddhists today argue that Buddhism is an ally and partner of science. Some will say that you should bear in mind that the Buddha didn't aim to reform the world but to enable people to leave it as well as to properly live in it.

You may use two currently popular phrases: **letting go**, and **loving yourself**. On both a philosophical level and a personal level, Buddhism represents the ultimate letting go. And loving yourself truly is a Buddhist gateway to loving everything indiscriminately and transcending yourself.

There is a contrast between the simplicity of the Buddha's try-it-and-see and the mass of theory that his various followers have built up over thousands of years. However, remember that for

Buddhists, absolute truth is inconceivable. So, in Buddhism, there can be no fixed dogma, only provisional and partial teachings, which are aimed at the capacities of the audiences being addressed. If you decide to adhere to a particular school of Buddhist teaching it doesn't mean you are rejecting any of the other streams of thought. It just means that you have decided that the ideas you have embraced are the best for you.

Remember the words of the Dalai Lama. "I believe there is an important distinction to be made between religion and spirituality. Religion I take to be concerned with faith in the claims of one faith tradition or another. Spirituality I take to be concerned with those qualities of human spirit ... which bring happiness both to self and others. While ritual and prayer, along with questions of Nirvana and salvation, are directly connected to religious faith, these inner qualities need not be however". (Dalai Lama *Ethics for the New Millenium*, Little Brown and Company 1999, page 22).

You don't have to be religious to be good, but to be good (or skilful or whatever you want to call it) is the first experimental step in the Buddhist religion. When dying the Buddha said, "Work out your own salvation with diligence. Be lamps unto yourself". Ignore the talk and get on with the walk. That would be the Buddha's advice.

Chapter 11

A Note on Chinese Religions

Confucianism, Taoism and Chinese Buddhism have developed and exist within a context of Chinese popular religion and traditional culture and you need to know a little about that.

There are considerable **differences between Western and Chinese thinking**. In the West there is more emphasis on materialism, and also on individual rights and freedom. Chinese culture puts more emphasis on humanism rather than materialism, and on human responsibility rather than individual freedom and differentiation. Another distinction is that the West has for long taken the view that the secular and the religious are best kept separate, whereas the traditional Chinese view was not to intentionally distinguish between such matters. In other words, not to compartmentalize philosophy, ethics, education, politics, religion, economics and the other human sciences. There is also a tendency in Chinese culture to be relaxed about mixing one belief system with another, and for an individual to be able to commit to more than one doctrine. Confucianism, Taoism and Buddhism have thus had a considerable effect on one another in China's history, despite times of conflict between their followers, and all have been affected by and have affected popular religion.

The traditional Chinese universe consists of Earth and Tian/ Sky/Heaven and Humankind. And everything in it is made of **qi**. This is the vital energy of which everything consists, and which operates under the influence of Yin-Yang, of which I will say more later. Thus, everything belongs in a way to the same family, being one substance, and identically subject to the principles of the universe.

Chinese traditionally believe in a **spirit world**. This shares the same substance, qi, as our material world. This is not a

Heaven/Hell world. It is much like our own world, run by a bureaucracy that can be petitioned, and even bribed with gifts. It is populated by gods, ghosts and our ancestors. The bureaucratic functions are undertaken by various gods. Each Chinese residential area has its own god, who will have his own temple or shrine and who will be processed round town on special occasions. The gods have to be looked after, by means of our rituals, prayers and gifts. In return they have to respond to prayers which are within their area of authority. There are some gods who operate outside the bureaucracy, with their own source of authority. Examples are the god of good fortune, the god of prosperity and the god of longevity. Attention to the gods has little to do with religious thoughts and everything to do with worldly advantage. A god who fails to give benefit may find himself neglected.

Traditionally, Chinese religion believes that we have **two souls**. The **po soul** is associated with the body. After death it sinks into the earth and dissipates with the flesh. It is important that the po soul finds its way to the underworld and may need help from the living to do that. If it does not, it may become a ghost and may roam the world causing trouble.

The **hun soul** is the ethereal soul and ascends into the spirit world. The hun dissipates after about seven to nine generations. So when we die we continue to live as spirits, but our Chinese souls are not immortal. From this you will appreciate the Chinese traditional concern about how to achieve immortality. It is possible for a hun soul to become a god, a promotion as a result of an exemplary life. The family altar is an important part of the traditional Chinese dwelling house, and the ancestors are there venerated in the form of inscribed ancestral tablets. An untended and angry ancestor is not a good idea.

You need to appreciate that for the Chinese our **ancestors** don't just live in the past, they live now. They give us a sense of continuity: we ourselves will be part of them in the future. Our life is just one link in a long chain. This is a different way to the Western way of looking at continuity and eternity. We owe everything to our ancestors who have, as it were, bequeathed our body to us. Our filial piety is due to them. So, regular sacrifice to the ancestors may be usual as a spiritual and moral reunion. There has also been a belief that this communication and respect can bring benefits to the spirits and blessings to the living. A family must look after its own ancestors. The celestial bureaucrats may be petitioned for their benefit. Both Confucianism and Taoism are set within these traditional beliefs. Confucianism, other than in its respect for ancestors pays less attention to the afterlife. Taoism has more concern about it, as you will see.

The Cultural Revolution involved a war against religion in all its forms. But China is experiencing **a revival of traditional religious beliefs,** whether Confucian, Taoist, Buddhist or by way of popular religion, all of which are alive and well in Chinese communities abroad.

Chapter 12

Confucianism

To consider Confucianism you will have come to the conclusions:

- that spirit exists,
- that there are universal values and that goodness is a principle of the universe,
- that you live in some way after death.

Confucianism is an ancient system which in its day dominated China and then greatly influenced Vietnam, Korea and Japan. What we call Confucianism is not so called in East Asia. The word used there can perhaps be best translated as 'the tradition of Scholars'. Confucius, over time, came to be seen by Chinese scholars as the epitome of their type, the sage teacher, the preeminent one of them. The West, attuned to systems involving founders of revelatory religions, often seems to see Confucius as such a creator of a religion. And indeed there have been periods in the past when Confucius was worshipped as a sort of god. However, Confucius, who lived from 551 to 479 BCE, considered that he was transmitting an old established culture rather than setting up a new religion. There is no central body in charge of Confucian thinking. There are different schools of thought, with ancient roots, yet being developed by Confucian thinkers, and adapting to changing circumstances. The present stage of Confucianism is known as Modern New Confucianism, and the main schools of thought are called Modern New Idealism and Modern New Rationalism. In this chapter I am much indebted to the works of Professor Xinzhong Yao.

A question often raised is whether Confucianism is a philosophy or a religion. An answer is that it can be either. More of this later.

I have already spoken of differences which can make it difficult for Westerners to understand Chinese religious thinking. Another major problem for a Westerner wishing to understand Confucianism arises from the difficulty of translating certain words. I will try to reduce that problem by using the Chinese word for certain ideas rather than an English word. Just one example may explain.

Through the ages an important aspect of the Confucian view of existence has been the idea of '**Tian**'. In Chinese the word literally means 'sky'. Conventionally, 'Tian' is translated into English as 'Heaven'. That word inevitably picks up Western cultural ideas of what 'Heaven' is, and so can give an incorrect idea of the meaning for Confucianism.

The Confucian universe consists of Tian, Earth and Humanity. Within Confucianism there has been little consensus as to exactly what Tian is, but there have been a lot of views. Here they are.

- The destination of our ancestors.
- Some supreme being which orders existence (an idea which has not survived to the modern world).
- The supreme judge and sanction of human behavior.
- The source of morality, the moral imperative, the foundation of 'ought'.
- The universal principle.
- Ultimate reality.
- Nature.
- Natural Law.
- A transcendental power which harmonizes the physical and the non physical.
- Something which is essentially good, and the source of goodness.
- Something which relates and responds to human behavior, or something which does not do that.

- The origin of the world, the inner nature of all things, that which brings the world into being and by which the world runs its course, that being called 'Principle' by some Confucian teachers.
- The innate heart/mind in us.
- In a more general sense, that which determines the course of human life.

You will already begin to appreciate how there is argument as to whether Confucianism is a religion or a philosophy, for that will depend upon which schools of Confucian thought adhere to which selection of the above.

Equally you can appreciate the disadvantage of calling Tian 'Heaven'. What are a Westerner's first thoughts on seeing that word? Paradise, and the question of what happens after death. Well, Confucianism isn't going to give you much enlightenment about that. The Chinese spiritual tradition has always been more interested in the effect of the physical/spiritual interplay on life in this world rather than in the next. When asked about the spirit world, Confucius said that what was needed was to concentrate on how to behave here.

Confucianism deals with how these three aspects, Tian, Earth and Humanity, fit and work together. It is in their nature to be in harmony. Tian generates and has created life, Earth nourishes it, but it is Humanity that can perfect the relationship. Humankind is the central factor. Humanity can be educated and perfected, and can transform the world. And this is how we can find eternal meaning in our brief lives.

It is that perfecting that Confucianism aims at. That's what the **'Way'** is about. The 'Way' is the translation of the word 'Dao', or 'Tao'. There is a Way of Heaven, a Way of Earth and a Way of Humans. There is no clear line to be drawn between these; they are so closely related to one another. We need to find what the Way is, and to follow it, to restore the harmony of the world and indeed of the universe. It is our individual responsibility to practice the Way in our personal life.

To some extent we are limited by fate. The Way is the source of the meaning and value of human life. However, to some extent, whether it prevails or falls into disuse is a matter of destiny. Within the framework of destiny, the ordering of Earth's affairs by Tian, we have to find and practice the Way. Confucius said, "If I am understood at all, it is, perhaps, by Heaven (Tian)" (*Analects* 14:35: in this chapter I use the translation of D.C.Lau). There is a belief in the justice of Tian. We are subject to fate. Our task, within that, is to fulfill our mission, the duties that our life has given us.

You will note that this is not a religion for those who would like to believe they will meet their pet dog in Heaven or in another earthly life. There is no reincarnation and only humans can relate to Tian.

You will also note the humanistic emphasis of the religion. The future isn't in the hands of an omnipotent God and the balance between Tian and Earth, and a better life is, to a significant extent, in the hands of humans.

Thus the object of life is to fully develop your own nature, which will put you in harmony with the universe. Someone who achieves this is referred to as a '**sage**'. In principle, everyone has the capacity to become a sage. Some Confucians believe that one who has achieved sagehood can share in Tian's function to coordinate the universe.

Of the Confucian **virtues** the most important is '**Ren**'. This has a wide meaning. It could be translated as 'love, goodness, benevolence, kindness', and other such words. The most accepted translation is 'humaneness'. This virtue deals mainly with how people relate to one another. To it, Confucianism attaches two other ideas. One is that of reciprocity, of the Golden Rule, of not doing to others what you would not want done to yourself. The other is the idea of '**Zhong**', roughly translated as 'loyalty'. This means that 'One who wishes to establish oneself must first establish others; one who wished to be prominent oneself must first help others to be prominent'. This is how to follow the Way, and as you can see it involves fitting your own self in with that of others. Other Confucian virtues are right-eousness, propriety and wisdom, but it is humaneness which is the principal one, and which runs through the others. Humaneness is perhaps best spelled humanness. How to be good is how to be human and vice versa.

Which brings us to 'Li'. Li has to do with the How of finding and following the Way. It is yet another word not easy to translate. In Confucianism's earlier days it could mean ritual. It could mean the rules of propriety or, to use a currently more fashionable term, appropriate behavior. It could mean a moral code. Subsequently its meaning broadened out as differing schools of thought developed in Confucianism. Now it includes the basic principles of the universe, which underlie the universe's rules, including those of morality. In practical terms Li reduces to proper conduct between parties. With a description of that complexity you will not be surprised that this is a word I will keep in its Chinese form.

The Confucian idea is that if we follow Li we will be following the Way. If we do that, the world will be peaceful and orderly. Harmony will reach through our personal lives and through society. This is more than just the seeking of practical advantage. It is a spiritual and moral union of the world of spirit and that of matter. Confucius was once reminded of the need to pray to the spirits. He first asked if there was such a thing as prayer, and then said, "In that case I have long been offering my prayers."(*Analects* 7:35). In other words, prayer was action, the pursuit of the Way. On another occasion Confucius said, "When you have offended against Heaven [Tian], there is nowhere you can turn to in your prayers" (*Analects* 3:13).

We had better have a brief look at how Confucianism deals

with Li in its practical **social context**. Confucianism takes the family as the basic social unit, and so sees it as society's cornerstone. If the family setup is right, so will society be. Within the family the relationships are, in order of significance, parent and child, husband and wife, sibling and sibling. Beyond the family is the relationship between ruler and ruled. "If only everyone loved his parents and treated his elders with deference, the whole world would be at peace" (Book of Mengzi 46:28), said the Confucian sage Mengzi (also known as Mencius, 372-289 BCE). For the purpose of an explanation of what Confucianism might offer in the present day we will gloss over its historical disregard for the place of women. The secret is for everyone to cultivate themselves and their virtues and so to fulfill their roles in the family and in society. This will produce a happy and healthy society of happy citizens. Historically, Confucianism was used by China's rulers to underwrite their position. Yet Confucianism held that only those with love and affection in their heart were entitled to rule and that only humane and virtuous rulers could make the state prosperous.

To Western ears the word **ritual** may have negative connotations. It may help you to appreciate its significance within Confucianism if you think about what Western society might term 'performative utterance'. A good example lies within the wedding ceremony, and the significance of uttering the words 'I do'. They are words of ritual which make something happen. Such acts form part of the fabric of society. Many of our daily acts, shaking hands and so on, are acts of ritual, and are deeply part of how we deal with one another. Go through a day thinking about whether what you do, whether replying to an invitation or buying a round of drinks, is ritualistic, and you may feel that Confucius was onto something.

Next, a glance at how Confucianism deals with the issue of **good and evil**. For Confucians the Way is good. What harmonizes with it is good. What obstructs it is bad. Evil isn't a separate force, it is just what gets in the way of good and the good of the Way. It is the attribute of actions which are not in conformity with the Way.

However, Confucians have two main lines of thought about the **relationship of humans to goodness**. One tradition thinks that humans are innately good. They just need to develop themselves and their true nature. Others consider that good behavior is not innate in us, and that the task of Confucianism is to take humans' nature, and by conscious action to harmonize it with the Way. Confucianism has had various ideas about humanity's moral nature, but these are the two major ideas that have passed down to the present.

You can see from this how important education and social rules of behavior have been to Confucianism.

A central idea of Confucianism is the desirability of **harmony and unity** within the universe. This involves a unity of humanity with some sort of universal principle. To the extent that this unity is obtained, humans can move to a higher plane, achieve a transcendent state. That is, to become a sage, to achieve a state of consciousness of being 'one body with Heaven and Earth'. This is Confucianism's view of immortality. Everyone has it in them to achieve this and if it is done it has to be done in this life. So it is on this life that we must concentrate. The theme of unity, of connection, runs through our lives. We need to harmonize our inner virtue with the external merit in which it should manifest itself. We need to harmonize the moral law with the natural order, for they are fundamentally the same thing. We need to achieve a situation where knowledge and action are united and become more than the sum of their parts. If we can do all this we will have achieved humaneness, which is an aspect of the universal principle. This all has to be done on the broad canvas of fate, fate being a context rather than a straightjacket. From the point of view of humanity as a whole, such conduct has the potential to bring together the spiritual and the secular, and to unify the nature and the destiny of humanity. So, the Confucian concentration on the self merges seamlessly with a view and agenda for society and citizenship.

How do we do all this? By **self-cultivation**, which is central to Confucianism. You have to look into yourself and improve yourself. You will seek the knowledge available from the words of Confucian sages. Confucianism deals with the argument that all this might be selfish by pointing out that your knowledge and virtue must be extended to everyone else, used for their benefit. Sagehood leads to what Confucianism terms 'kingliness', that is to say the regulation of other people, the achieving of peace and harmony in society. You will see that here lie other ideas of unity, the unity of the individual with society, and the unity of humanity with the universe.

Confucianism has no agreed formula for **becoming a sage.** Some take the view that it requires a slow accumulation of learning. Others say that it can be a sudden realization. Not surprisingly, those who take the second view tend to emphasize that sagehood is available to all.

Self-cultivation requires 'carefulness when alone'. Above all, it requires '**cheng**'. Cheng is translated as 'sincerity' but it means much more than what that word means to a Westerner. It means absence of fault, honesty, seriousness, being true to yourself and to the nature of being. So, you will wish to conduct yourself accordingly as you practice virtue and accumulate good deeds. You will wish to look into yourself to find your true nature.

You may practice '**quiet sitting**'. As Zhu Xi, a Confucian teacher of the twelfth century put it, "Tranquility nourishes the root of activity and activity is to put tranquility into action." (W. Chan's *Source Book of Chinese Philosophy*: 608, Princeton University Press). Confucians distinguish quiet sitting from the Buddhist and Taoist practice of meditation, on the grounds that it is connected with this world rather than aiming to forget it, and with perfecting the self rather than forgetting it.

As with most religions, Confucianism developed within a tradition of **ritual and sacrifice**. Some kind of sacrifice, an offering of food and drink, may still be put before a statue or picture of Confucius, or another sage, as a reminder of their great virtue. And semi-annual public sacrifices to Confucius take place still in temples of Confucius in China and Taiwan as well as in Japan and South Korea, notably at the National Confucian Academy in Seoul. The practice of worshipping Confucius as some sort of god, a product of times when Confucianism was a state religion, has not survived.

This is a very **different** sort of religion to what you will be accustomed to if you have been raised in a Western cultural tradition. There is no salvation: humans can only help themselves or help others to help themselves. Westerners are also used to seeing religion as a structure which involves them behaving in a 'good' way in this life so they can enjoy a blissful experience in the next. Confucianism doesn't have that emphasis. It concentrates on this life. If you become a sage, it will be in this life. There is a next life, but it is very different from the Western idea of an afterlife. These are ways of looking at things that can disconcert a Westerner, perhaps even into feeling that this can't be a proper religion.

Confucianism has a considerable body of **sacred and ancient writings**. The Five Classics include the *I Ching*, a book on divination well known in the West, the *Book of Poetry* said to be selected by Confucius for the purpose of education, the *Book of History*, the earliest history book and a foundation of Confucian politics and philosophy, the *Book of Rites*, and the *Spring and Autumn Annals*, another history, pointed at the issue of government. There are four other major texts as follows. The *Analects of Confucius* (or *Lun Yu*) is a collection of Confucius's sayings and his conversations with his followers. The *Great Learning* explains how to learn and practice the 'Great Way' and the progression from self-cultivation to the government of others.

The *Doctrine of the Mean* deals with self-cultivation and becoming a sage. The *Book of Mengzi* records the theories of Mengzi, a sage second only to Confucius.

For Confucians, learning has much more than academic value. It is the study of the Way of Heaven. Confucius said that a person of virtue who studies the Way loves his fellow men (*Analects* 17:4). In the long history of Confucianism the sacred texts have, at different times, been approached dogmatically and, conversely, deepened by interpretation. When Confucianism was the state religion of China, the Civil Service examinations were based on the Confucian writings.

This book aims to tell you what is on offer now. Accordingly it does not go into the history of Confucianism, nor many of the variations in its teaching that have been more emphasized in the past. Hopefully, this short chapter will give you a feeling of how Confucianism 'works', and whether you are sufficiently attracted to look into it in more detail.

If you are, you will wish to consider the two paths of thought of **modern Confucianism**: Modern New Idealism and Modern New Rationalism. The division of ideas between Idealists and Rationalists developed the best part of a thousand years ago. Both traditions see Tian as an ultimate reality, a transcendental power which harmonizes the physical and non physical, and the source of morality and of 'ought'.

Modern New Idealism is within a tradition which identifies Tian with our Heart/Mind, and believes that there is a responsive relationship between Tian and Earth. In other words, that what happens in Tian can affect what happens in Earth, and that what happens on Earth can produce a response from Tian. Heart/Mind is the same as, is the substance of, humaneness. It is the ultimate reality. If we can realize it in ourselves we will have transcended ourselves and achieved a unity with the ultimate. Given its nature, Heart/Mind, humaneness, is within each of us, so we all have the possibility of sagehood, we are all innately good, we all know what is good and can learn to be good. The twelfth-century Confucian thinker Lu Jiuyuan said, "The universe is my mind and my mind is the universe." (W.Chan's *Source Book*: 579). Other more modern thinkers have spoken of the idea of an inner spirit which comes from Tian and is embodied in morality and politics. Others emphasize the issue of awakening moral consciousness. Others equate Heart/Mind with truth, goodness and beauty. The basic idea is that there is a responsive connection between us and our world, and Tian, Heaven, which centers on a common reality which Tian embodies and which resides deep inside each of us. Our task is to connect with that, to harmonize ourselves with something inside ourselves.

Modern New Rationalism, on the other hand, belongs to a tradition which sees Tian as nature, natural law, something which does not respond to human behavior. The Rationalist tradition of thought saw Li as being identified with the law of nature. For the Rationalists, Li, natural law, which they called 'principle', is what we have to connect with and follow. It is what brings everything into being. It is what governs how the world runs its course. Together with the qi, which everything consists of, it operates the universe. It is as if qi is the seed and principle, the potential for growth. Our task in helping sort this out is to work at getting rid of those things which obscure our connection with principle, natural law, Li. In this way we harmonize ourselves with the Way, with something outside ourselves. The Rationalist tradition emphasizes the need for learning, so the necessary knowledge and understanding can be attained.

Within these broad categories Confucian thinkers seek to develop Confucianism into something that can change and survive in the modern world.

Confucianism has been an important religion in **Korea and Japan**, as well as China. In Korea the Rationalist school was dominant and the Idealist tradition had little influence. In Japan the Rationalists were more established than the Idealists, being sponsored by the royal house. However, Idealism was and is influential as well. In Japan Confucianism found an affinity with the native Shinto tradition. Confucian ethics slotted in well with the Shinto religion. It was also seen as blending with Buddhism. Unlike in other countries, Confucianism in Japan played a part in modernization.

Despite Confucianism's lack of enquiry into the nature of the afterlife, this has played a significant part in the faith, by virtue of the importance placed on relations with one's ancestors. This tradition of respect for ancestors predates Confucianism and, as I have explained, is a common East Asian tradition. Mediums or shamans may be used to communicate with the dead. This may be far from modern Confucianism but is part of the communal traditions within which Confucianism has coexisted.

Of the many decayed Confucian **temples** some have been restored, and even a few new ones built. These are used to honor, to venerate, Confucius and other masters and scholars of the tradition, often by ceremonies of sacrifice. In the past, temples were public spaces and were also used as public schools for such things as training in music and in ritual. Civil service exam results used to be posted up in them.

As with every religion, Confucianism has its **festivals**. The Clear and Bright festival demonstrates family unity and remembers the dead. The Double Fifth festival is a time to avert danger from the family (the famous 'dragon boat' races take place on this festival.) The Autumn festival celebrates the harvest, the moon and the seeking of immortality. As to rites of passage, the significant ones are death and marriage. At death, you become an ancestor. On marriage, traditionally, you become married at the moment when you both bow before the ancestral tablets of the groom, so introducing the bride to the groom's ancestors.

Historically, there has been a close relationship between Confucianism and government. In its earlier days it saw Tian as incorporating the will of the people, by which the legitimacy of a government was confirmed. The idea of harmony implies change, yet in reality Confucianism was often used to justify the status quo. So did the fundamental Confucian idea that it was possible to incorporate 'Heavenly' principles into human codes of behavior and activity. The faith had an obvious appeal to the educated and to the political class, not to say the rulers. Ally that with the fact that Confucianism existed within an authoritarian culture, and has so largely existed until the twentieth century, and you can see how it became so identified with power structures. As those crumbled, that caused understandable damage to support for the belief system which ideologically underwrote the failing politics. Simultaneously it suffered the attack of ideological materialism.

Confucianism had a bad twentieth century. Its natural tendency to become associated with rigid social and political forms was particularly evident at the end of the nineteenth century. As a state religion in China it was damaged by the fall of the Manchu Qing dynasty in 1911. In both China and Korea it was identified as a barrier to modernity and economic progress. In the Cultural Revolution it was cruelly persecuted, to the point where mainland China had become the least Confucian country within the religion's former ambit. For similar reasons the development of modern Confucian thinking has taken place largely outside China, notably in Hong Kong, Taiwan and the USA.

As to **numbers**, much depends on where the line is drawn between Confucianism and Chinese traditional religion. The latest edition of Encyclopedia Britannica gives an estimate of over 5 million but notes that that is the number of Confucians outside China.

It is difficult to forecast the **future of Confucianism**. However, you may feel it offers much that is relevant to modern society. It is a belief system which supports the idea of good citizenship as a main plank of belief and practice. Certainly, within

Confucianism's traditional geographical area, the new economic confidence is marked by a greater cultural confidence, and a search for cultural roots. Since the 1980s this has increasingly offered Confucianism a relevance it has lacked for many years. In various Chinese communities in East Asia a number of Confucian organizations have been set up with the aim of restoring the religious functions of Confucianism. In 1994 the Graduate's Society of Beijing University published a manifesto calling on all students to start with cultivating good habits and moral virtues. Confucian academies in China are now praised as centers of learning and education. There have been suggestions in Japan and Singapore that Confucian ethics be incorporated into the school curriculum. This may all be part of the next step in the system's evolution and coming to terms with Western influences. For yourself, you may welcome Confucianism as a belief system which puts in its place an individualism which may have got out of control, by balancing it with an ethic of responsibility linked to a system of morality underwritten by a concept of the spiritual harmonization of the universe. You may also be attracted by a belief system that preaches the harmony of humanity and nature and which could dovetail in with modern environmental concerns. At the center of Confucianism is that search for unity which, in one way or another, seems to be the foundation and desire of all religions.

As with all faiths, there are different views as to the nature of Confucianism, both within it, and from its critics and scholars. Some argue that Confucianism is inherently inconsistent with modernization. There is also an argument that Confucianism is incompatible with democracy, or the Western idea of that. Some say that despite the emphasis on harmony, the reliance on self-cultivation is insufficient for Confucianism to underwrite a society capable of eliminating social conflict. History has yet to play these discussions out. However, these are discussions concerning the social and political utility of the faith and you may feel that while they are important they are secondary in a choice of whether this belief system fits the way you think and how you want to live inside yourself.

Harvard Professor and Confucian thinker Tu Wei-ming says, (in *Our Religions*, HarperCollins, pp221-2), "Since we help Heaven to realize itself through our self-discovery and self-understanding in day-to-day living, the ultimate meaning of life is found in our ordinary, human existence."

Chapter 13

Taoism

It is probably best if you read the chapter on Confucianism before you read this one.

To consider **Taoism**, which is also called Daoism, that being the way 'Taoism' is pronounced, you will have come to the conclusions:

- that spirit exists,
- that there are universal values and that goodness is a principle of the universe,
- and that you live in some way after death.

Taoism is **an ancient religion** which developed in China and which is nearly as old as Confucianism. Taoism also became rooted elsewhere in East Asia, notably in Korea and Japan, and also Thailand, Laos and Vietnam. It is mainly identified with China, not least because its texts are written in classical Chinese.

Taoism has been badly served by nineteenth- and most of twentieth-century **Western scholarship**. This tended to see Taoism as having had an early 'classical' period of thought, which later degenerated into superstitious practices. Modern scholarship sees Taoism today as a coherent tradition, albeit one which it is difficult to define. Taoist texts are voluminous, many are as yet untranslated from the Chinese, and scholars have more ground to cover before they can assert the certainty which their predecessors claimed, and put an end to scholarly acrimony. None of this is made easier by the fact that at times in Taoism's history it has been difficult to find a dividing line between it and Chinese folk religion.

Taoism follows the traditional Chinese calendar, and so Taoist festivals may follow the same cycles as traditional Chinese culture.

Within East Asia Taoism has taken many forms. It has changed to fit itself to the times, and will continue to do so. It has borrowed from other religions, changing itself accordingly. Bear in mind that a current leading scholar of Taoism, Russell Kirkland, has recently said, "Are there, or have there ever been, ideas or practices that 'were generally agreed upon' by all, or even most Taoists? The data with which I am familiar today leads me to say no." If you are a Western reader you will be used to the idea of believers struggling to remain true to some original message. Taoism isn't like that. It doesn't have a single dominant scripture, or any central hierarchy. Nor do Taoists agree to disagree. They just understand that others may see things differently. Russell Kirkland adds that "vestiges of nearly every Taoist idea and practice ever attested in China endure in the minds and lives of someone in East Asia today". This chapter, to be of use, has to simplify, and cannot express all the variations within Taoist thought. So, remember that as you read it, and treat it as an introduction rather than a definitive summary.

The word 'Tao' means '**the Way**'. What is the Way? Perhaps we can start with a passage from the *Tao te Ching*, the most famous Taoist text, reputedly more than two thousand years old, and one of the world's most translated writings.

"There is a being – in chaos yet complete. It preceded Heaven and earth. Silent, it was, and solitary; Standing alone, never changing. Moving around, yet never ending. Consider it the mother of Heaven and earth. I do not know its name. To call it something I say Tao. Forced to give it a name, I say great. Great – says it departs. Depart – says it is far. Far away – says it returns. Therefore Tao is great, Heaven is great, earth is great, humans too, are great. In the universe there are four 'greats'. And humans make their residence in the whole of them. Humans are modelled on earth. Earth is modelled on Heaven. Heaven is modelled on Tao. Tao is modelled on its own spontaneity." 'Spontaneity' is the Chinese word 'ziran', which strictly but less poetically translates as 'self-so'. In other words, Tao, the Way, is its own foundation, manifesting itself as a process of transformation.

That translation is by Livia Kohn adapted by James Miller in his book *Daoism* published by Oneworld in 2003. Let's have another translation of this extract, one by D.C.Lau.

There is a thing confusedly formed, born before Heaven and earth. Silent and void it stands alone and does not change, goes round and does not weary. It is capable of being the mother of the world. I know not its name so I style it 'the way'. I give it the makeshift name of 'the great'. Being great, it is further described as receding, receding, it is described as far away, being far away, it is described as turning back. Hence the way is great; Heaven is great; earth is great; the king is also great. Within the realm there are four things that are great and the king counts as one. Man models himself on earth, earth on Heaven, Heaven on the way, and the way on that which is naturally so.

Reading two versions may give you a better sense of the original. It may also give you some appreciation of the limitations of a literal reading of a translated text.

The *Tao te Ching* also says, "The Tao that can be named is not the eternal Tao". Like the wisdom of the Jewish Kabbalah it cannot be reduced to words or known consciously but only absorbed.

The Way is a pathway of communication between Earth, Heaven and humankind, the process which governs their relationships. It is what explains the world to a Taoist. Change is constant. James Miller in his book 'Daoism', to which this chapter is much indebted, describes the Way as filled with life, a 'cosmic heartbeat'. Taoism seeks harmony between Heaven, Earth and humankind, not a static harmony but a dynamic harmony that lies behind the development of the universe. A secondary meaning of Tao in Chinese is 'to speak', and the Way is an active form of communication between Heaven, Earth and humankind. It is the power that lies behind things, which wells up in them. It is the basis of the universe. It is the whole, and as it goes into every part so it makes every part contain something of the whole, like the DNA of each individual cell containing the complete DNA of the whole organism, another analogy for which more thanks to James Miller.

That leads us on to **the Taoist view of the body**. Some other religions have the idea of a soul which is distinct from body. Taoists don't have that idea. They see us as a whole, a single organism. We understand with our whole body, not just our mind. Our body is related to the cosmos, it is a microcosm of the universe. Gods, spirit beings, can reside in it and can direct its functioning. So what we do with our body can be of as much concern as what our minds believe or our hearts feel. It is the vitality that flows through the body that we must cultivate.

You can see from this that bodily disciplines can have a deeper meaning within this religion. The Taoist idea of body thus brings together what might otherwise be seen as disparate aspects of Taoist practice.

This Chinese universe consists of **qi**, vital energy. This is the basic energy of the universe. Everything consists of qi. It condenses into matter. We and all things are made of qi. So far as our bodies are concerned, if the qi flows we live, if it stops moving then we are dead. Qi can be cultivated so we can live better and longer. We are born with a stock of qi which we slowly use up, and we derive further qi from food and effort.

Within the Way, the vital energy, qi, undergoes constant

change in a pattern. We have already referred to the 'cosmic heartbeat'. This pattern is that of **yin and yang**. These words literally refer respectively to the shady side of a hill and the sunny side of a hill. They are sometimes, wrongly, seen as opposing qualities. They are complementary: together they encompass a whole, but the balance between them in that whole varies. Often yin and yang are seen as male and female.

On a cosmic level, the Way brings all things into being, and it then reverts them back into non being. It has an eternal cyclic pattern.

Traditionally the Chinese have not seen the world in terms of atoms, but in terms of energies that operate in phases and cycles. There are interconnections and resonances. James Miller compares the resonance between the qi of things as being like the wave resonance of the sound from a guitar string. You yourself may think this idea has its own resonance with modern physics grappling with quantum theory and string theory.

Everything in the universe has its own 'de', a word which translates as 'power' and 'virtue'. De is the inherent potentiality and embodiment of the Dao, especially as expressed by human beings. If this de is allowed to flourish, order and harmony result. However, humans have the capacity to ignore de, which causes a lot of problems. 'De' is also related to the Chinese character for 'to attain'. So you could say that for a Taoist, virtue is the power obtained when the Way is attained. For Taoists, the search for the Way can transform both their lives and their environment. Everything can grow and develop if it is properly nourished and looked after.

Here the Taoist idea of **'wuwei'** comes into play. Wuwei literally means 'without action'. This is different from inaction, though the difference is subtle. The idea is that the Tao is spontaneous and we just need to let it flourish. We should take no action contrary to nature. Wuwei embodies a paradox of Taoism, namely that things flourish best if let be, yet the Way is to be actively sought. In turn this links in with Taoist ideas of embracing simplicity and decreasing desires.

This idea is sometimes adopted and adapted by what one might call New Age Taoists, who most scholars would regard as not being Taoists at all. The 'Tao of Pooh' is an example of this. Pooh lets the world go by and doesn't bother too much about understanding it.

So, how do we actually do this nourishing? James Miller calls Taoists the gardeners of the cosmos. This gardening, this nourishing, is done by **communal ritual** and **self-cultivation**. This is all part of the harmonious communication between Heaven, Earth and humans. You may be attracted by the traditional Taoist care and concern for the environment which is part of this harmony. Early Taoism gave instructions on draining roads, not letting marshes dry up and so on.

Self-cultivation is not a selfish exercise. It involves not just you, but the Tao which enfolds you and everything else. It is the cultivation of the reality of the Tao. Russell Kirkland uses the word **'biospiritual'** to describe Taoist practices which concentrate on the physical body.

That brings us to the issue of **death**. Chinese traditional belief has a preoccupation with death and longevity, and so does Taoism, which has a wide spread of views on the subject. Taoism has a concern for the afterlife which is absent from Confucianism. Some Taoist texts refer to reincarnation, although Taoism is not generally regarded as a reincarnation religion. Some Taoists believe in the possibility of a physical immortality which seems to ignore the difference between the living and dead. In the past there have been Taoist accounts of persons being physically taken up into 'Heaven'. Others see immortality as involving the keeping together of the two souls, which both go to 'Heaven', so avoiding the underworld. Others think the body of a perfected person can be transmuted into a transfigured celestial being impervious to nature and maybe with supernatural powers.

There is also the idea that this state can be achieved while still alive. Some believe a sage may live for a thousand years and then ascend. Generally speaking, Taoist views on death accept the eventual death of the physical body. Confusion may have been caused by the translation of the word 'hsien'. Hsien is a goal of Taoist life, and has been much translated as 'immortality'. Many current Taoist scholars prefer to use the word 'transcendent'. Saying that death can be transcended is very different from saying it can be avoided. There is no clear unified teaching on these issues and Taoists have seemed content for the matter to be surrounded with ambiguity. The Taoist quest seems to be for a higher state of existence rather than mere immortality, but that word sticks to the faith, and the idea of physical immortality is within the tradition. Generally, the object is to achieve a transcendent state, an enhanced reality, by means of moral, spiritual and cognitive growth. This can achieve a state which will not be extinguished by death.

Another idea deep within Chinese tradition is that of **fate/destiny/givenness of life. To this Taoism adds the idea that our cultivation of our nature may influence our destiny**. So, back to self-cultivation, the development of what is inside ourselves. This involves becoming more real. Many people lead fruitless lives, out of touch with their own reality. The first step in becoming more real is to learn what is fruitless living and what is true living. Unlike some other religions it is not a matter of thinking certain thoughts and trying to put them into action. The Taoist seeks to change his or her awareness of things. This is a slow process. Taoism doesn't believe in the sudden awareness that, say, Zen Buddhism offers. Nor does it see the change sought as a change of consciousness, without reference to the body and to the surrounding world. The awareness sought is that of mind, body and spirit, and of the realities surrounding them.

So, Taoists don't have an idea of an enclosed separated **self**. For them an understanding of self involves a holistic understanding which includes other people and the realities in which the self is embedded. Taoist practices are designed to achieve that understanding of one's body/heart/mind/spirit/energy, and the social, political and physical framework of one's life. This **holistic perspective** of Taoism is very different from that of most other belief systems.

Another idea within Taoism, one of a number, and you will have to take your choice, is that the universe has developed out of nothing or **non being** so that paradoxically nothing is the place where power and life are made. In a famous image of the *Tao te Ching* the empty center of the wheel's hub is what the wheel circulates around, and the empty center of the vase is what gives it its use. "Thirty spokes share one hub. Adapt the nothing therein to the purpose in hand, and you will have the use of the cart. Knead clay in order to make a vessel. Adapt the nothing therein to the purpose in hand, and you will have the use of the vessel."(verse 11, trans. D.C.Lau).

Other Taoist teachers have seen the origin of everything as **life energy** itself, concluding that the important thing is to conserve our energy as much as possible, notably by diminishing our desires.

Taoism has given and taken ideas from Chinese folk religion, Buddhism and Confucianism, and vice versa. Its texts are subject to a wide range of interpretations. In East Asia it is not uncommon for a person to adhere to more than one belief system. In particular most lay people do not identify themselves as exclusively Taoist or Confucian. Over six hundred years ago, the **Three Teachings movement** sought to build a religion by combining elements of Taoism, Confucianism and Buddhism. In some temples in Taiwan incense is offered to Confucius, the revered Taoist master Laozi and the Buddha. In the Taoist White Cloud Temple in Beijing you will see statues of Confucius and the Neo-Confucian Zhu Xi. You may see an even bigger mixture in Chinese neighborhood temples run by lay people.

Most Taoists believe that within existence, within the Tao, the Way, **humanity** is particularly important. We are a unique set of capacities, and as such can be regarded as a high point. We have the potential capacity to direct the continuing evolution of the universe, of Heaven and Earth. We have the capacity to find a transformation within us, which will enable us to do this. And we can be the mediators between Heaven and Earth.

Who are **the spirit residents of the Taoist cosmos**? There are **gods**. These are a mixed bunch. Some have been taken over from Chinese folk religion. Some are gods of natural formations such as rivers, caves and particularly mountains, sacred places where qi is found in quantity. The gods include eminent people worthy of veneration. There is an abundance of gods. Among other things they run the celestial bureaucracy. Taoism reveres **Laozi,** the name given to the person or persons said to have written the *Tao te Ching* or *Daode Jing*. Many Taoist movements have regarded him as a manifestation of the Way itself. Some Taoists treat him as being a god and as important as the values set out in the *Daode Jing*. There are also the **immortals**, those who have transcended death, who have realized the Tao. They are free of the concerns of both humans and of gods, and don't have to concern themselves with either the human or the celestial bureaucracies. The Chinese word for deity and spirit is the same.

There are two principal schools of Taoism, **The Way of Celestial Masters**, and The Way of Complete Perfection. The Way of Celestial Masters is also called the Way of Orthodox Unity. This was the first organized Taoist religious system. Its basis was that there was a vast celestial bureaucracy, just like an earthly government. The Taoist priests had privileged access to this bureaucracy, and would intercede for people, to seek the help of spiritual powers. Petitions would be submitted, as they might be on earth. **The Way of Complete Perfection** is a monastic tradition. It encourages people to become renunciants and live a life of complete religious commitment. Today this tradition is dominated by the Dragon Gate (Longman) branch at the White Cloud monastery in Beijing. There have been other Taoist schools, but they have died out or have had their ideas absorbed by the two remaining schools.

Two other ideas found in Chinese traditional belief and Taoism, as well as elsewhere in the world, are the ideas of **shamanism** and of the **medium**. The shamanism idea is that a person's spirit may travel and communicate with spirits. The medium idea is that a spirit may enter into a person and communicate with them. Many Taoists reject mediumism. Shamanism is an important aspect of Taoism.

Now, on to how all this can work out in practice.

The quest for physical immortality was well established before Taoism, and flourished within Taoism for centuries. **Outer alchemy** was the search for a formula you could swallow which would do the trick. At the time it seemed a sensible idea. The theory was that if you could process a physical substance back to its original pre-evolutionary condition, you would be restoring it to its purest form. It was thought that if you ingested this your body would in consequence be restored to its purest, and so immortal, form. Unfortunately, a favorite material of the alchemists was mercury, which led to a lot of disappointed people dying earlier than they might otherwise have done. There were some side benefits, such as advances in Chinese medicine, and the invention of gunpowder, if you think that was an advantage. Outer alchemy wasn't all chemistry. The correct mental attitude was necessary if it were to work. Perhaps the promotion of the sale of health foods and vitamins echoes this tradition.

Internal alchemy is of more relevance to the modern world, and is alive and well. This evolved on the basis that the energy of the body could be refined to a purer condition, so a person could achieve a pure and transcendent state. In other words, rather than make the body physically immortal, it aims to transform the physical form into immortal pure spirit. Internal alchemy was developed largely within The Way of Complete Perfection, the monastic school. The individual must first physically cultivate themselves: mind and body are both important.

Another technique, prominent in the Shangqing Highest Clarity School, which was absorbed into the practice of The Way of Celestial Masters, was and is that of **visualization**. This added a personal quest for transcendence to the School's bureaucratic emphasis. It involves shamanism. The method is to visualize a journey of one's spirit to the gods, and notably in the constellation of the Great Bear/Big Dipper. This is done in a state of meditation. A sacred chart may be used to find the way in the spirit world.

One purpose of such a journey might be to petition the gods, the influential and powerful spirits in Heaven, and negotiate with them. That could include the matter of the state of one's ancestors. Another aim might be to absorb the qi and light of the stars as a purer form of energy for oneself. It might be that you would invite the gods to go into your inner organs and energy systems. Bear in mind that Taoists see the interior of the body as a microcosm of the universe. These methods of visualization are still in use, though they tend to concentrate on the body's brain rather than other organs, an effect of Western influence. In the West these methods are likely to be presented as psycho energetic practices, or as health and fitness techniques.

Taoist rituals take three major forms: Zhai (fasts), Jiao (offerings) and Jie (ordinations). **Zhai** are rituals, usually public, organized by Taoist priests and involving purification. The body is purified by bathing and fasting, and the heart by the confession of sins, and then there is a communal feast to celebrate the reestablishing of harmony between the gods and the people. The main current Taoist ritual is the **Jiao** offering. In this an altar is put up, and written invitations are sent to the gods, who come down to the altar. There, incense is offered and the sponsors of the ritual have an audience with the gods. When the ritual is over, the altar is taken down and everyone goes home. The jiao can last from a day to a week, depending on its importance, and may be accompanied by music and dance. The sponsors will pay for it, and it will be directed by a Taoist priest.

Taoist priests intercede with the celestial bureaucracy. They use written petitions and talismans to do this. Lay people hire Tao priests for these services. Some priests live as hermits or in monasteries and concentrate on self-cultivation. The monasteries are open to all lay people who wish to pursue practices of self-cultivation. Some priests may marry and live with their families, and perform rites in the community. These rites may be the rituals I have discussed or perhaps rites of healing or of exorcism. Some priests manage local spirits rather in the manner of a shaman, going out of their bodies to communicate with the spirits. Others have considerable training and can summon hosts of divinities. The burial ceremony is particularly important, being the most significant Chinese life ritual. It is important that the soul going to the underworld successfully makes the journey. Taoist priests may enter the spirit world to facilitate this.

A common Taoist view has been that spirit agents in the body report your **sins** to Heaven and that these sins reduce your life span. So the removal of the stain of your own sin is important.

It was also thought that sin blocked the communication between Earth, Heaven and humans. This blockage could accumulate, hanging over humanity. The blockage could cause natural disasters. So, confessing one's sins both helped restore harmony in the world and helped heal the penitent. Thus, **the confession of sins** developed as a ritual way to promote harmony, as well as to heal the sick and lengthen life.

In the West the most well-known form of qi cultivation is perhaps that of **T'ai Chi**. This is often associated with Taoism although some scholars take the view that there is no connection. T'ai Chi's modern form probably dates back no further than the nineteenth century, and it was at first a martial art form. In principle it can be looked at in a number of ways. It can be seen as a mix of assertive yang movements and receptive yin movements in interplay with one another. It can be seen as a guiding of your qi through your body. It can be seen as a ritual dance embodying the yin yang form of the Way. One of the largest T'ai Chi organizations in the world is centered in Toronto. It promotes the health benefits of T'ai Chi, and has a large Taoist temple tucked away on an upper floor. To many in the West, T'ai Chi appears to be simply a form of exercise.

Another qi practice is that of **Qigong**, which means qi-skill. This involves exercises to guide and circulate the qi throughout the body. The idea is that this will make the body healthier. You can do it to yourself, or have someone do it to you. The exercise may involve physical movement or may be just internal. The major Qigong organization is Falun Gong, which is outlawed in China. Again, Quigong is associated with Taoism in the Western mind.

Feng Shui is another art which is associated with Taoism, although not strictly part of it.

In the past, Taoism has had **political aspects**. It is possible to see its progress as embodying a pursuit of harmony between the universe, the body and the state. There were times when Taoism gained the favor of China's rulers, and was the official religion of the court.

There is a multitude of **Taoist texts**. The earliest and best known is the already quoted *Tao te Ching*, a collection of aphorisms, many enigmatic, which talk of the Way and of de. The *Zhuangzi* is another text, popular though less important to Taoist thought. It gives a view of the perfected person as someone unconcerned about politics, business and what might happen to him. Another one is the *Neiye*, or 'inward training', now seen as important to the development of longevity practices and breath meditation. The training is that of the body's energy systems. Well known is the *I-Ching* or *Book of Changes*, an ancient divination manual. You could argue that the Taoist themes of social harmony, mystical realization and biospiritual cultivation are there in these ancient texts.

For Taoists **writing can be a form of communication with gods**. Taoists believe that some texts have been revealed by the highest deities. In China today spirit writing is still practiced. Offerings are made to a spirit who descends into a stick held by two mediums and which draws letters in the sand. Such practice might take place within or outside a Taoist context.

As well as sacred charts and diagrams, used to guide Taoist priests in the spirit world, much use is made of **talismans**. These involve the use of writing or symbols to enable a priest to communicate with the spirit world. They are usually on paper, but may be gestured in the air. A written talisman may be put to the spirits by burning. Talismans may be used to cure or exorcise, for protection, for invoking deities, for journeying in the lands of spirit.

Another way of looking at Taoism, albeit one which Taoist scholars might frown on, is to classify it by the different **practices** it has. Thus, one grouping would be ceremonial Taoism, using ritual to communicate with sacred powers which govern human destiny. Another would be divinational Taoism, seeing patterns of change in the workings of the universe. Another is magical Taoism, involving channeling power from the spirit world. Another is internal alchemism, seeking to change the whole self to achieve health, long life and transcendence. Another grouping would be what might be called karma Taoism, the idea that good works accumulate merit, reward and long life; and bad deeds retribution, ill health and early death.

Taoism has influenced **Chinese art**, particularly landscape painting and calligraphy. In calligraphy the brush was seen as having the creative force of qi. In painting, the artist sought to understand the inner reality of the subject before starting to actually paint.

You are likely to read elsewhere that at times and in some places Taoism has been involved with Chinese **sexual yoga**, a practice which had nothing to do with pleasure, for sexual alchemy requires one to be free of desire. However, Louis Komjathy, a well-known scholar of Taoism says there is very little evidence to connect Taoism with this Chinese court practice, despite the fact such a link has 'become a Western fantasy'.

At the risk of oversimplification, it might be said that in **social** terms Taoism was for the most part dominated by the well-to-do classes. Taoists were often leaders in the development of the physical and biological sciences, and in Chinese pharmacology and medicine.

As to **numbers**, much depends on how one defines Taoism: adherents.com confirms that it is difficult to estimate. Figures seem to vary largely between thirty and fifty million.

Taoism is rooted not just in China (including Taiwan), but in Korea, Singapore and Japan. The Yao people of Thailand, Laos and Vietnam practice their own form of Taoism. Communism bore hard on Taoism, treating it as a superstition which should be banned. Since 1980 there has been a degree of toleration of world creeds in China but great hostility to popular practices such as shamanism and magic. China's Religious Affairs Bureau now regulates the activities of Taoist, Buddhist, Protestant, Chinese Catholic and Islamic religions. Taoist monasteries and temples have been reestablished, but only with government permission. The fate of Falun Gong shows what happens to movements that try to operate outside the state's authority. This authoritarian situation is a familiar one for China and for Taoism which, after all, itself had a period of dominance in the past as the religion of the Chinese court.

The flip side of the twentieth-century vicissitudes of Taoism under Communism has been its spreading over the world by virtue of the emigration of millions of Chinese. Thus it has permeated **the West**. How it will ultimately adjust to Western ideas is not clear. Many Taoist practices thrive in the West (and elsewhere) shorn of their religious/philosophical context.

Scholars struggle to define Taoism, with its multitude of variation. You may find it exciting ground to investigate, particularly if you are already into T'ai Chi and other health practices with Chinese roots. You may be attracted by a holistic view which fits in well with environmental concerns. You may welcome Taoism's tolerance and breadth of belief. Or you may feel that this religion is too ethnic, too Chinese, for you. You may feel Taoism has surprising and unexpected views which contrast with the attitude of a creator God religion which you may have been brought up in. Or you may feel it is too bound up with what you might regard as superstition. You may find attractive the idea of a faith that underwrites the idea of living in touch with nature's rhythms and the flow of one's own true nature.

Chapter 14

Shintoism

To consider this religion you will believe:

- that spirit **exists**,
- in universal values
- and you will almost certainly be Japanese, or someone who is to marry a Japanese.

Shintoism is **the ethnic religion of Japan**. It is part of Japanese national life. From shortly after 1868 until 1945 it was Japan's official religion. During this time obedience to the Emperor, who was seen as a living god, was held to be the noblest ideal.

Shintoism believes that nature is governed by spirit entities. These are called **kami**. The religion is also called 'the way of the gods'. The word Shinto derives from two words, 'shen' (spirit) and 'tao' (way).

A central idea of Shintoism is '**wa**' or benign harmony. This is something which is inherent in human nature and in nature itself. What helps wa is good and what disrupts it is bad. Humans require rules of behavior to maintain wa. Chaos will result without such rules.

This way of looking at things reinforces and is reinforced by the traditional Japanese view that **the group** has priority over the individual.

Another reinforcing structure is the idea of 'tatemae' or '**face**'. This idea is that a person should maintain the face they **present** to the outside world. If you fail to do this you will bring shame on yourself, and indeed on a group to which you belong, a social or work group for example. Atonement has to be given for loss of face. Shame **and** suicide are much linked in Japan. If a

Japanese company fails in its role in some way, all its employees may feel shame.

To all this has to be added another important group to which a Japanese belongs, namely your **ancestors**, your extended family. The veneration of this family is an important part of Shintoism and of Japanese tradition.

Purification and **renewal** are ideas which constantly appear in Shintoism. Renewal reflects the cycles of nature. Purification is to do with the restoration of the balance, the harmony, of nature in ourselves.

Shinto is a religion concerned with this life. It has little concern with the afterlife.

At this point we must talk about other religions which have established themselves in Japan. In about the sixth century CE **Buddhism, Confucianism** and **Taoism** all appeared there. All of them affected Shintoism, particularly Mahayana Buddhism. Indeed many if not most Japanese believers regard themselves as both Shintoists and Buddhists. These other religions fill the gap of Shintoism's lack of concern for the afterlife. Many Japanese will have a Shinto wedding and a Buddhist funeral. It could be said that this early accommodation of Shintoism to other religions prevented it from developing into a religion more concerned with an afterlife. Japanese seem to be able to live happily with the contradictions which belief in two religions or more may involve.

Back to the **kami** or spirits, which have their own realm and which oversee nature, including human life. Buddhist and Taoist deities are often included, the Buddha Amida for example. Kami vary greatly in their nature and power. Some are gods and may be very powerful, the Sun god for example. Some deities were originally human. Some of them can take human form. Some constitute a class of thing, the god of trees for example. Some represent an abstract quality in nature, the god of growth for example. Gods are just one type of kami. There are myriads of kami. They may be spirits of the neighborhood, of birds or beasts, the thunder, the echo and so on and so on. Some kami may be friendly. Some may not be. Some may be demons. Some unfriendly spirits, often animal spirits, can possess you, in which case you had better get exorcised quickly. Some are harmful ghosts, and you can protect yourself from those by ritual.

Many natural features are regarded as sacred. Mount Fuji is regarded as a deity. Most shrines are placed in natural settings. Shintoism has a profound reverence for nature.

Kami also include your ancestors, and you will be such a kami one day. Your descendants will revere you at the household shrine, and sustain you with offerings. They will have a duty to you not to bring shame upon themselves and so on you. Your job will be to bless and protect them. After thirty-three years you will lose your individual identity and merge with the family's collective spirit.

Shintoism's view of good and evil is that everything has gentle/positive characteristics and rough/negative character-istics. Depending on the circumstances either may be manifested. This applies both to living and non living things. Even demons may have their positive aspect. Bad things aren't a product of evil, but a result of an interruption of wa, a disruption of the natural harmony of things.

Since many, many kamis have a **shrine**, you will be accus-tomed to attending Shinto shrines, which are marked by a sacred gateway. The shrine will have an image of the kami. Before you approach this you must purify yourself. You will do this by pouring water over your hands and rinsing your mouth with water. This ritually cleanses you both inside and out and restores your body's inner balance. In the shrine you will pray and make offerings. Your prayer is likely to be asking for something or giving thanks for something. There is a solemn quietness. Traditionally your daily worship has been very much an individual thing, but since the war there is more of a tendency for people to worship together.

In an act of renewal, shrines are rebuilt periodically. In the same way you will annually replace the small shrine you have at home. The two oldest and most sacred shrines are those at Ise and Izumo. You are likely to go there on pilgrimage.

Shrines are managed by members of the shrine elders' association. The priests are paid officials. A major shrine may have numbers of priests, a small shrine may have none and the priest's role may be undertaken by one of the elders. Most shrines are very local in their identity. There is an Association of Shinto Shrines, of which many devotees will be unaware: overall organization is very loose.

Shrines are centers of **rituals and festivals**, which you may attend. Dancing and singing may be involved. A shrine will have an annual festival at which a portable shrine, which may contain the kami's image, is carried in procession, to sanctify the neighborhood. Other annual festivals are those of the New Year, and of Obon, the Buddhist day of the annual return of the dead to their homes. Rituals to do with birth take place at shrines. Shinto priests perform the traditional Japanese wedding ceremony wherever that takes place.

If you are female you will be pleased at Shintoism's postwar increasing acceptance of **the role of women**. By the turn of the century about ten percent of priests were women and an increasing number of shrines permit young women as well as young men to carry the portable shrines at festivals.

In the last two hundred years many other spiritual groupings have developed in Japan. These are referred to as the **New Religions**, and for convenience I will deal with them in this chapter. While most of them have grown out of Shintoism, they may be heavily influenced by Buddhism, Taoism, Confucianism and Christianity, and even Western occultism, for there is a strain of occultism and magic in Shintoism.

The oldest New Religion is **Heavenly Truth**, founded in 1838, with now about two million adherents. It takes a spirit/kami hierarchy from Shintoism and an idea of salvation and an underworld structure from Pure Land Mahayana Buddhism. It is established in Japanese overseas communities.

Value Creating Society came out of Buddhist tradition in the 1920s.

The Syncretic House of Growth aims to overcome disease and suffering.

PL(Perfect Liberty) **Kyodan** sees life as art, and religion as a way for people to realize this. It claims two million adherents.

Dancing Religion is based on revelations of its founder in the last century, and is noted for a form of dancing which encourages a state of not self.

Shintoism, and indeed Japanese Buddhism, reaches into Japanese custom to the extent that many **secular** people in the increasingly secularized Japanese society may be involved in its rituals at some time in the year. If you have a close connection with Japan you will not avoid it.

Part III

God Religions

Chapter 15

Zoroastrianism

To consider Zoroastrianism you will take the view:

- that spirit exists,
- that there is one creator God,
- that it is good and all-knowing,
- that it is eternal,
- that there is another uncreated and powerful spirit being which is evil but without creative power in the material world,
- and that you have a soul, quite separate from God.

Some say the founder of Zoroastrianism saw his new religion as a future world faith. In any event, it came to be seen as **an ethnic religion**, and there aren't that many followers now. Estimates vary widely, from one to two hundred thousand, to over three million (see adherents.com). In its time Zoroastrianism was the religion of three successive Persian empires, over a period of more than one thousand years. It was the major world religion at the time of the birth of Jesus Christ, but eventually lost most of its followers to Islam, and then more to the Baha'i Faith.

So, why talk about it? Well, Zoroastrianism is **one of the most ancient living religions** of the world, over three thousand years old, predating Christianity, and sharing certain historical roots with Hinduism, and it has had great influence on other religions. It also has some unusual ideas, the chief of which is that evil is an independent force and that the Devil, like God, has always existed.

Zoroastrianism is a **revealed faith** and a **salvation faith**. Sometime between 1500 and 1200 BCE the prophet Zoroaster is said to have had a number of visions, and the religion is based on these.

There are two uncreated spirits, **Ahura Mazda**, God, who is good and **Angra Mainyu**, the Devil, who is bad. Ahura Mazda created the spiritual world and then out of that created the physical world. Both were perfect. The idea that the physical world is in essence perfect is an important one for Zoroastrianism. Essentially, the body is as important as the soul. The problem with the physical world is that it has been spoiled by Angra Mainyu. Angra Mainyu has always existed. He has creative power in the spiritual world but no creative power in the physical world. Within the spiritual world Angra Mainyu has been able to create a negative counter creation, within the material world his evil just clings like a parasite. Thus Zoroastrians see Angra Mainyu as a destructive force opposed to Ahura Mazda's spiritual creation and who is the source of all evil and imperfection in the material world.

Ahura Mazda created both the spiritual world and the physical world to be **a battleground** within which he could defeat Angra Mainyu. So it was, and Angra Mainyu attacked and spoiled creation and brought evil into it. The good news is that Ahura Mazda will eventually be successful in this battle and that we have to help Him in it, so the evil in creation can be ended forever.

Thus, **in this religion humankind has a quite different role** compared with most religions. We can help God restore creation to its perfect state, when evil will be completely eliminated. Angra Mainyu may have always existed, but he will lose. It is significant that Zoroastrians pray standing up, not kneeling or abasing themselves before the God they seek to help. They can hold their heads up, responsible not just for the fate of their own spirit but, in a small way, for the fate of the world, so evil in it can be ended.

Apart from helping God, there is the issue of **personal**

salvation. When we die, our good and bad thoughts, words and deeds are judged and weighed in the balance, and accordingly we go to Heaven ('the house of welcome') or Hell. This judgment is a mechanical process. Good and bad thoughts, words and deeds are added up and you go to Heaven or Hell or, if the balance is even, to an intermediate neutral limbo, a 'place of the mixed ones'. These states are temporary, for when God has triumphed over the Devil we will be reunited with our bodies and judged again. Then we are purified. For the good that is not painful, but the more bad things we have done the more painful is the process of purification. The really evil will thereby suffer a second death and perish off the face of the earth. By the end of all this, Angra Mainyu will be defeated, powerless and evicted from creation. All his products will go away, and we will live forever in a physical world restored to its original perfection. Evil may continue to exist, but outside creation as it was in the beginning, and so will not matter. You will note that this is **not a religion of forgiveness**. If you haven't lived your life properly you have to pay for it. There are no fatted calves for prodigal sons and there is no point in praying for your sins to be forgiven (although in practice many Zoroastrians may do so).

This sequence, of a judgment after death, then Heaven or Hell, then the resurrection of the body and a last judgment, history having an end, and then eternal life for the reunited body and soul in the company of God, may be familiar to you from a number of religions. Well, Zoroaster was the first to teach this sequence of ideas.

Zoroastrians also believe that in the final struggle with the Devil, a human savior, a **Saoshyant**, 'one who will be strong', will be born, and will drive evil out of the material world. He will be a posthumous son of Zoroaster and born of a virgin, and will come at a time of apparent calamity.

The idea that the devil is an uncreated spiritual entity and the source and cause of **evil** gets round the problem that other religions have in explaining how a good God can have a creation with evil in it. It is also a ready explanation for the problem of **catastrophe and injustice**.

A counterpart of this is that **the Zoroastrian God is not omnipotent**. Otherwise he would not have needed to create the spiritual and physical worlds to assist in the defeat of Angra Mainyu.

Free will is an important element in Zoroastrianism. It is because we know the difference between right and wrong and can exercise free will that we can help God. Not only does man exercise free will but God and the Devil made a choice between good and evil, albeit not a surprising choice given their natures.

Within spiritual creation God is immanent in the form of his Holy spirit, **Spenta Mainyu**, and He has manifested various of His attributes as the six holy immortals, great spirits, the **Amesha Spentas**. The first is Good Purpose, followed by Best Righteousness. Then there is Holy Devotion, to what is good and just. Then Desirable Dominion, which for God is his kingdom and power and for humanity is the power which should be exercised for righteousness. Then Health, and Long Life. Zoroastrians may pray to these immortals, for these things to be given. The Amesha Spentas have in turn created a number of lesser beings. Collectively, all these spirit beings are called **yazatas** ('worthy of worship').

The Devil has created his own band of evil spirits, the **daevas**, who chose evil.

The purpose of humanity's existence is that of creation itself, namely **the defeat of evil**. We must cherish all that is good in creation, in our fellow beings, in the world around us, by good thoughts, good words and good deeds, complying with Asha, the natural law, universal principle, of order, justice, righteousness and truth.

A word of warning. In the interest of simplicity this brief chapter glosses over a number of scholarly differences as to details of the faith.

The Zoroastrian scriptures are known as the **Avesta**. Some of these are said to be the words of God. These tend to be the most enigmatic of the scriptures. There are also other texts, written in middle Persian. During various persecutions of Zoroastrians some scriptures were lost, and those that survive were written down relatively late. Zoroastrians tend not to seek a literal interpretation of their scriptures, which were combined with an oral tradition handed down within the priesthood.

The primary role of Zoroastrian **priests** is to pray and perform rituals for devotees, who pay the priests for doing this and to keep the temple fire burning. Rituals aim to strengthen Ahura Mazda and His creation. Private prayer aims to strengthen the individual in the fight against evil. Prayers are preformulated in the ancient language of the Avesta but if you have a special wish you may have that in mind as you pray, and your selection of the text may also depend on your wish. Some yazatas have special functions. For example, there is one who women pray to for a pregnancy or good birth.

Zoroastrians of both sexes who have been initiated, usually as children between the ages of seven and fifteen, wear a cord round their waists, wound round three times, knotted front and back and known as the **kusti**. This is tied over an inner shirt of white cotton, the **sudra**, which has a small purse sewn into it, to remind you to continually fill its emptiness with good thoughts, words and deeds. The cord is tied and untied repeatedly when as a Zoroastrian you **pray** five times a day, a weapon in the fight against evil. There are six important **festivals** a year, the most important being that of Fravardigan at the vernal equinox when day and night are of equal length, the New Year and Muktad, when the souls of the dead are praised and invoked.

Fire is important in Zoroastrian worship, and they have been wrongly regarded as fire worshippers. The idea is that light equates to good and dark to evil, and that fire represents the energy of the creator. The attention to the invaluable hearth fire of ancient times evolved to the holy fire of the **imageless** Zoroastrian temples. All fire is sacred, from the sun to the household fire. The holiest fire of the Parsees, in Gujarat in India, has been kept burning for more than one thousand years. Zoroastrians will seek to pray before some sort of light, be it fire, the sun, the moon, a candle, an electric bulb or otherwise.

God made the world perfect. Anything which blemishes it, like dirt and disease, is the work of the Devil. That is the idea behind Zoroastrianism's traditional concern with personal **cleanliness**. This reaches out into concern for the preparation of **food**, for the **environment**, for the **welfare of animals**. In the past many rules grew up about ritual purity, food preparation and so on, which would now be observed only by strict Zoroastrians. The idea of ritual purity is also behind the rule that non Zoroastrians may not enter fire-temples.

Zoroastrians are concerned about not polluting the earth, because it is a holy creation. It was this currently fashionable idea which was behind their method of disposing of **their dead**. This was to expose the corpse on a tower and let the creatures of the air eat the polluting flesh, after which the powdered bones were thrown into a pit at the center of the tower. Zoroastrians still have 'towers of silence' in India. There is nowadays a shortage of vultures, and not all Zoroastrians follow the practice.

Work is a duty, and laziness, as opposed to relaxation, is frowned on.

Creatures harmful to man, such as wasps, scorpions, animals of prey, are also unclean and made by Angra Mainyu. So you will not think twice about killing such '**khrafstra**', and would seek to avoid touching them alive, and even more so if dead.

Today Zoroastrianism has two main centers. One is in Iran, its homeland, in the desert cities of Yadz and Kerman and in Tehran, where they are referred to as **Guebors**. Following the Muslim conquest of Iran in the mid seventh century CE a group of Zoroastrian refugees from Iran eventually arrived in India and became known as the **Parsis** or **Parsees**, now the best known group of Zoroastrians. Some differences in ritual and belief have evolved between the two groups. There are also Zoroastrian communities in Pakistan, East Africa, Hong Kong, Australia, Canada, the USA, the UK and elsewhere. Zoroastrian communities have Zoroastrian Associations, and the first World Zoroastrian Congress was held in 1960, to create a forum for common discussion.

Over the last century the control of the religion has passed increasingly into the hand of its **layman** believers, there being now an acute shortage of priests.

Zoroastrianism has had **no ascetics and no monasteries**. Their duty is to marry, have children, to enjoy and expand God's creation, and fight evil.

Zoroastrianism is not a missionary religion. According to some liberals, mainly in the West, it may be possible to **convert** to become a Zoroastrian, but not a Parsee, which is a matter of birth.

Women have traditionally had equality with men within the religion, despite the fact that they cannot be priests.

If outsiders were to summarise the **Zoroastrian lifestyle** in the last century or so they would use words such as 'education', 'reputation', 'prosperity' and 'charity'. Zoroastrians tend to hold respected positions in society, and in politics sometimes, out of proportion to their numbers. Their devotion to education plus their reputation for honesty and keeping their word has made them prosper economically. The lay control of their religious community has directed much of its energies into social and philanthropic work. Charity is a way of fighting evil.

It may be from all this that you will feel that this is a not a faith for an outsider to join. It is menaced by secularism, its birthrate is falling, it has not come to grips with the issue of how to deal with the spouses and children of those marrying out of the religion, nor as to whether conversion into the religion is acceptable. There is a wide range of opinion on ritual and observance. Matters are not helped by a century or so of misinterpretation of the faith's beliefs encouraged by Western scholars. Nonetheless it is a religion with some interesting and indeed unique ideas, and ones which in some ways sit well with a modern, environmentally conscious, humane and prosperous world. The faith is oriented to family and community. As a Zoroastrian you have a duty to expand God's material as well as spiritual creation, to marry and have children, and to enjoy creation. Misery drives out the divine, and happiness is central to your task. You are not an unimportant speck in the universe, but someone doing your bit in the universal war, which is going to be won, which uses happiness to secure happiness. Despite Zoroastrianism's small modern base it is an important faith with some distinct ideas.

Chapter 16

Judaism

For this, your basic decisions will have been:

- that spirit exists;
- that there is a creator God, just one,
- that He is good,
- and eternal,
- and all-knowing,
- and all-powerful,
- and who cares for you individually, and is potentially interventionist;
- and that you have a soul, which is separate from God but is an element of the essence of God.

Judaism says that God has a special relationship with the Jewish people, and has a **covenant** or binding agreement made with them at Mount Sinai and that, as a foundation of this, God has revealed to them His laws and commandments.

Nowadays, there are plenty of secular Jews who do not practice the rituals of Judaism. And it is possible, although not that easy, for a non Jewish person to convert to Judaism. All you gentile (non Jewish), uncircumcised men may have certain thoughts about that, and you will have the answer later.

The Jews' part of the covenant with God is to keep his laws as revealed to them through Moses at Sinai, and to bring holiness into every aspect of their lives, which can perhaps be seen as a ritual to honor an ever present God.

According to the Hebrew Bible God made not one but three covenants with humans. The first was with Noah when God promised there wouldn't be another flood and gave Noah a set of laws for all humanity. These are referred to as the Noahide laws. The second covenant was a promise given to Abraham concerning the part of his descendants in history. The third was the covenant with the people of Israel, later the Jews, given to Moses at Mount Sinai together with God's law and commandments.

So, Judaism's idea is that **God has chosen the Jews** and will look after them, but he has done so through love and so that they will remind everyone of his love for everyone and the necessity of obedience to his Law. This Law was given to the Jews to follow for the benefit of everyone. The aim is not that everyone should become Jewish but that they should conform to God's will. The Jews are chosen but they are not thereby necessarily better than other nations. They just have a different task, to be a holy nation, set apart. As the Hebrew Bible's book of Exodus says, 'Indeed the whole earth is mine, but you shall be for me a priestly kingdom and a holy nation.'

Traditional Jewish interpretation says that all nations were offered the Torah, or Law, but only the Jews accepted. Deuteronomy, the fifth book of the Hebrew Bible, records that God's choice was made from love rather than because Israel particularly deserved it. Jews aren't into the business of denying salvation to others, or even seeing life in terms of salvation. They are exclusive in the sense that God has chosen them for a task, but not exclusive in the way of some Christian groupings.

You can see from this that Judaism is very much a communal religion. God chose the Jewish people, not particular individuals. Group worship is a central part of Judaism. Its laws are deeply bound up with a daily way of life and ritual, shared by all Jews to a greater or lesser extent. Each Jew is asked to realize, in his thoughts and acts, the covenant with God.

Non Jews may be familiar with the oft repeated Christian assertion that Judaism adheres to harsh values found in the Old Testament and the phrase '**an eye for an eye**, a tooth for a tooth' is often quoted. In fact, so far as Judaism is concerned, this related to the law of damages, of compensation. For example, the Talmud, a principal text of Jewish law, suggested that if an eye be put out, the compensation be judged by pretending the victim was a slave and calculating how much the injury would have reduced his value. The only injury that this approach could not sort out would be if the victim had been killed, so in that case only the death penalty would do. Otherwise the view was not so different from the world of daytime TV adverts for personal injury claims.

As an historical aside, I remember, when young, hearing New Testament Christian Bible stories read out talking of the **Pharisees** and the **Sadducees**. Who they were I didn't know, but I was given the impression they were a bad lot. The principal difference between these two ancient Jewish groupings was that the Pharisees believed that the soul was immortal and the Sadducees believed that the soul died with the death of the body. The Pharisees' view won. The Pharisees then vied with another Jewish grouping, the followers of Christ.

A trap for those wishing to understand Judaism is to see it in the context of Christianity, possibly because of the common use of the Hebrew Bible, which Christians term the Old Testament. However, it is possible to reduce Christianity to a precise doctrine and theology. Not so with Judaism, apart from the belief in the nature of its one God, the covenant with the Jewish people, the role of the prophets, the Messiah and the resurrection of the dead. A 1937 conference of American Reform Rabbis tried to agree on a definition of Judaism. The best they could do was, 'Judaism is the historical religious experience of the Jewish people.' A famous story in the Talmud has a prospective convert ask a Rabbi to teach him the whole of the Torah (the first five books of the Hebrew Bible). The Rabbi says, "That which is hateful to you do not do to your neighbor. This is the whole of the Torah. The rest is commentary. Go and study it." [*Tractate*

Shabbath 31]. Since **Judaism has such a limited theology**, Jews can have a wide range of opinion on matters that would be more rigidly defined in other religions. It is what you do that matters rather than what you believe.

Nonetheless, if you wish to convert to Judaism you may find yourself, (depending on which denomination you join and how religious you are), having to submit to **a multitude of rules** which affect all aspects of your daily life. And if you are a true convert you will embrace this happily. Worship for Jews is largely a matter of obedience, done out of love. **The Law** is both a commandment and a blessing.

Thus 'doing good' for an Orthodox Jew includes fasting on Yom Kippur and praying in the synagogue, and 'evil' includes eating pork and switching on the light on the Sabbath.

As for what God's laws are, they are set out in a number of texts, principally in the Book of Leviticus. This is where the authority resides, not in any person or group of people. These written records are sometimes referred to overall as **the Torah**, using the word in its most general sense. However, the Torah is strictly the first and most important record, consisting of the first five books of **the Tanakh**, or what Christians would call the Old Testament, perhaps better referred to as the Hebrew Bible. Traditionally, Judaism regards this as the word of God as told to Moses, the first and greatest of God's prophets, who is the means by which God has spoken. Then there is the rest of the Hebrew Bible. Then there is the later oral tradition, long ago reduced to writing, in the **Mishnah** (derived from the word for 'to investigate'), and then **the Talmud**. The law which you, as a Jew, must follow, is set out in these books. There are also extensive further works of commentary and interpretation. The idea is not so much that what is in the Torah is good but that it is in the Torah because it is good. The written Torah cannot be altered, but it is subject to considerable interpretation and that interpretation can evolve.

Before we go into more details about these rules, there are a few other points you should take on board.

One is Judaism's attitude to the idea of an **afterlife**. That road of thought is sometimes treated as a bit of a distraction by Judaism. If you become a Jew, your concern will be to live a life here of which God will approve. Judaism is in this sense a this-worldly religion. Good and evil will respectively be rewarded and punished, but exactly what happens after death is God's business and subject to many different beliefs within Judaism.

Like most God religions, Judaism struggles with the issue of **evil**. Isaiah 45.7 suggests that evil was indeed created by God. Generally Judaism sees evil as an inclination of man, termed the yetzer-ha-ra. Although this inclination can lead to wrongdoing it is none the less essential since it gives life its driving power, albeit one with a disadvantage. It is sometimes referred to as the 'leaven in the dough'. The bread would be unpalatable without it but it can cause over fermentation. It cannot be destroyed, but man must struggle against its adverse effects, and the Torah is his best help. Kabbalah, of which more below, has its own ideas on the issue of evil.

As a Jew you may believe in **the Messiah** and in Messianic times to come. The idea of the Messiah is that he will be a human 'anointed' by God. He will come before the end of time and make the final judgment of everyone.

Next, consider the words of one of history's most famous rabbis, Maimonides: "Our sages and prophets did not long for the Messianic age in order that they might rule the world and dominate the gentiles, the only thing they wanted was to be free for Jews to involve themselves with the Torah and its wisdom." (*Laws of Kings and Wars 12:4*). Non Orthodox Jews (of which more below) put the emphasis on a Messianic age rather than on an individual person.

Above all, you will believe that **God is just and fair**. That may not seem a surprising idea, but Judaism was one of the first religions to adopt it.

The mere history of most religions is not particularly helpful in telling you what they have to offer now. But Judaism has its history at its center, for it is a **history** in which Jews perceive a divine purpose. So, a thumbnail sketch of how they see their history may be appropriate. Judaism holds that the Jewish people are descended from one Abraham. Much later, Abraham's descendants moved to Egypt where they were enslaved. After some centuries they got away and their leader, Moses, led them to what is now Israel and Jordan, which in due course became the Kingdom of Israel. It was on this journey that God made a covenant with Moses and his people, the Israelites, and gave him the Ten Commandments. After the death of King Solomon, Israel split into two kingdoms, Israel in the north and Judah in the south. Later, the Assyrians conquered and enslaved the northern biblical Kingdom of Israel and with the eclipse of Assyrian power the southern biblical Kingdom of Judah fell to the Babylonians who destroyed the Temple in Jerusalem. Many inhabitants were then exiled to Babylon. By now we can refer to the Israelites as the Jews. Later the Jews came under Roman domination. So the idea of being dispersed, and also seeking a way back to a homeland is deep in the history of Judaism. The Judaic interpretation of history sees well-being as the result of obedience to God and disaster as a result of disobedience.

Thus, ritual has a deeper significance than in many religions, being part of a way of life which has bound Jews together for many centuries and through which they have worshipped together. The law may be found in every aspect of daily life.

It is for these reasons that this chapter will describe details of daily life and ritual which may be ignored when dealing with other religions.

The Torah contains 613 commandments. A lot of these are obsolete. For example, some deal with the rituals of the Temple in Jerusalem, destroyed early in the Common Era (or early AD). Others applied to farmers in ancient Israel. Less than 300 apply today, but that is still a lot. The best known ones are the **Ten Commandments** which are listed as follows.

I am the Lord your God.
You shall have no other Gods before me, and you shall not make idols.
You shall not wrongly use the name of God.
Remember the Sabbath day and keep it holy.
Honor your father and mother.
You shall not murder.
You shall not commit adultery.
Do not steal.
Do not bear false witness against your neighbor.
Do not covet your neighbor's wife, or neighbor's possessions.

Will God forgive you if you break these commandments? Yes, if your repentance is sincere and provided you don't repeat previous sins and failings. As a Jew you will observe the penitential season ending on Yom Kippur and during which you will review your deeds. Note that if you sin against another you should seek that person's forgiveness before atoning to God.

What else will you be in for? Well, the other rules divide into those where the reason is obvious (such as not bearing a grudge), and those (such as not eating some kinds of meat) where the reason is not obvious, but which are in the Torah and so must be obeyed.

There are a number of denominations within Judaism. The chief ones are: **Orthodox, Conservative (mainly in the USA), Reform and Liberal**. The difference between them is the extent to which they are prepared to modify the rules in the Torah to fit in with modern life. This in turn arises from the view taken of the origin of the Torah. Is it God's word, or is it a human document which expresses what the writers of the time believed was God's will for humanity? Those who believe it is God's word take the view that no changes can be made and that the rules in the Torah must be obeyed in their entirety. Orthodox Jews believe that. Those who believe the Torah is a human document believe that it can be interpreted and some of its strictures ignored with a clear conscience. So when the rules of Judaic life are described here, their application to you may depend on which denomination you join.

This is not the place to go into different theories of biblical origination which separate **Orthodox** Jews from other denominations. Suffice it to say that the Orthodox stick firmly to the traditional rules. Of course, as with all religions, you will find some members less rigorous in observance than others.

There are also Jewish groups which are sometimes called **Ultra Orthodox** by others, particularly those outside Judaism. Another term is **Traditional Orthodox**. These include the ones where the men all wear hats and black clothes and have ringlets. They tend to be very observant indeed of the rules, and have some extras of their own. For example, a man may not be alone with any woman another than his wife. Even holding hands when others are present is considered immodest. If you are a woman, don't expect such a Jew to shake hands with you. Don't be offended, it's nothing personal. Traditional Orthodoxy is influenced by the Kabbalah tradition, of which more shortly. Some Traditional Orthodox groupings seek to segregate themselves from non Jews, many don't.

The main differentiating idea behind **Reform** Judaism is that the Torah, rather than being God's word, is what the writers of the time believed to be God's will for humanity. Since humans can make mistakes, Reform Judaism believes that the interpretation of the Torah can be tested against new knowledge and understanding. If a practice no longer serves a purpose it can be abandoned. Moral laws are forever, but not so other laws. Some Reform Jews are radical in this approach. Others, more 'traditional', are not. Reform Judaism in the USA tends to be more radical than that in the UK. Reform Judaism in particular believes in the complete equality of men and women in every aspect of Jewish observance and practice.

Liberal Jews have historically been even less orthodox than Reform.

Conservative Judaism broke away, not from Orthodox Judaism, but from the Reform movement, was a creative response to both Orthodox and Reform Judaism in the USA, and tries to bridge the gap between them. It embraces a wide range of traditional Jewish opinion, and accepts modern methods of study of the text of the Bible. It examines history to see if given laws go back to the beginnings of Judaism. If they do they are sacrosanct, but if not then change is possible.

Reconstructionist Jews are a smallish minority who believe that Judaism is an evolving religious civilization, not a religion revealed by God.

Karaites are a small grouping that accord sole authority to what is in the first five books of the Bible. There are some Jewish groups, the **Messianic Judaism** movement for example, who practice Jewish traditional practices but who believe Jesus was the Messiah. Another example of that is the **American Jews for Jesus**. There are even Jewish pagans, humanists and spiritualist style groups. These are minority groupings. They are included to show that if you want to join the Jewish people you will find a slot somewhere.

We can now consider the various ideas within Judaism about **what happens after death**. Orthodox and many Conservative Jews believe that the soul lives after death and that after the coming of the Messiah the dead will be resurrected. However, many Jews don't believe in the resurrection of the body. That is the position of most Reform Jews. There is general agreement that a soul living after death is dealt with according to how its life was lived, the righteous to Heaven, the unrighteous to Hell. However, there have been many different views as to the nature of Hell. These have ranged from annihilation of the soul, to a perpetual life in Hell, to a stay for just twelve months. This last became the dominant view. And some Jews don't believe in the ideas of Heaven and Hell. Some Jews, notably some of those who follow the Kabbalah tradition, of which more below, believe in reincarnation. Some Jews believe that we live in some way after death, but only in this world. For example, through the continuation of the dispersed atoms of our body, or through our genes, our children, or through our social group or nation or through Jewry, or through influence or through deeds. Note that a belief that your soul doesn't live after your death does not require you to believe that God does not exist. Also, there are Jewish atheists. In the last hundred years or so Judaism has evolved so that a significant number of Jews believe that you can be a good Jew without believing in God, drawing instead on centuries of Jewish tradition, history and practice. Any summary of Jewish views of life after death is likely to be inadequate. You can see that as a Jew there is a great variation of view open to you, depending on which grouping you join. I repeat: the important thing for a religious Jew is not to concentrate on what might be but to live a life in accordance with God's laws and values.

Now some words about the **Kabbalah** (the 'inherited tradition' or 'that which has been received'). You have probably come across the term already, perhaps in connection with the pop star Madonna. This is a mode of Jewish thought and belief which is traditionally associated with mysticism, although many followers of Kabbalah aren't mystics. Some people see Kabbalah as associated with magic.

The tradition fully developed in the thirteenth century, though it has also been said to have been founded on a tradition handed down secretly, much of it orally, the suggestion being that it dates back to early Judaism, the idea being that the teaching was ancient but that it could only be received when the people were ready.

Kabbalah is controversial and has been seen as dangerous to study, being easily misunderstood. Its followers see its teachings as the true inner meaning of Judaism. The word is loosely used to describe a number of traditions of Jewish mysticism. The central idea of Kabbalah is to find out how God is present in the world and to develop ways of connecting with Him here.

Of **Kabbalistic texts**, the best known are the *Sefer Yezira* or *Book of Creation*, the *Book Bahir*, and the *Zohar* or *Book of Radiance*. The second- or third-century *Book of Creation* highlights the idea that the universe was created by the power of divine speech, so generating a preoccupation with the significance of letters, and that there is a harmony which binds the words and letters of the sacred texts and all aspects of existence. The enigmatic *Bahir*, dating to the eleventh or twelfth century although ascribed by tradition to the first century, develops the idea that divine power is divided into ten powers or spheres and introduces the idea of reincarnation. The *Zohar*, the major text of Kabbalah, dates to the thirteenth century, when Kabbalah was fully developed, but is ascribed by some followers to the second century or even the time of Elijah, and has the idea that the flow of spirituality which comes from these divine powers links everything.

Thus each of these **divine powers** is an aspect of an otherwise unknowable God (En Sof, 'there is no end'). These aspects (**sefiroth**) emanate from God. The last aspect, the Shekinah, is that by which God becomes present in the world and active in everything which exists. This Shekinah is seen as the female aspect of God. The sefiroth are often illustrated in the form of an upside down tree. The idea is that the roots are based in the incomprehensible God and the branches are in the world. The sap runs from En Sof to give the tree life. The flow of spirituality which comes from these divine powers, these sefiroth, links everything. If the flow is weakened, so is everything and evil becomes stronger. We weaken or strengthen the flow by our behavior in relation to the commandments. God gave the commandments to enable the people of Israel, and others, to sustain this flow of divine sustenance. This is a dynamic process which can put right the things that have flawed creation. This trend in Kabbalah thinking was conservative, since it was a further reason to concentrate on following the rules, to which it gave a new dimension, and so was wedded to what would now be called Orthodoxy. The process could be seen to operate not just individually, but communally, perhaps even nationally. This sense of collective responsibility has permeated Judaism. Later, these ideas became linked in with the idea that the Messiah would appear when humanity's behavior had had a sufficient effect upon the divine flow.

Consider the **creation** story adopted by Lurianic Kabbalah, a tradition founded by one Isaac Luria in the sixteenth century. In this, God withdrew, shrank into Himself, as it were, to make way for the world. God then filled the emptiness with divine light. But the pipes carrying the light shattered under the strain. Sparks of the divine light were dispersed. Some returned to God, others were trapped in the Godless realm. Later, Adam could have fixed it, but sinned. The divine sparks were trapped in material objects. A suggestion was thus that God was not omnipotent. Indeed Lurian Kabbalism suggested that during this imperfect creation God's Din, or Stern Judgment, had become separated from His other attributes, including His mercy. Some Kabbalists envisioned the divine presence on earth as a woman tragically separated from the Godhead and exiled with human beings in the material world. Here were answers as to how the world was riddled with distress and evil. And by the observance of the law the Kabbalists could restore the Shekinah to the Godhead, and the world to its proper state.

The Lurian version of creation was quite incompatible with the *Genesis* Biblical account, and is an illustration of how little dogma there is in Judaism. Jews are free to have many variations of belief as long as they follow God's laws.

202

Later, a form of Kabbalah known as **Hasidism** saw these sparks of the divine in everything. So you could experience God in the smallest actions of your daily life. Everyone could do it. It was a mystical approach to following God's laws.

Next, a new form of Hasidism, **Habad Hasidism**, took the view that only God existed. Only our limited perceptions made us think that the world was real. We had to go deep into our inner world to reach the center and the truth.

The practice of the Kabbalah turned the search for God inwards in a **mystical** way. The Kabbalists recognized that God was unknowable but believed that He could be experienced in mystical meditation on the scriptures. Various methods, techniques and exercises were used, sometimes accompanied by vigils and fasts. The overall idea was to find the presence of God in yourself and perhaps in everything.

The majority view was that the specific ideas of the Kabbalah were **not to be taken literally**, but that they were an attempt to explain what could not be rationally explained. An eighteenth-century text has Luria say, "We only speak in a parabolic (like a parable) way to satisfy the needs of comprehension, but a wise person will understand by himself that this does not reflect an actual representation of divine reality" [*Kanfei Yonah* 1786 by Moses Jonah]. Another such commentary says, "... one must say that the Divine Contraction is not meant literally ... The obvious truth is that it is a metaphor used to promote understanding". [*Shomer Emunim* 1736 by Joseph Irgas]. A minority did take a literal approach. If you are interested in Kabbalah you need to weigh that up. Bearing all that in mind, the Kabbalah was seen as easily misunderstood and came to be seen as something which should be studied only by those with sufficient learning and adequate guidance.

During the nineteenth and first half of the twentieth century, Reform Jews, Conservatives, Reconstructionists and Modern Orthodox Jews rejected any interest in the Kabbalah.

So, what of **the Kabbalah today**? Its ideas have influenced Judaism generally, brought more spirituality to Judaism and have prevailed in Traditional Orthodoxy.

Some ideas from the Kabbalistic tradition have found their way into **other faiths**, notably Christianity, something which started in the fifteenth century. Christians experimented with the significance of language, letters and divine names. This became associated with magic and numerology. Generally, the Kabbalah had associations that made it disregarded by mainstream Western thought in the nineteenth and much of the twentieth century.

Strangely, this separation of the Kabbalah from Judaism later returned to Jewish tradition in the form of people who saw it as **an alternative to Judaism**. You could say it became allied to forms of secular Jewish spirituality.

Since the nineteen seventies many **New Age groups** have used Kabbalah material and ideas, particularly, the idea of a cosmic harmony. The organization which Madonna joined is the **Center for the Study of Kabbalah**, founded in California and now worldwide. Within this, self-styled Orthodox 'rabbis' seek to teach the traditional Jewish life to secularized Jews, but the organization attracts all sorts of seekers of spirituality, many of them Christians. It is New Age in attitude. There is also a tendency for magicians and some healers to call themselves Kabbalists.

Since Kabbalah has so influenced **Traditional Orthodoxy** this may be the place to say a bit more about that. There are a number of traditions within Traditional Orthodoxy. Generally, they are all faithful to the idea that everything is linked with the flow of divine power. **Hasidism** ('the pious ones') emphasizes the mystical tradition, concentrating on the joy that accompanies the doing of religious deeds with the correct spirit of devotion. The message is 'there is no place from which He is absent'. It also has the idea that the way to approach God is through a mediator, who is regarded as a messenger of God, and who passes this role on within his family. Such a person is called a Tzaddik or Rebbe, and each such dynasty has a group of followers who have a deep belief in the bond holding them together. **Habad Hasidism** was largely centered in Russia, and in Israel developed an anti-secular political aspect. An active subgroup is referred to as Lubavitch Hasidism, Lubavitch being a town in Russia.

Some followers of Kabbalah in focusing on a coming Messianic Age associate that with Zionism.

That only scratches the surface of the Kabbalah and involves many generalizations, but it does give an indication of the wide range of views that this much used word can be attached to, both within and outside Judaism.

If you are attracted to Judaism, then the main areas where your choice of denomination will make a significant practical difference to you are as follows: getting married, getting divorced, worship, and your daily life within your family and community.

So, on to **the rules**. We all have to eat, so maybe food is a good place to start. It is also a key way of finding how observant of the faith a Jew is. The issue is, is food 'kosher'? **Kosher** means 'right' or 'fit' or 'clean'. In other words, the food which is not forbidden. So the question is, what is forbidden?

Why all this fuss about food? Well, it is in the Torah, in the Law. It is a way to holiness. It is a discipline, not having what you want when you wish. The Talmud says, '… the altar atoned for Israel, but now a man's table atones for him' [*Tractate Berakoth* 55]. A man's table is like an altar. When you eat you demonstrate your belief in God.

Onwards to the menu. There are lists of birds and animals which may not be eaten. You may, if you wish, eat duck, goose, chicken and turkey but not other birds. You may not eat fish that do not have fins and easily removed scales: so, goodbye prawns, scallops, and mussels. Animals must chew the cud and have cloven feet. No bacon sandwiches. Milk and eggs must be from a kosher species. And a kosher beast must be slaughtered appropriately, the throat cut and the blood drained out. Animal lovers should be reassured. The cut removes the blood supply to the brain. So the animal loses consciousness almost immediately. There are also rules about preparing food. Milk and meat cannot be mixed when making the meal, nor eaten straight after one another. If you have taken milk you mustn't eat meat for another thirty minutes, and if you have eaten meat you must wait longer than that before you take milk. There are other rules, but this is enough to give you the idea of what you could be signing up to in this aspect of your daily life.

You will note the word 'could'. Some Jews may sometimes eat non kosher food. Conservative Jews are allowed to judge whether the food (and other) regulations add to or take away from the person's spiritual development. Reform Jews used to deny these rules as purposeless and even harmful, but now it is left to the individual – some do, some don't, more don't than do. Liberal Jews are much the same as Reform Jews here. Reconstructionists, who you might expect not to follow these rules at all, may follow some of them for reason of tradition.

As with all religions, Judaism has its special days, or as Leviticus says **'appointed festivals'**. Judaism's attitude to these is that they are times when the eternal, spiritual world can be glimpsed.

The observation of **the Sabbath** is very important. After all, it is in the Ten Commandments. It will affect your weekly life. You should be aware of the details. To Jews, the Sabbath is not a duty but a gift from God. If you don't like the prospect of it, you're looking in the wrong corner. For Jews, the Sabbath is the Saturday, but it starts at sunset on Friday night. So, just before Friday sunset, the mother of the house, with any young children, will light two Shabbat (Sabbath) candles. Other members of the family will be welcoming the Sabbath in the synagogue. After that the family has their meal at home. There is special food, and often guests, especially those without a family. To all denominations the Sabbath is important. On the Saturday morning there is the main and family oriented service. The rest of the day is for relaxation and study, apart from the afternoon and evening service. As the Sabbath ends shortly after sunset, there is a special ceremony to end it, Havdalah, which symbolically separates the holy day from the other days of the week. Orthodox Jews should not drive on the Sabbath. Better not to go to the synagogue than to drive. This would be ignored by Reform and Liberal and many Conservative Jews. As usual, be prepared to engage with rules that you need to accept with loving obedience.

Another area involves the situation of **women**. From the start, Reform allowed men and women to pray together and in 1972 Reform had its first woman rabbi, followed by Reconstructionists and then by Conservatives. Within Orthodoxy, however, women play no part in public worship in the synagogue and sit separately, and women rabbis are not accepted. Within Ultra-Orthodoxy, and for some Orthodox Jews, rules of 'family purity' apply. A concept is that menstrual blood defiles ritual purity: so, no sex during your period and for seven clear days afterwards, and a ritual bath immersion. This is not an anti sex thing. Procreation is emphasized by Judaism, and the sexual duties of spouses are approved. Sex on the Sabbath is definitely not regarded as work.

There is no need to go into the details of weddings, but **divorce** needs a mention. Judaism has always allowed divorce. However, the husband can withhold his consent, for only he can initiate a religious divorce. He can't stop a civil divorce, but he can stop a religious one. In Israel, where only religious divorce counts, the court can ultimately imprison a husband for his refusal, but cannot insist on his consent. One man spent more than thirty years in jail for this reason. Nor can a husband's consent to a religious divorce be forced outside Israel although religious courts will make very strenuous efforts to persuade a recalcitrant husband to comply. However, Reform will if necessary grant a divorce without the husband's consent if the couple already have a civil divorce. Liberal Judaism recommends a religious divorce but will permit the remarriage of a Jew who only has a civil divorce.

For male Jews, **circumcision** is a must, unless there is a powerful medical reason against it, such as hemophilia. The ceremony is performed on the eighth day after birth. It is a religious ceremony rather than an operation, and is performed by a trained expert known as a mohel. For Jews it has a spiritual dimension, as does so much Jewish ritual observance. That may be difficult for a non Jew to understand. It is part of the covenant, the promise, the relationship, between God and the Jews, going back to Abraham who is said to be the first to perform the ritual. And yes, if you are a male convert you must be circumcised, unless you have that convincing medical reason not to.

So, if you wish to **convert** to Orthodox Judaism, you will have to accept and embrace the Law in its entirety. Your daily life is going to be much affected. It may in practice be difficult to live in the same household as someone who does not share your belief. However, much depends on which denomination you convert to. All denominations accept converts, although Orthodoxy makes it extremely hard. The stricter the denomination, the more searching the enquiry as to your motives is likely to be, and the more demanding the instruction you will have to undergo. The non Orthodox groupings are less demanding both in their conversion procedures and the requirements of your daily life. Note that Judaism is a **non missionary** religion. It isn't going to seek you out to convert you.

It should be added that there is one exception that all denominations make to most of the rules, and that is actions necessary for the preservation of life. If you have a heart attack on the

Sabbath an ambulance may be called to come and get you.

A word needs to be said about the role of **the rabbi**. The rabbi's role is to be an expert in and a teacher of the texts of Judaism. A rabbi will have pastoral skills, and care for his congregation, but that is an accompaniment to his main task. The pastoral aspect, although not unimportant for the Orthodox Rabbi, will have more emphasis within Reform and Liberal Judaism. The use of sermons may be more emphasized by the Reform/Liberal side of Judaism.

As a Jew, as with many religions, you will have a belief that each individual life is sacred. As to **birth control**, Liberal and Reform Jews can decide for themselves, and Conservatives accept most sorts of birth control. For the Orthodox, it is forbidden unless the potential mother's health is seriously threatened.

If a pregnant mother's life is in danger, an **abortion** is permitted and indeed required by Orthodoxy, but otherwise no abortion. The Israeli state permits abortion in cases of rape, incest, serious deformity and pregnancy in underage girls. Non Orthodoxy permits abortion only in these and serious circumstances.

If you are a non Jew thinking of marrying a Jew you need to face the possible consequences. If you are a Jew thinking of marrying a non Jew you will be well aware what those consequences can be. As usual, it will depend upon the denomination involved. Formerly a Jew '**marrying out**' had to leave family and community. Your family said the prayers for the dead for you. Some still do. Given that history, even modern non observant Jewish parents are likely to feel dismay at a child marrying out. You can readily see the practical problems that marriage to an unconverted gentile can place in the way of conventional Jewish household life, depending on the denomination.

A word about **Zionism**. Zionism stems from Judaism's long held belief that Jews would one day return to the biblical land of Israel from which the Jews had been exiled by the Romans, and within which Jews can live a full Jewish life. This is a political movement. You can be a Jew and not be a Zionist, and be a Zionist and not be a Jew. A significant body of Israelis are not Zionists. A minority of ultra Orthodox Jews take the view that God took Israel from them because they had been unfaithful to the covenant with him, and are anti Zionist. Some ultra Orthodox Jews see a modern political state as preempting God, Who they believe will restore a religious Jewish state with the advent of the Messiah. Zionists are a mixed bunch. Many are secular and at odds with religious Judaism. In the last fifty years there have emerged in Israel a number of ultra Orthodox movements which combine religion with Zionism. Within these there is an extreme element. However, if you are inclined to Judaism your view of the politics of Israel need not affect your decision, other than as to whether you join a Jewish grouping with a particular political view.

Who is a Jew? I had much trouble with this one. The technical answer seems to be someone who has a Jewish mother. But then, what about converts? Bearing those in mind, it seemed to me that a distinction could be drawn between the Jewish religion and a Jewish race. That got me into hot water with a learned rabbi who told me that only Nazis thought in terms of a Jewish race. But if religion is the only criterion of Jewishness then what about non religious Jews? How do you get round that? You could enlarge your definition of religion to include those who don't believe in God, or in spirit, or in life after death. That would do it. But it would leave you with a definition of religion that wasn't much use in other respects. The problem is the growth of secularism. Before that, being a Jew involved being religious. It seems to me, therefore, that what has happened is that Judaism has, with the growth of secularism, evolved beyond what is usually under-stood as religion. Religion is within it but isn't compulsory. Perhaps Judaism can be seen as a cultural tradition which binds its followers in some semi transcendental network. Is that much different from the views of Reconstructionists? Such an answer gets round the sensitive issue of whether there is a Jewish race as well as a Jewish religion. Although it still leaves the issue of the requirement of a Jewish mother which is pretty near to the idea of race. Anyway, the message of this paragraph is, don't think that the issue of who is a Jew is simple.

Note that if you propose to marry a Jew and convert, then you should take advice as to the Jewish status of your potential children, a status which may vary according to whether you are a man or woman.

Numbers are uncertain. There may be about fourteen to fifteen million Jews worldwide perhaps more, of whom about six and a half million live in Israel. You may have heard the expression 'Sephardic Jew'. Sephardic Jews were the descendants of the Jews who were expelled from Spain, Sefarad as they called it then, at the end of the fifteenth century. Many of them went to either North Africa or the Balkan provinces of the Ottoman Empire. Some settled in Palestine. The term has thus been extended to Jews of Middle Eastern descent. Ashkenazic Jews are those of Central or Eastern European descent.

Finally, I have been struck by similarities between parts of Judaism, and **non Abrahamic religions**. The Orthodox death/messiah/ resurrection of the body sequence is found hundreds of years earlier in Zoroastrianism. Other comparisons can be made with ideas from Kabbalah. The Kabbalah has the idea that sin can shorten your life, and that idea is present in Taoism. The Kabbalah idea of divine sparks caught up with matter echoes the Jain idea of how the spirit/soul/jiva is caught up with matter/ajiva: the spirit's task being to release itself from this material embrace. It also echoes the Jain idea of karma. The idea of interdependence between human beings and divine powers, and of a relationship between 'Heaven' and earth which can affect society generally is found in Confucianism, and particularly in Taoism. I think a major problem in explaining or understanding Judaism is that it is so often seen through a Christian perspective. To understand it you need to appreciate how different it is.

Chapter 17

Hinduism

To be attracted to Hinduism you will have come to the conclusion:

- that there is a creator God, or that you're not sure, or even perhaps that there isn't one: however, the overwhelming majority of Hindus will believe there is such a God;
- that there is only one such God;
- and that such a God is good and all-powerful and all-knowing is everywhere and is eternal and has personality and may be interventionist – or not;
- that goodness is a principle of the universe;
- that you have an immortal soul;
- that if God exists your soul is identical, or that although it is that it is somehow separate from God, or that it is quite separate from God;
- that God can be worshipped as a person, or not;
- that you believe in reincarnation;
- that you believe in karma.

Hindus believe that there are **many ways of reaching God**, and that each is as valid as every other. There is little conflict between Hindus over great differences of view. To Hindus such differences are no more than the infinite aspects of God.

An important and central idea of Hinduism is that of **dharma**. This is 'right action'. It is a value system governing behavior, a religious code of conduct: truth, righteousness, duty, law and justice. Unlike Abrahamic religions, this is not a system of rules revealed by God to humankind, or something which requires doctrinal agreement between those who seek to practice it. For humans it involves love, detachment, honesty, selfless work, and a desire to get closer to God. This value system is just part of existence, how it is, a natural law. Just as the dharma of fire could be said to be to provide heat, so the dharma of humankind is to follow these principles. As a Hindu you will see your religion more as a matter of how you conduct yourself than of your belief. It is your mode of conduct and the values deciding your behavior that are paramount. Thus dharma is a way of life, a mode of thought. The way it actually applies to how we live is subtle and difficult to define and I will talk more of that later.

To a non Hindu, your first contact with the religion may give an impression that it has many varied and exotic gods. However, Hinduism believes only in **one God**. It is just that It has many faces and aspects. The one God is known as **Brahman**. Often It is described as 'truth, consciousness, bliss'. Hindu sages have said that the infinite cannot be described, and that the nearest description that can be given of Brahman is to say what it is not.

As a Hindu you will believe in reincarnation: a cycle of birth, death and rebirth. The bit of you that makes this journey is your eternal soul, or **atman**, your true self. For the vast majority of Hindus who believe in God the relationship between atman and Brahman, the soul and God, has been compared with that of salt dissolved in water.

An important element in this project is **karma**. The idea of karma is that all our actions which are done with attachment to their fruits have a consequence which manifests itself, often in a later life, a law of cause and effect. It may manifest itself in how you are reincarnated (not necessarily as a human being), your personality, your family, your characteristics, or simply what happens to you. Good and bad deeds don't just cancel one another out for we have to experience the fruits of all our actions. Lasting happiness can only be found from escaping the bonds of karma and the cycle of birth and death and rebirth, a cycle known as **samsara**. Thus, the reason to follow your dharma is that it can lead you to **moksha**, or freedom from the cycle of death and rebirth. You need to appreciate the Hindu idea of **attachment**. Attachment is what it says. It is a connection, something that attaches to your actions and so to you. That something is desire. So karma attaches to all actions done with attachment, which are attached to desire. The man who can act without desire, without attachment, is free. As Krishna, an incarnation of the god Vishnu, says in the Hindu text, the *Bhagavad Gita*, "You have the right to action alone. You never have the right to the fruit. Do not be motivated to act because of the fruit. But don't be motivated to not acting either." (2.47: here I use the Penguin translation by Bibeck Debroy). The key is to overcome the thirst for desire.

If you become a Hindu you will have to decide on **the relationship between God and your soul**. For most religions that is a choice which decides whether you join or not. Within Hinduism it is merely a choice within the religion.

If you are a Hindu who believes in God (most of them) your choice is between a number of ideas. One is that our souls are part of God or more accurately that our souls have an absolute identity with God. This is a **monistic** idea. Another is that our souls are separate from God, which is a **dualistic** idea. If and when we break out of the cycle of reincarnation then if we have an absolute identity with God we cannot be distinguished from It. Some Hindus believe this. Otherwise, there are two alternatives. One is that we are in the company of God, but quite separate. Or we can be part of or identical with God and yet somehow separate from God, as a prominent school of Hinduism believes.

Your decision here also involves the decision as to whether God has a personality. If your soul on release from reincarnation will be identical with God, then God is not separate from you, and is not a separate living personality. If God and your soul are separate in some way, then God is an independent being, and can be worshipped as such. You could describe the two views as God being an infinite principle, and God being the supreme personal being.

If you believe in the infinite principle idea, you will be looking into your soul to find its innermost core, and to become fully aware of that. If you believe in the supreme being, you will be cultivating your relationship with and love for God.

As a Hindu you can, if you wish, take the view that not only are you as it were, part of God, but that everything is part of God. So if you wish to worship God you can do so by attaching your devotion to anything, even a lump of wood.

Traditionally Hindus believe that there are **four principal stages in life**. First there is the stage of discipline and education, the stage of knowledge which gives you the training for service to humankind. Next is the life of the householder and worker. That is followed by a retreat from that life and a loosening of bonds. Finally, there is the stage of complete renunciation of material things although many do not do that. This view means that your daily objectives and values may differ according to your time of life. So, for example, the accumulation of material prosperity is seen, in its place, as a worthy task. Indeed, there are many activities of daily life that Hinduism can see as having a religious dimension that other religions would regard otherwise.

As a Hindu, your prime objective is to achieve moksha or liberation and to end the cycle of rebirth. As a Hindu, you have a number of choices as to what would be the best method for you, in your daily life, to achieve that. There are a number of methods or paths to choose from. They are referred to as **yogas**.

Raja yoga is the path of meditation. Through meditation you will seek direct experience of spiritual truth. The object is oneness with Brahman, or God. Raja yoga involves a system of mental discipline. This leads on to the purification of the physical body, focusing on physical postures and control. Out of this developed **Hatha yoga**, which focuses first on the body and then on the mind.

Jnana yoga is the path of knowledge. It will appeal to those with an intellectual approach to their religion. If you choose this you will concentrate on seeing what is real (connected with your true self) and what is not, on disconnecting yourself from the pleasure of this world, concentrating on your mental discipline and on your driving desire for moshka.

The path of **Karma yoga** seeks to be free by acting without attachment to the result of your actions. This will free you from the chains of karma. If you succeed, you will purify your heart, free yourself from your ego, find humility and see God in everyone.

Bhakti yoga sees your love and devotion for God as the path. You will worship God as a divine personal being. Rather than trying to merge your consciousness with God, as with Raja or Jnana Yoga, you will concentrate on a loving relationship with God. You will pray, and sing devotional hymns and chant God's names, in order to purify your mind and actions.

You don't necessarily have to choose only one method or yoga. You can combine them. So, for example, a follower of Karma Yoga may take a Bakhti approach and offer the result of every action to God. The method you embrace may depend on the philosophy of Hinduism that you follow and I will explain more about that shortly.

For those of you brought up within a Western culture, a few comments on the use of the word '**yoga**' may be helpful. The word's root means to join or unite, and you can see how that relates to the idea of the unity of the soul with the divine. So the word is used, as it has been above, to mean a path to this end. It is also the name given to one of the six major traditions of Hindu philosophy, of which more later. Finally, Hatha yoga, mentioned above, has become known in the West as 'Yoga', and usually practiced there with a concentration just on its physical aspect.

It is said of Hinduism that it has grown like a tree. It is one of the oldest religions, with its roots more than two and a half thousand years old. It has no prophets. Many of its believers regard it as having existed forever, and to be a statement of eternal truths. It is free from a formal theology. However, that freedom does not mean that Hindus do not have a variety of theological views as to how individuals relate to the universe. It just means they have a choice of view. To understand the variety of choice this religion gives you, of the range of religious lifestyle it offers, you need to appreciate the ideas, varied as they are, that underlie the different ways of seeking to be close to God or indeed of being an atheist. As always where religion is concerned, to summarize is to simplify, and sometimes in a way which could be accused of oversimplification. Nonetheless, this chapter tries to explain the underlying ideas of Hinduism, in the most general way. Let us now consider the principal philosophical systems of Hinduism, as follows.

First, **Nyaya**. The word means logical analysis. Nyaya is concerned about how we know about anything. There are a number of ways. One is perception, the evidence of our senses. One is inference, the conclusions we can draw. One is analogy. One is credible testimony, which includes the authority of Indian 'scripture'. Nyaya philosophy seeks to distinguish between a true knowledge and a false knowledge. It is usually combined with the philosophy of another school. Indeed, all Hinduism's philosophical traditions accept the fundamental principles of Nyaya logic.

Next comes **Vaiseshika**, which is closely allied to Nyaya. It believes the universe is made of nine substances. The material elements are earth, water, fire and air. The others are: space, time, ether, mind and soul. Vaiseshika has a God, separate from mankind, a dualistic God. This God created the world. An interesting aspect of this school is that it holds that the nine constituents existed before the creation of the world. So, God created the world but not its constituents.

Samkhya sees the universe as consisting of two things,

purusha and **prakriti**, which have existed forever. Purusha consists of selves or spirits, entities of consciousness, let us call it soul. Prakriti consists of everything else, everything that nature can consist of, let us call it non soul. It is capable of change, it is the substance of evolution, of development. Samkhya believes in cause and effect, but believes the effect is present in the cause: so development is inherent in prakriti. How does this development work? The idea is that soul draws non soul to itself like a magnet, and this focusing produces spiritual awareness. Following that individual consciousness evolves. Next comes the elements, then the organs of perception, and then mind. Everything else is produced by various combinations of these things. However, pain is caused by soul being caught up with non soul. In particular there are three strands, or **gunas**, of non soul that coil round soul and imprison it. These gunas are sattva, rajas and tamas. Each of them binds the purusha, or soul, with attachment. **Sattva** is a tendency to goodness, balance, order, purity: and it binds through attachment to knowledge and happiness. **Raja** is a tendency to desire: and it binds through attachment to action, passion, craving. **Tamas** is a tendency to ignorance: and binds through attachment to error, darkness, sloth. These tendencies of nature compete with one another. In this evolution of the world, the self and the non self get mixed up and the intellect confuses the self as to where it belongs. However, if and when the knowledge of this distinction is truly understood, then the soul is no longer bound by the prakriti or non soul, and is free from rebirth. Knowledge gives freedom. And so a follower of Samkhya would concentrate on jnana yoga, the path of knowledge. Samkhya discourages external ritual. It holds that the key to moksha lies in the purification of the thinking process. And you don't have to believe in God.

Yoga is Samkhya plus God: an all-knowing, all-powerful but non personal and non creator God. Every so often It dissolves the universe and starts the process of evolution again, not unlike modern physics' idea of the big bang and the big crunch. This school is associated with a system of mental and physical exercises and discipline. These contribute to achieving a state of freedom: it is not only a question of knowledge, as in Samkhya. The method of discipline can be used in other schools too.

Mimansa concentrates on the interpretation of the ritual parts of the Vedas. Followers don't believe in a creator God but do believe in gods who reward people's meritorious actions, and who can give people gifts suitable to their offerings. Karma operates and gods follow the deeds of a person. You are liberated when your karma is exhausted, when all its fruits have been experienced and when you have stopped more karma being generated by your actions.

Vedanta is the most influential tradition. It embraces both monism and dualism, in other words the idea that our souls are what you might see as part of God, and the idea that they are separate. The majority of Hindus follow some version of this group of ideas.

In this system the non dualistic, or monistic idea is that we have an absolute identity with God, and has the consequence that when and if we end our cycle of rebirth we realize that the material world is only a manifestation of God, the highest reality, and so is an illusion. In practice you have to first realize this intellectually and then base your life on this truth and realize it in practice. Otherwise you are in bondage to ignorance. This view is known as **Advaita**. It sees jnana, the way of knowledge, as the main path to liberation.

A different interpretation of the Vedanta school is that the highest form of spirit and soul and matter form reality. The idea is that everything is within God, but that our souls are different from God in some way, so that when you achieve moksha, release from the cycle of rebirth, you are still separate. This is called **Vishishtadvaita**, or qualified non dualism. The practical importance of this idea is that it gives a philosophical basis for Bhakti, which is the path to liberation for followers of this school. You will remember that Bhakti yoga is the path of devotion. Devotion requires two separate elements: the devotee, and the thing worshipped. So this idea of Hindu classical philosophy underpins Bhakti, for by being separate from God we are able to worship It, and we can receive or cling to Its grace. Bhakti is the most popular religious path of Hinduism. It usually identifies the god Vishnu, Lord Vishnu, with God. Followers of Vishna are called Vaishnavites. For Vishishtadvaita all yogas may be helpful but the path of Bhakti is essential. In the form of an absolute, unqualified surrender to God it can lead to a swift liberation. Liberation consists of attaining a nature like that of God. But it all depends on God's grace. I will speak more of Bhakti later.

Dvaita is also centered on Vishnu as the supreme being. He controls sentient and insentient things, which have a different nature to him. They are real. God is independent reality. Everything else is dependent reality and is controlled by God. The nature of soul is bliss and pure intelligence and its bondage arises from a sense of independence of conduct and is a product of ignorance. Bliss comes naturally on liberation. And on liberation we are separate from God. Bhakti is the path to this, but assisted by the other paths.

These are the main traditions of Hinduism but there are plenty of other variations. Not least is pure materialism. So if you are a materialist, don't ignore Hinduism. The **Carvaka** system, also known as **Lokayata**, rejects the ideas of soul, God and any afterlife or rebirth. Only material objects are real. Your object is to enjoy as much pleasure as you can.

For those who do believe in rebirth there is little guidance on what happens **between incarnations**. However, some Hindu writings refer to temporary stays in various Heavens and Hells. The soul is born into such a place if it has accumulated certain kinds of bad or good karma. When that karma is exhausted, the soul moves on to its next incarnation. Similarly, you can be reborn as a non human, which is very bad news so far as moksha is concerned.

So, where have we got to? As a Hindu you have an eternal soul/spirit, which is involved in a cycle of death and rebirth, linked in with karma. Your object is to be free of karma and rebirth, and for your spirit to be at one with the principle of the universe. The principle of the universe may simply be an infinity of spirits like yours, but for nearly all Hindus it will be God. You achieve this object by right action. This always involves love, detachment, honesty and selfless work. You may combine this with an inward looking concentration on finding God in yourself. Or you may seek to find it in your ordinary life, doing what may be appropriate to the stage of life that you are in, for what is appropriate for a young person may be different for an old person. In this task you may use different methods of approach. You may try meditation and mental discipline. This may appeal to you more if your approach is looking inward, but you can use it even if that is not your approach. There may be an aspect of physical discipline. You may concentrate on disconnecting yourself from the apparent pleasure of this world and trying to see what is real, what is your true self. You may seek to act without attachment to the results of your actions, to disconnect yourself from desire for their results. And/or you can concentrate on your love and devotion for God to help you. Pick and mix. When you escape reincarnation, what may you find? There's quite a choice within Hinduism, according to your fancy and belief. You may find there is no God and that you are free within a universe without God. You may find you have an absolute identity with God and merged into That. You may find you are part of God, but separate from It in some way. Or completely separate. You may simply cease to exist in which case you will have wasted time that you could have spent seeking pleasure.

To put it a bit more technically: Your atman is involved in samsara, and the course of that depends on your actions and on karma. Your object is to achieve moksha. For your actions to lead to this you must follow dharma as it applies to you and your life situations. Your path will be some combination of any, or all, or one of raja yoga, jnana yoga, karma yoga or bhakti yoga. When you achieve moksha, Hinduism gives you a number of choices. You may find yourself in the universe of Vaishesika/Nyaya, or that of Samkhya, or that of Yoga, or that of Vedanta's Advaita, or Vishishtadvaita or Dvaita. And if the Carvaka system is right you won't be there at all after your death. And, of course, remember (if you believe in God) that there are many ways to God, and that the matters set out above are only the major threads of the thick and ancient rope of Hinduism.

What a range of ideas about the universe is available to you in this religion. Everything from ideas for sophisticated intellects, to those for people who prefer unsophisticated ideas. Consider a list of some of them.

Pantheism.

Panentheism.

A monistic view of the relationship between humankind and God.

A dualistic view of the relationship between humankind and God.

A world made by God from nothing.

A world fashioned by God from pre-existing and eternal substances.

A world of matter and spirit, evolved without the necessity of God.

A world which is just an aspect of God, and in some sense not really real.

A world in which only matter is real.

You can see that this is a flexible and (mostly) tolerant religion which has room for most views about the makeup of the universe. Conduct is the most important thing in this religion. However, there is a treasure trove of ideas if you have an intellectual approach to religion, and if you aren't interested in ideas there is a rich variety of worship and rituals. Furthermore, nobody is likely to knock on your door and try to persuade you to a particular point of view. Hinduism is not a missionary religion. After all, as a Hindu you will take the view that spiritual goals can be realized through any religion which is practiced sincerely. As the incarnation of the god Vishnu, Lord Krishna, says in an ancient text, "Whoever worships me, in whatever way, I entertain them in that way. Everywhere men follow in my path." (*Bhagavad Gita*, Ch4.11).

Another tradition is **Tantra**, elements of which can be found in most Hindu denominations. Tantra concentrates on methods to identify internally with the divine that is within us, and so could be described as mystical. The method may be yoga, or may be the use of mantras, or the use of visualizations of the deity. Tantra is also found in Buddhism and Jainism. A minority of devotees have practiced sexual rites, on the basis that as well as procreation and pleasure, sex has the purpose of liberation. This aspect has been seized upon in the West. If you put 'Tantra' ('a loom') into Google, the first page that comes up will mostly consist of sites with a sexual connotation. Those who seek to practice Tantra in this way may care to consider that the tradition emphasizes the need for a guru, meditative practice, and rules of conduct. It has been said that if you get into Tantra without that lot, you are confusing Tantric bliss with ordinary orgasmic pleasure.

Like most religions Hinduism has its **sacred texts**. The oldest of these are collectively referred to as the **Vedas** (Veda means knowledge). The Vedas probably date between 1200 BCE and 1000 BCE, though scholars have different opinions and some say 1500 BCE. In any event they are the oldest religious known texts. Originally the Vedas weren't written down, and were transmitted orally for perhaps a thousand years. The Vedic religion was based on sacrifice. The Vedas contain collections of hymns and melodies to the gods, rules as to how sacrifices should be conducted, magical formulae, and discourses on philosophy. The philosophical sections are known as Upanishads. Their present form is thought to date from 400 BCE to 200 BCE. A number of the prominent ideas within Hinduism are found in the **Upanishads**, such as the idea of Brahman the universal soul, and atman the individual soul, and that they are identical, ideas of reincarnation and karma, and the possible liberation from this cycle, ideas that renunciation might be a path to this liberation, and ideas of theism. Within the Upanishads can be seen a movement from the fearful worship of gods to a consideration of what was inside the individual. They are considered to be self-existent knowledge that has been discovered, although some Hindus consider them to have been revealed by God. There is more on the Upanishads on the website.

Other Hindu texts are considered to be inspired. One is the *Ramayana* which was composed some time after 500 BCE. This portrays the ideals of human behavior for everyone to emulate combined with a recognition that even the most virtuous have weaknesses. Its stories are not taken as literal by most Hindus, it is their point that is important.

The major sacred epic, the *Mahabharata*, also composed some time after 500 BCE, looks at what is within us, the 'self', and the nature of its unity with the outside world, the 'other'. It demonstrates that until we have a right relationship with our self, we cannot have a right relationship with the other, which is inseparable from our self. The question is, how?

This brings us back to dharma. Hindu writings give **four sources for the basis of dharma**. The Vedas. The behavior and practice of good people. The prompting of your own mind and conscience. And the inspired ancient Hindu epics.

I have described **dharma** earlier as a sort of natural law but it is subtler than just a moral code. Hinduism distinguishes between everlasting dharma that is universal and one's own dharma which is the personal implementation of dharma in one's life. This personal implementation is at the center of the *Mahabharata* whose epic stories are accounts of how dharma may apply in individual situations and apparent moral dilemmas.

Dharma cannot properly be appreciated without also understanding the idea of sila. **Sila** is inner coherence, a right relationship between one's self and everything else. The Western tradition would ask, what is happiness. The Hindu tradition would ask, what is a happy person like? Every human attribute has a place and a value, but for Hinduism that place and value has meaning only in its relation with other attributes. So, if you take one element on its own it will lose itself. Take for example the pursuit of pleasure, or the pursuit of provision for your family. Pursue those in isolation and they will be lost. The issue is to know the true place of everything. Opposing truths need to be taken into account. Non violence is necessary but violence is necessary sometimes. Unrestrained pleasure will kill itself, true self-interest requires the serving of others' interests. Furthermore, conflicts are not just between right and wrong, but between right and right, moral dilemmas.

Thus "In case of conflict between one dharma and another, one should reflect on their relative weight, and then act accordingly; what does not denigrate and obstruct the others is dharma." (*Vana-parva* 131.12 trans. Chaturvedi Badrinath, which I use in the following). Wealth should be earned through dharma, sexual matters should be subject to dharma. The value of an act does not just depend upon motive, but upon the given place and given time. This is Hinduism's form of relativism. "Sacrifice the individual for the sake of the family; the family for the sake of the region: and sacrifice the world for the sake of the soul." (*Udyoga-parva* 37.17). Work that one out!

Back to 'Sila' (inner coherence), and the Hindu explanatory parable of Prahlada (*Santi-parva* 124). In this a great Emperor was approached by the lord of the Hindu gods, to whom he said, "Ask for whatever you wish and it shall be given". The god asked for his Sila, and the Emperor had to agree. Then a column of light in a human form came out of his body. "I am Sila", it said. So far, so good. Unfortunately, another column of light emerged and said, "I am Dharma. I too am leaving you, for I live where Sila lives". Then three more columns left. Truth said he followed Dharma. Good Conduct said he followed Truth. Strength said he followed Good Conduct. Then emerged the form of a woman. "Who are you?" said the Emperor. "I am Sri, all that is desirable in human life. I lived in you, but you have abandoned me; and I, too, am leaving you, for I live where strength is." The Emperor's inner being now emptied, Sri said to him, "Dharma, Truth, Wealth, Strength, and I – all of us are rooted in Sila. Of that, there is no doubt".

The **Bhagavad Gita**, or Song of the Lord is a good read. Part of the **Mahabharata**, this poem is set just before the start of a battle and takes the form of a conversation between a great warrior and his charioteer, who is really Krishna, an incarnation of Vishnu, who is believed by many Hindus to be God. It talks of the paths of devotion, knowledge, and selfless action. It concentrates on action and attachment and explores how moral conflicts are struggled with within the context of dharma to achieve inner coherence.

There are many **other scriptures**. Some consist of devotional philosophy or musical poetry. In most Hindu ceremonies, sacred texts, when spoken, are usually recited from memory.

As a Hindu you are likely to be involved in **image worship**, of a statue or picture. This is different from idolatry. The idea is that it is God that is being worshipped, not the physical object. Many Hindus think that God is present in everything, and so can be worshipped in anything. Some Hindus think that an image needs to be consecrated in order to become an incarnation of divinity on earth. Some Hindus take the view that the physical object of devotion is simply a reminder of God. The end result is that when you go to a Hindu temple you will be surrounded by images and pictures, and you will also find these in shrines within the homes of Hindus.

When the Hindu God is viewed as the supreme being It is called **Ishvara**. But It has many faces, presenting Itself in many different forms. Some of these are '**gods**'. Some of these gods have in turn manifested themselves by incarnating themselves as human beings on a number of occasions. Such human beings are called **avatars**. Brahman, God, is often said to be beyond comprehension. However, in assuming the forms of gods and avatars, God makes Itself accessible to humankind. So you will see many images of these gods and avatars, and may well worship them. In addition, these accessible gods can be interventionist. You can pray to them for things.

K. M. Sen's *Hinduism* (Penguin at page 35) refers to a conversation three hundred years ago between the French traveler Francois Bernier and some Hindu pandits of Banaras on the subject of images. The pandits said, "Images are admitted in our temples, because we conceive that prayers are offered up with more devotion when there is something before the eyes that fixes the mind; but in fact we acknowledge that God alone is absolute, that He only is the omnipotent Lord."

If you don't like the idea of image worship at all, don't let that put you off Hinduism. There are a few Hindu groupings which do not believe in worshipping God through images, and you can seek those out.

The majority of Hindus follow the methods of **Bhakti** devotion and are not too concerned with theological intricacies and prefer religious exuberance. They tend to worship Vishnu or Shiva or the mother god or perhaps Krishna, of whom more shortly. A few words on the intricacies of Bhakti worship may be helpful. Most worshippers are likely to be involved in the lower level of Bhakti. This is love of the deity with mixed motives, entailing a self-centered element, hoping for something, health, a job, prosperity and so on. This is fine so far as it goes. It's better than ungodly existence but it produces karma which will delay liberation. Selfless Bhakti is better.

There are a number of Bhakti methods. Examples are, to chant and ponder on the divine attributes or on the divine forms. Another is to concentrate on admiring and attending to a murti, an image of a god. Another is to visualize a form of the deity. Yet another is to relate to the deity as if you were a familiar servant. Or as an intimate friend. Or as a parent or a child of a deity. Or as a lover. There are many other ways, but you get the picture. You might visualize being merged with the deity, or being in a state of painful separation from it. The majority approach is one of an intimate and loving communion with the deity.

Now, at last, we get to the bit which is most people's first introduction to Hinduism, and which is the source of much misunderstanding of the religion, namely the multiplicity of **Hindu gods**. No number can be put on how many there are of these. There are as many spiritual paths as there are spiritual seekers, and potentially as many gods. As always, any description of a particular god plucks specifics out of a sea of variations.

The most important gods are Vishnu, Shiva and a manifestation of the divine in female shape, sometimes referred to as the Goddess, who is worshipped in a number of forms, which can be considered as separate gods. In these gods lie the functions which maintain the universe, namely creation, preservation and destruction. Historically, creation was regarded as the job of the god **Brahma** (note the different spelling to Brahman). However, Brahma is less worshipped now, and creation, preservation and destruction can today be seen as functions within any of the principal gods, depending on the worshipper.

Vishnu has always been seen as the preserver of the universe. His avatars have saved humankind from disasters or tyrants.

When you see his image it will have four hands. These are likely to hold a lotus (his favorite flower), a conch, a discus and a mace. His vehicle is an eagle, a bird which his followers, therefore, regard as sacred. Vishnu's worshippers see him as the greatest god, indeed as God.

Vishnu has had many avatars. As a giant fish, Matsya, he saved Manu, a figure like the Noah of Abrahamic writings, when all others perished in a great flood. As **Rama** he performed acts of valor in the war against the king of Lanka, as set out in the epic *Ramayana*. Vishnu's followers regard Buddha as Vishnu's incarnation. His most worshipped avatar is **Krishna**. A good illustration of the variety of Hindu belief is that some traditions regard Krishna as the supreme deity. Vishnu's next avatar will come at the end of this age.

Shiva is the destroyer. This is not negative, for regeneration and change requires destruction. This dynamic is reflected in Shiva's contrasting characteristics. He is fierce and benevolent, he is ascetic and austere and yet a dancer and husband. He is often worshipped in the form of the lingam and yoni, the male and female sexual organs. When you look at his image it has four arms. In one variation, one upper hand holds a drum, to control the rhythm of creation, and the other holds the flame of destruction. The lower hands are empty, but one offers protection and one salvation. One of Shiva's feet dances on the demon of ignorance, the other is raised.

The Goddess, the female principle, the mother, is worshipped in many forms. In her own right she is known as **Shakti**. She is also referred to as **Durga**. In the form of the goddesses **Parvati** and **Kali**, she is a wife of Shiva. In the form of **Lakshmi** she is often regarded as the wife of Vishnu, and her avatars are the wives of Vishnu's avatars.

Durga is both a warrior and a producer of crops. Her image holds weapons, and shows her slaying a demon. By it, is the lion which she rides.

Lakshmi is the goddess of wealth and good fortune. She also signifies beauty, love and grace. Her popularity will not surprise you. Remember that for Hindus the pursuit of material gain can be a godly pursuit as long as it is appropriate to your stage in life and consistent with the general rules of behavior. Lakshmi doesn't stay long with those who are lazy or who only desire her wealth. Lakshmi is also referred to as **Shri**. She is also capable of giving that greatest of wealth, liberation from the cycle of death and rebirth. Lakshmi's four armed image shows her rising from the lotus flower with which she is associated. Her upper two hands hold lotus flowers. Of her lower two hands, one bestows gold coins, and the other gives blessing.

Kali is the goddess of time and of the transformation that is death. Remember that death to someone who believes in reincarnation is a different prospect to one who believes in a single life. Kali represents a strange mixture, which includes both violence and motherly love. For the ignorant she creates fear, for others she removes the fear of death. Kali's image is striking. A necklace or girdle of human arms hangs from her, and she has a necklace of decapitated heads, or skulls.

Another striking image is that of the god **Ganesh**, who has the head of an elephant. Ganesh is another popular god, being a remover of obstacles and difficulties. He is a god of good luck, wisdom and learning. Ganesh's image shows his body as human and pink. Of his four arms, three hands may hold respectively a goad or axe, a snare, and sweetmeats, and the fourth offers protection and blessing. A rat attends on him, so Ganesh's followers regard rats as sacred.

Ganesh is the child of Parvati. One account is that Parvati made him, fully formed as a young boy, from the scurf of her body, and in Shiva's absence. When Shiva returned the boy barred his way, and an angry Shiva cut his head off. When Parvati explained the situation, Shiva promised to replace the head and sent his men to bring the head of anyone found sleeping with their head pointing north. They came back with the head of a baby elephant, and that was that.

Another striking image you are likely to see is that of **Hanuman**, shown as a strong monkey with human hands and feet. With one hand he holds a club, with the other he holds a mountain. In the epic *Ramayana*, Hanuman helps Rama and performs heroic deeds. One of these involves finding herbs to heal the wounded. These herbs are on a distant mountain. When he gets there Hanuman can't identify which herbs are the ones needed. So he brings the whole mountain back. Not surprisingly, he is the patron of physical strength. He is regarded as a guardian spirit and a model of human devotion to God. His followers regard the Hanuman monkey as sacred.

Saraswati is the goddess of knowledge, music and the creative arts. Students pray to her before exams.

As well as many other higher gods there are numerous **lesser and local deities**, and in Indian country areas these may mean more to the villagers who worship them. There may be spirits in trees or at crossroads who have to be given offerings so they give protection. Nor is divinity confined to gods, avatars or spirits. Natural objects may be considered as divine, such as the sun, moon, and planets and certain rivers and lakes. And remember that many Hindus see God in everything, so everything can be worshipped. At Indian village level Hinduism may blend seamlessly into polytheistic folk religion.

There are a number of groupings of Hindus which you might regard as **denominations**. Those who devote themselves to the god Vishnu are termed **Vaishnavites**, to Shiva, **Shaivites** and to the mother god in one or other of her forms, **Shaktas**. Although Hinduism is noted for its toleration, some devotees regard their own grouping and god as superior to others.

The majority of Hindus live in India, and in India you will repeatedly meet the idea and phenomenon of **caste**, which is also bound up with the history of Hinduism. The idea of caste was that you were born into a class of persons. In earlier Hindu times, there were deemed to be four classes. There were priests and religious teachers (the Brahmin caste); kings, warriors and aristo-crats; traders, merchants and professionals; and servants; and those who worked on the land. As times passed, so there came to be many more subdivisions. These can be seen as supportive groupings, or they can be seen as social class barriers. Within Hinduism there was been a tendency for the intellectual element, particularly those who followed the path of knowledge, to support caste. Those who embraced Bhakti, the path of faith, tended to be liberal on the point of caste. In early Hinduism there are notable examples of low caste spiritual exemplars. In modern India there is legislation against caste barriers, and positive discrimination in favor of those of low caste. However, the positive discrimination has caused much resentment and in some ways strengthened caste feeling. Caste traditionally used to influence a person's dharma, or code of behavior, and caste can still affect the form of a family's religious practice. The more educated and middle class in India now tend to pay less attention to caste.

Hinduism does not have a trained and ordained **priesthood**. Individuals study under a teacher, who may be called a guru or swami. Teachers are also found in monasteries. There are many influential Hindu teachers with considerable followings. Some followers regard their gurus as incarnations of divinity. As a student learns and develops he may seek some priestly function. It will depend on his scholarship and inclinations and his abilities and what others think of those. Some will seek the life of meditation and/or become religious mendicants, sadhus (holy men), ascetics. Some will become teachers. Some will conduct religious rituals in temples and elsewhere.

Temples are often regarded by Hindus as a bit of Heaven on earth. They are the home of the images (murtis) within. The word 'murti' is perhaps better translated as 'embodiment' or 'form'. The temple priests are the murtis' servants, and look after them as if they were humans. They wake them, bathe them, dress them and offer them food. At times the temple will close so the gods may rest. At night they are put to sleep. Worshippers visit as their guests, and ring a bell to announce they are there. At festivals the images are brought out to visit the worshippers, and are carried in procession so people can worship them and make offerings to them. Hindus don't have to go to temples. When they do, the meaningful part of their worship is being in the presence of God in the form of the image. An offering of something may be made to the image and then returned, 'blessed', and with the god's favor within it. A Hindu may go every day to the temple, or may go just at festivals. Procedures within temples may vary, depending on whether the temple belongs to a particular grouping or is non sectarian, or depending on which part of the country it is in.

You can see from this that in India the function of **the temple and the temple priests** is different, for example, from the Christian church building and its priest. The temple priests are employees of the temple, looking after the images and carefully performing certain rituals. They do not have a teaching or pastoral role. At the temple you will have singing of devotional poems and songs, chanting, perhaps dancing, rather than sermons. I say 'in India', because in Western societies the temple has developed more of a congregational and social role.

Subject to that, Hindu worship is mainly on an individual basis. The home will have a shrine, with a chosen image. The word for worship is **puja**. Modern Hinduism developed from an ancient religion based on sacrifice, the idea that the gods should be looked after and pleased by gifts so they would favor the devotees with good crops and good fortune. The daily puja at the household shrine will start with mantras, sacred prayers, recited usually by the head of the household. Then each person will offer flowers, rice, grain and prayers to the image. Mantras are prayers or chants. The idea is that they help you focus on holy thoughts or on your feeling of devotion. Many Hindus practice ritual chanting. The most familiar example of this for those in the West may be the Hare Krishna chant of the Gaudiya Vaishnava tradition.

Ritual is an important part of Hinduism and there are an enormous number of Hindu ceremonies open to you. If you performed all of them it would keep you busy all year. However, Hindus generally confine themselves to a chosen few. One grouping, the Bauls, do not perform any ceremonies at all.

As in most religions, Hinduism has rituals for the individual's steps in life: birth, coming of age, marriage, death and other events. There are as many as sixteen **rites of passage** which can be celebrated, ranging from baby's first solid food, to the 'sacred thread' coming of age ceremony, to the retirement stage of life, to cremation. Some of these rituals are quite informal and may be done at home (not cremation!).

Again, as in most religions, Hinduism has its **festivals**. The extent to which a Hindu participates in a festival may depend on which god that person is devoted to. For example the birthdays of the god Ganesh and of Vishna's avatars Rama and Krishna are important festivals, but notably for their devotees. Divali, the festival of lights, is the most widely observed festival. Another one is Navaratri (nine nights). Some other festivals may only be celebrated in certain parts of the country.

As a Hindu you don't have to make **pilgrimages**, but a lot of Hindus do. In India there are lots of holy places to make a pilgrimage to.

Each family may adopt a different system of worship: which god it devotes itself to, which temple is attended to view the god's image, how various festivals are celebrated, which rites of passage are celebrated. This is likely to depend on the family's social category and caste. If you are thinking of becoming a Hindu, be aware what this may involve for you.

If you have a thing against **cremation** you had better look elsewhere. As a Hindu you will be cremated, unless you are under five or a eunuch or a religious mendicant.

As for behavior, you have seen what 'right action', dharma, requires of you. Since you probably believe God permeates everything you will **respect all life**. You don't have to be a **vegetarian** but estimates of the number of vegetarians in India range from twenty to forty percent. Most Hindus nowadays don't actually worship cows, but they are honored, and in most states of India cow slaughter is banned. As always, practice varies considerably from place to place in India.

The idea of **ritual pollution** is a tradition of Hinduism. It includes leather, so shoes are left outside the house. It includes blood, hence ritual purification and other rules in relation to childbirth and menstruation. It is the origin of the untouchables, people whose jobs made their touch polluting to those of higher caste, a concept now legislated against in modern India. It is usual to cleanse the body before ritual and before cooking. The mouth may be cleansed before saying mantras, on the basis that impure acts and thoughts leave the mouth and saliva unclean. The influence of all this on your daily life will depend on your family's position and your country and the extent to which your family is Westernized.

Setting out the detail of **daily life** as a Hindu is difficult in that many aspects may derive not from the Hindu religion itself but from the cultural traditions of its devotees. So, one could say that in a traditional Indian household men eat first or that many girls accept or have to accept arranged marriages and so on. However, this book tries to confine itself to those aspects which have an overtly religious basis. If you are joining a Hindu family you will need to get a good idea of how they run their household before you commit yourself.

Homosexuality tends to be a taboo subject. It is acknowledged in Hindu scripture. Whether this approves or condemns is a matter of argument. Hinduism does not approve of **divorce**. **Birth control** is accepted. So is **abortion**, despite a traditional rule against willful abortion. **Suicide** is accepted but if it is to avoid suffering it is not approved of. Nor is mercy killing. **Alcohol** is polluting but acceptable. The ban in some Indian states is on social grounds.

Although Hinduism is traditionally a non missionary religion, **there are some groupings which do proselytize**. The best known is probably the Hare Krishna movement. Another is Arya Samaj, a back-to-basics movement of the nineteenth century which rejected the idea of caste. The Transcendental Meditation movement, which seeks followers, is based on Vedanta teaching, but its method can be used independently of Hindu philosophy.

A caveat also needs to be put against the statement that Hinduism is a religion of **toleration**. While its doctrinal tolerance is notable, there has been less tolerance in matters of practice, something which overlaps with issues of caste. And note that since before Indian Independence there has been a growth of a Hindu nationalism which is hostile to other traditions, a political rather than a religious development.

As to **numbers**, Hinduism is the third largest religion, after Christianity and Islam. There are about a billion Hindus. Roughly 890 million of these live in India. Most of the rest live in Nepal, Sri Lanka, Bangladesh, Indonesia, Malaysia and in a Western diaspora.

Finally, back to **dharma**, which will be the practical basis of your life if you become a Hindu. It will require selfless service to others, honesty, love, detachment, and a journey to become closer to God/the universal principle. The word is often used loosely to mean religion but you can see how it is much more than just that. To understand dharma is to understand the meaning of life and to be at one with the self.

Chapter 18

Christianity

To arrive at this door, you have decided:

- that spirit exists,
- that there is a creator God, just one,
- that it is good,
- and all-knowing,
- and all-powerful,
- and eternal,
- and it cares for you personally and is interventionist;
- and that you have an immortal soul,
- which is in some way in the creator's, 'image', but separate from God.

Christians agree that **God is beyond our understanding**. We cannot know His essence.

However, Christianity takes the view that **we can understand God's powers**, what he does. Because of this, Christianity can say that its God is the only one, has always existed and always will, is all-powerful and can do anything, is all-knowing and even knows our thoughts, is the creator of everything, is to be found everywhere and is good.

Likewise, Christians also believe that **God is concerned about each one of us**. And that He intervenes in our world. Sometimes this involves miracles. Christians believe that sometimes God answers our prayers, that if we ask for something he may arrange it. But perhaps the biggest way God intervenes in our lives is to forgive us.

Christians also believe that they know more about God because He took human shape in the form of Jesus Christ. St

John's Gospel says, "The Word was made flesh and dwelt among us." **The Word** is an expression then used to describe God's presence in the world. Jesus is a historical figure who was born in Palestine about two thousand years ago and put to death by crucifixion, at the age of thirty-three it is said. As a Christian you will believe that Jesus then rose from the dead and went to Heaven. We know quite a lot about Jesus. So Christians are able to think of God in His human form and feel closer to Him because of that.

Most Christians (Christian Unitarians are an exception) believe that God is three distinct persons yet that they are all the same one. God the Father is the God we cannot comprehend because He is outside our understanding. Next is God the Son. This is God made man, the Word made flesh, Jesus, being God and yet fully human at the same time. And third, coming from God the Father and God the Son, is God the Holy Ghost or Holy Spirit. The Holy Spirit is God's continuing presence in the world. These three aspects of God in one are known as the **Holy Trinity**. There have been differences of opinion as to just how these three aspects relate to one another and I will be looking at those later. A consideration of exactly what Christ was and just how he relates to God goes to the very heart of Christianity.

As a Christian you will believe that Christ was crucified as a sacrifice to save mankind. But from what? Well, shortly after God created the world, things went wrong in what the Bible calls the Garden of Eden, or for those who see that as a mythical representation of a truth, in an early stage of human existence. Man sinned in a way that made it impossible for his soul to be close to God. Christ's **crucifixion** removed that barrier.

Accordingly, the **principal festivals** of Christianity are Christmas and Easter. Christmas celebrates the birth of Jesus Christ. Easter celebrates his death (Good Friday), and resurrection (Easter Sunday).

Jesus was born of **Mary** and many Christians believe that she was a virgin, that God fathered her child by divine intervention and that her nominal husband Joseph did not exercise his matrimonial rights.

You will see the **Bible**, which consists of the New and the Old Testaments, as the primary and divinely inspired source of knowledge about God. The Hebrew Bible is adopted by Christians as their Old Testament. The New Testament gives accounts of Jesus' life on earth and of his apostles thereafter.

Within Christianity there is an ongoing disagreement between those who confine themselves to the literal meaning of the Bible's words and those who do not. Before deciding which side to come down on in that discussion, you need to appreciate that the **literal interpretation** is a relatively modern phenomenon. For well over a thousand years the approach was to start with the literal meaning of the words, then move on to the moral sense and then to the spiritual sense, the connection with God that was hidden in the page. The corresponding use of allegorical interpretation of the Bible is not some modern development but an ancient and longstanding approach.

As a Christian you will believe in **Heaven**. Many, many Christians also believe in **Hell**. You will believe that how you live your life will decide how you live on after death and that God can enable or assist you to secure your passage to Heaven. Christians have different views as to what Heaven and Hell are like.

Many Christians believe that **the end of the world** will take a particular form. Christ will return, the dead will be physically resurrected in some way and everyone will be judged by God and the good ones will live forever in a new Heaven and a new improved Earth, with their bodies and souls reunited. There is disagreement within Christianity concerning the detail of this and some Christians don't believe this bit at all. The general idea seems to be that the resurrected body won't be a warts-and-all affair but some sort of new and improved matter.

Christianity sees **the body** as important and fought an early war of ideas against those who suggested that matter was inherently evil. The body and soul are in union both in life and following resurrection, and in resurrection the body will be purified.

Christianity emphasizes God's love. **God is love**. That's a bit of a platitude, isn't it? I will do my best to explain how this idea of God's love permeates and underpins Christian thought. In the meantime, consider how the Holy Trinity can be seen as love given, love received and love shared. Also, consider Matthew 22.36-40 (NLT Tyndale), where Jesus is asked which commandment is greatest. 'Jesus replied, "You must love the Lord your God with all your heart, all your soul, and all your mind. This is the first and greatest commandment. A second is equally important, Love your neighbor as yourself. The entire law and all the demands of the prophets are based on these two commandments."' Jesus here puts both these commands on an equal footing. You can't properly love God and not your neighbor for to love God is_to love your neighbor.

With God's love comes His mercy and **forgiveness**. Whatever you have done, you can be forgiven if you truly repent. Forgiveness is an important and attractive feature of Christianity. You can be forgiven not just on judgment after death but in this life. However many times you fall down you can get up again. Christ told Saint Peter that before the cock crowed he would betray Him. St Peter did so and nevertheless was retrospectively considered the first Pope. The parable of the prodigal son is another example. However, there are differences of opinion, notably within Protestantism, as to just how forgiveness works.

Christians believe in God's **Grace**, a sort of connection with God, a gift from Him, which the individual can connect to, tap and find strength from. It is by tapping into this that you can benefit from Christ's sacrifice to help us achieve salvation and get to Heaven. There are differences between Christian Churches as to the exact nature of this Grace.

Another possible connection with God lies in **the sacraments**.

These are ways of encountering God and His Grace which are marked by a sacred ceremony. Christians disagree as to the number of sacraments and just how they work. Most Christians believe in the sacraments of baptism and the Eucharist or communion. Many Protestants see even these as just symbolic conventions.

And, like most religions that believe in God, Christianity emphasizes the desirability and power of **prayer**, your ability and chance to speak to God directly.

As a Christian you will have to lead your life in a certain way. This is best summarised by **the Ten Commandments** set out in the Hebrew Bible/Old Testament. Different Christian groupings have slightly different interpretations of the commandments and as to how they should be listed. You have almost certainly heard the commandments before but here they are again together with some comments.

- I am the Lord your God. You shall have no other gods before me.
- You shall not make any carved images. (The images found in many churches are seen as devices for paying honor to God and not worshipped for themselves. Some Christian groupings criticise this use of images.)
- You shall not wrongly use the name of God.
- Remember the Sabbath day and keep it holy. (Nearly all Christians have come to regard Sunday as the Sabbath. Observance of the Sabbath, by church attendance, not working and so on can vary with denomination.)
- Honor your father and mother. (This is sometimes interpreted as an injunction to obey lawful authority.)
- You shall not murder.
- You shall not commit adultery. (Strictly speaking this just forbids having sex when one or both of you are married to someone else. It is usually extended to include sex outside marriage and lust generally.)

- Do not steal.
- Do not bear false witness against your neighbor. (This is interpreted as including lying.)
- Do not covet your neighbor's wife. (Just to make it doubly clear.)
- Do not covet your neighbor's possessions.

St Augustine of Hippo said that the last two of these commandments govern private thoughts, the first five our relationship with God, and the rest public relations between people. Incidentally, should you have noticed that there are eleven rather than ten commandments set out above, the reason is that Catholics and Lutherans list them differently from other Christian groupings and setting them out in this way avoids having to choose between the two methods. Catholics and Lutherans merge the first two commandments above and other Churches merge the last two.

A useful addendum to the commandments, to illustrate what you are in for, if you are willing, is a list of the seven deadly sins and the seven virtues. Here they are.

The seven deadly sins are:

- Lust
- Gluttony
- Anger
- Pride/vanity
- Laziness/sloth
- Envy
- Greed/ covetousness

Lust and gluttony are sometimes called the disreputable but warm-hearted sins of the flesh. They are distortions of virtues. The same applies to anger. There is righteous anger. Christ overturned the moneylenders' tables in the temple. The other four deadly sins are sometimes called the respectable but cold-hearted sins of the spirit and are more complicated. They are self-consuming and self-destructive and cause great damage to others on the way. Pride is a sin which underlies others. It establishes us as our own judge. It suggests we are enough for our own needs and then attacks us through our own strengths. The other three sins, namely covetousness, envy and sloth, are easily hidden as virtues. Sloth or laziness can hide in the form of tolerance as an end in itself. Envy hates to see others happy and can hide as concern for justice and fairness. It can lead to possessiveness. It leads to joylessness and consumes its owner. Greed/covetousness/avarice can hide as business efficiency. Of all the deadly sins it is the one that can force others to act in the same way.

Let us take a more positive angle and consider **the seven virtues**.

- Chastity. Can this be better expressed as 'purity of soul'? Can it be untangled from sex?
- Temperance. There's a word with a lot of baggage. 'Self-restraint' may suit you better.
- Charity. Do you prefer the word 'giving'?
- Diligence. 'Integrity' may be more in keeping with our modern vocabulary.
- Meekness. That's another word which has outlived its time. What does it mean in our present? 'Calmness', 'composure', 'acceptance', 'serenity'?
- Kindness.
- Humility.

It is interesting that the vocabulary of virtue has become more dated than that of sin.

For a slightly different angle, there are **the four cardinal virtues** (from 'cardo' a hinge): courage, temperance, justice, and intelligent action which we acquire by habitual action.

Finally there are **the three theological virtues**: faith, hope and love (charity being love given) which are the gifts of God to us.

The area that may concern the seeking unbeliever more than any other in the search within Christianity is that of **sex**. The issues are: sex outside marriage, divorce, same sex physical relationships, and abortion. There is also the issue of contraception.

As to **abortion**, generally the Yes answer lies within the more or most liberal area of Christianity and the No answer lies within the conservative and mainstream area. Questions are: when is the fetus a human being, when does it have a soul, when is a termination murder, are a woman's rights over her body greater than the rights of the fetus inside her?

As for **contraception**, the argument against it is that it is sinful to prevent life in this way. The Catholic Church is the principal one that takes this firm line. While it is true to say that millions of Catholics ignore this you may well wish to avoid a life of sin by joining some other Christian denomination if you wish to use contraception.

The Catholic Church also takes a strong stand against **divorce**. Those whom God has joined together let no man put asunder.

Same sex relationships are more complicated. Generally, Christian Churches do not condemn homosexual orientation per se. But they do largely agree that homosexual sexual acts are sinful. If you are gay you will find some churches that will welcome and accept you and your way of life. One choice is the liberal end of the Anglican Church (in the USA the Episcopal Church). Or you could join the United Church of Christ, a USA evangelical reformed Church with a congregational tradition, whose General Synod has come out in favor of equal marriage rights for all regardless of gender.

Given the wide variety of theological views adopted by the

numerous groups following what they see as Christ's teachings it will now be necessary to look at these groups individually so you can try to choose between them.

First, **a one-paragraph history**. In 451 CE, at the Council of Chalcedon, a meeting of bishops, mainstream Christianity agreed on an interpretation of the Trinity whereby it was held that God the Father, God the Son and God the Holy Ghost were of the same nature and being. A number of groupings had slightly different ideas and went their own way. We will meet them again shortly. Christianity had already become the religion of the Roman Empire, which became separately administered as a Greek speaking Eastern Empire and a Latin speaking Western empire. Following the fall of the Western Roman Empire the Western Church continued to be centered in Rome with the Bishop of Rome as its head. In 1054 the Eastern 'Greek' Church, known to us as the Orthodox Church, and the Western 'Latin' Church, known to us as the Catholic or Roman Catholic Church, acrimoniously split, but continued to recognise one another as valid Christian Churches. In the sixteenth century the movement within the Catholic Church known as the Reformation gave birth to Protestantism with its present myriad denominations. Throughout the history of Christianity, particularly in its early days, various ideas were developed and adopted or discarded by the Christian Churches. Discarded ideas became termed heresies, although in their day some heretical ideas were for some time, before their formal rejection, just one side of an ongoing discussion.

What of the Churches that went their own way after the Council of Chalcedon in 451? We can refer to them as **the non Chalcedon Churches**. Sometimes they are called the Oriental Orthodox Churches. The issue they split away on was the nature of the Trinity, or how God the Father related to Jesus Christ, God the Son. In particular, how did Jesus combine his human and his divine nature? The Chalcedon formula said that Christ was truly

God and truly man yet of the same substance. However, there were two differing lines of thought that weren't satisfied by this. One wanted more emphasis that Christ had two natures, divine and human. This was termed the Diophysite or Nestorian view. Another emphasised that Christ had but a single nature. That was termed the Monophysite or Miaphisite view. So if you come across any of those labels that gives you an idea as to what makes those Churches distinctive.

The Monophysite Churches regard themselves as Orthodox. Examples are the Syriac Orthodox Church, the Church of Armenia (also well established in the USA), the Coptic Church of Egypt and the Church of Ethiopia.

Diophysite Churches, regarding Christ in his human nature as the second Adam whose holiness we should do our best to imitate, have been treated badly by history. They are sometimes collectively referred to as the Church of the East, also as the Nestorian Church or the Assyrian Church of the East. nestorian.org suggests they number about 500,000 people.

The Non Chalcedon Churches have come to define themselves and pass their faith on by the transmission of a common pattern of worship and prayer rather than by doctrine and scripture. They tend to see themselves as the local represen-tatives of Christianity. You are unlikely to have close contact with them unless you have some geographical or cultural connection.

This is a good point to say more about heresies. **Heresies** were ideas that gained a following but which were ultimately rejected by the Church of the time. Heresies seem to arise mainly from two issues. One is the nature of the Trinity. The other is how it is that there is evil in a world created by a good God.

Trinity heresies include the ideas:

- that Christ was 'adopted' by God;
- that the Father, Son and Holy Spirit are just, as it were, different hats worn by God;

- that Christ is unlike the Father, being inferior or subordinate to Him;
- that the Holy Spirit is the pinnacle of the Trinity;
- that Christ had a body and soul but not a human mind.

People don't dwell much on the nature of the Trinity now, but you can see that it has been more of an issue in the past, and the contrast of these ideas may make you look at the idea of the Trinity with clearer eyes.

Heresies associated with the problem of evil are:

- that matter is bad and that the world was made by a Satanic creator;
- that there is no all-powerful good power but a battle between good and bad powers with humanity as its center;
- that material things are evil and so we must transcend the physical so we can achieve spiritual purity;
- that there is some kind of demigod, higher than man but lower than God, who did the creating of the world.

Following from this, a word about **Gnosticism**, a movement which embraced some of the above heresies. Victors write the history books, and the Church wrote its own version of Gnosticism, whose writings it largely destroyed. The postwar discovery of a number of Gnostic texts has enabled a wider view.

The word 'gnosis' means knowledge, so Gnostics were people who knew. They knew not in the sense of 'I know that two plus two equals four' but in the sense that 'I know John'. They held that there was the general knowledge of Christianity and then a secret knowledge (theirs) which involved an acquaintance ('gnosis') with God. This secret knowledge was obtained by inspiration. This setup of direct knowing access to God bypassed the Church with its growing structure of authority so it isn't surprising that it was so hostile to the movement, which was widely spread and pervasive.

The Gnostic scriptures now available make it clear that there was a wide range of beliefs among Gnostics. That's understandable given the view that becoming spiritually alive gave rise to what might be regarded as creative invention, for whoever received the spirit communicated with the divine. The Gnostic teacher Heraklion says (Frag. 39 in *Origen, COMM. JO.* 13.53), "people at first are led to believe in the Savior through others" but when they become mature "they no longer rely on mere human testimony."

Gnostic ideas of creation of the spiritual world generally involved complex emanations from the first principle rather than the Genesis accounts. Some texts talk of numerous Heavens with mystical passwords. The belief in a demiurge, an imperfect part-human part-divine emanation in the spiritual universe and creator of the material world, under God, was one common belief. Those who believed in a demiurge often saw the Church as offspring of the demiurge and themselves as children of the Father. The Church attacked the Gnostics as not believing in one God. But many and the more influential Gnostics did believe in one God, as the ultimate source of being.

Some Gnostics saw Christ's resurrection as symbolic not actual. The *Gnostic Gospel of Mary* sees the appearances of the resurrected Jesus as visions. The *Apocalypse of Peter* has Jesus say that he is the intellectual spirit filled with light. The *Gospel of Philip* sees the virgin birth as something to be understood symbolically. The *Acts of John* explain that Jesus was not human but a spiritual being who adapted himself to human perception. Generally, the role of women and the feminine was more acknowledged. Some Gnostics, such as the so called Heumetics, weren't Christians at all.

A leading theologian of the second century BCE, Valentinus, developed mystical Gnostic thought hiding behind allegory, so it sometimes seemed on the surface to be indistinguishable from mainstream Christianity, which annoyed some orthodox Christians no end. Valentinus is thought to have nearly become Pope. His followers developed his ideas, claimed St Paul as their theological ancestor and regarded their academic texts as equal to the New Testament. The Church still had an order of service for the forgiveness of his successors in the seventh century. Valentinus' *Gospel of Truth* talks of awakening from a nightmare state by acquaintance with the Father, who in the form of the Son Jesus resides in us, and uniting with and reposing in Him. There is a suggestion that the world may be an illusion, an element of predestination and a general anti-materialist view.

The school of St Thomas is strictly speaking not Gnostic, but is associated with Gnosticism. It concentrates on the belief that in knowing yourself at the deepest level you can come to know God, so that the self and the divine are identical. So potentially God's kingdom is already present without waiting for the last day. Some people seek to link this with Hindu thought and there are groups you can seek out if this takes your fancy.

Why all this about long defunct heresies? Well, the Gnostics found themselves in revolt against conventional institutions. Many people nowadays find themselves in a similar position. Old questions, debated vigorously in early Christian times, are being reopened. There is increasing interest in the Gnostic gospels as offering different interpretations of the teachings and significance of Christ. You will find English translations of Gnostic texts on earlychristianwritings.com.

However, do bear in mind that the Gnostic gospels are generally considered to be '**pseudepigraphic**' that is to say they are the product of a literary convention which attributes them to respected figures of the past. An obvious example is *The Three Tablets of Seth* (Adam's son). Also, if you choose to believe that any of the Gnostic gospels are inspired scripture, bear in mind that the Gnostics put the authority of their own experience before that claimed for scripture. And don't get excited that the bit in *The*

Gospel According to Philip which says Jesus was in the habit of kissing Mary Magdalene is an eyewitness account.

Before we move on to specific Churches, **a brief but important word about 'belief'**. We are used to belief meaning intellectual assent to a proposition. If you want to understand Christianity, its history and its development, you need to realize that this is a modern meaning that only came into being in the seventeenth century. If you read texts dating earlier than that date and sometimes later, the word has a different meaning. In the Greek New Testament Jesus talks of 'pistis' which meant loyalty, trust, engagement, commitment, in short, faith. When the New Testament was translated into Latin the word used for pistis was 'fides' which at the time meant loyalty. However, fides didn't have a verbal form so the Latin word 'credo' was used for that. When the Latin Bible was translated into Middle English the word credo was translated as 'beleven' which meant to value or hold dear. So when you read the word belief or believe in the Bible or pre-seventeenth-century texts it means loyalty, trust, engagement, commitment. That's a long way from our modern understanding of the word. In setting this out I have borrowed from Karen Armstrong, to whose many readable and scholarly works I am much indebted.

The Orthodox Church

I will deal next with the Orthodox Church. The Catholic Church has 1 billion members, which is a good claim for first attention. However, the Orthodox Church, whose name means 'right teaching/worship', claims with some justification to have kept more closely to the tradition of the early Church, so I deal with it first. That may also help correct a popular misconception that Orthodoxy is somehow Catholicism without the Pope.

Let's look first at **the way the Church is organized**. The Orthodox Church is decentralised, a family of self-governing Churches. There is a tendency for these Churches to have a

national and/or cultural emphasis but the Churches do not necessarily follow national boundaries. The largest is the Russian
Orthodox Church (100-150 million). The position of the Ukraine
in relation to this Church is complex and I won't address it here.
There is a Greek Orthodox Church (9 million). And there are
other Orthodox Churches such as the Church of Romania (23
million), the nationalistic Serbian Orthodox Church (8 million),
the Bulgarian National Church (8 million) which suffers from
having been particularly considered an organ of its former
communist regime, the Churches of Georgia (5 million), Poland
(750,000), Albania (160,000) and Cyprus (450,000), and some
smaller autonomous Churches. The heads of the individual
Churches are usually called Patriarchs. Some are called
Archbishop or Metropolitan. There are also four ancient non
national Patriarchates. The oldest, that of Constantinople (6
million), first in prestige among all the Churches, covers Turkey,
Crete, the Greeks and many of the Slavs abroad and, would you
believe it, Finland, since the Finnish faithful had to find a new
Orthodox home after the Russian revolution. The leader of this
Patriarchate is termed the Ecumenical or universal Patriarch, and
is a bit like the Archbishop of Canterbury within Anglicanism.
The other three ancient Patriarchates are those of Antioch
(750,000) which covers Syria and Lebanon, Alexandria (350,000)
which covers all Africa notably Uganda, Kenya and South Africa,
and Jerusalem (60,000). There is a multiplicity of branches of the
various Orthodox Churches throughout the world. In particular,
many Orthodox Churches are well established in the USA, the
largest grouping being the Greek Orthodox Archdiocese of
America, and there is an entirely independent Orthodox Church
in America (over 1 million) with Slavic roots.

Under each Orthodox Patriarch are the bishops and priests
and their helpers, the deacons. Being a deacon is a permanent
office, not necessarily a stepping stone to priesthood. Before the
eleventh century women could be deacons. Some Orthodox want

that to be revived, so watch that space. Priests have always been men. A small minority of the Orthodox would like that looked at more closely. There are no cardinals, a Catholic invention. Orthodox clergy may marry but bishops, traditionally chosen from monks, may not.

Some Churches which are Orthodox in their beliefs are affiliated to the Catholic Church. These Churches are called Uniate Churches. They include the Ukrainian Catholic Church, the Greek Catholic Church and any Church with Maronite, Malankarese or Malabarese in the title. Some of these are well established in the USA, notably the Ukrainian Catholic Church.

The Orthodox Churches see themselves as unified in diversity. The unity lies in the collective authority of the bishops, an idea close to that of the early Christian Church. This unity is seen as reflecting the unity of God in the Trinity and the celebration of the Eucharist is seen as the glue holding the Church together. Decisions of all the bishops in council together are deemed, once accepted by the whole Church, to be infallible. Such decisions are seen as God manifesting Himself. Orthodoxy sees the bishops as deriving their authority from what is known as the apostolic succession. Like the Catholic Church, Orthodoxy says that Jesus appointed his disciple Peter, seen as the first bishop of Rome, to run things after him, and the Church claims an unbroken line of succession of its bishops. It agrees that the Bishop of Rome occupies a premier position but only as first among equals. For Orthodoxy, all bishops share equally in the succession.

Note that the bishops and the people are an organic unity. You can't have one without the other. And all are linked with God, to be the Church, the Body of Christ, divine and human, visible and invisible, saints and angels included. The Church lives both in this age and the age to come after Judgment Day.

There is no **salvation** outside the Church. However, Orthodoxy gets round the problem of the good outsider by saying there may be members who are not visibly such and that membership is known to God alone. So if you do join up you can have the comfort of being in the true Church without the worry of there being deserving people condemned unreasonably to eternal discomfort.

When it comes to **the Trinity** the Orthodox Church and the Catholic Church have some different views. The Catholic Church introduced the idea that the Spirit 'proceeded', came from, both the Father and the Son rather than just from the Father or from the Father through the Son. Orthodoxy felt that idea downgraded the idea of the Spirit. If you attend Orthodox services you will hear constant references to the Holy Spirit. All Orthodox services start with the words, 'O Heavenly King, Comforter, Spirit of Truth, everywhere present and filling all things. Treasury of blessings and Giver-of-Life: come and abide in us, cleanse us of every impurity, and save our souls, O Good One.' Orthodoxy also felt that having the Spirit come from both the Father and the Son destroyed the balance of the three aspects and led to an emphasis on the abstract essence which the three persons shared rather than seeing the Father as the unifying aspect. This summarizes and oversimplifies a mass of theology, and will probably seem rarified disagreements to you. But they mattered deeply at the time and they need to be pointed out to you because of the part they played in separating Orthodoxy and Catholicism.

More important may seem the way that Orthodoxy is generally content not to explain the Trinity but to leave it as a mystery, on the basis that God is incomprehensible. Western Catholic Christianity has concentrated more on making God comprehensible, which has meant being more concerned with His human aspect. There is an inclination in the Western tradition to attribute human thoughts and ideas to God: He wants this, He forbids that, and so on. Orthodoxy's God remains mysterious. Orthodoxy seeks an intuitive rather than a rational understanding of the Trinity, whose contemplation is a religious experience.

The book of Genesis says that **God made us in His own image and likeness**. Orthodoxy sees image as a sort of kinship with God and likeness something which depends on our own moral choice. So we can find God within ourselves.

If we do this, we have the opportunity of **deification**, a union with God which retains our personal separateness. This goal is open to every Christian.

Orthodoxy believes in **the resurrection of the dead**, that Christ will return to judge the living and the dead and that if we are among the righteous we will be reunited with our transformed bodies. As humans we have a unity of body and soul and Christianity has traditionally believed that Christ saved and redeemed the whole person. Our soul can achieve deification but our body has to await the Last Day to achieve that.

However, **God is unknowable, so how do we attain union with Him?** Orthodoxy sees a difference between the unknowable essence of God and his knowable powers or energies, His divine energies, still God Himself, manifesting as Grace. This we can have contact with. As to how, Orthodoxy has a tradition of thinking about this unknowable God in terms of what He is not rather than what He is. This isn't just a point of view but also a method of prayer which seeks contact with what cannot be conceived. It is a meditative approach which may involve breathing techniques. For the Orthodox, prayer involves both mind and body. It is the whole being, body and soul, which prays. And the prayer, at its best, will fill the whole consciousness. A few quotes from the *Philokalia*, an anthology which is Orthodoxy's major spiritual text, are illustrative. "Blessed is the intellect that is completely free of form during prayer" says Evagrios, (*On Prayer*, sec.117-120). "Prayer is converse with God", says St Theodoros, (*A Century of Spiritual Texts*, sec. 60). "If we have not attained prayer that is free from thoughts, we have no weapon to fight with" says St Heychios the Priest, (*On Watchfulness and Holiness*, sec.21). I use the translations of the Faber edition by Bishop Kallistos Ware and others.

So generally, Orthodoxy is more introspective than Catholicism. The approach to prayer described above is prayer's highest form. As an Orthodox lay Christian your meditative prayer may involve the contemplation of an icon, or the repetition of a devotional phrase. The Jesus prayer, 'Lord Jesus Christ, son of the living God, have mercy on me.' is particularly used in this way. The power of God is present in the name of Jesus.

Unlike the Catholic Church, **the Orthodox Church was not so influenced by classical culture,** in particular by the thinking of Aristotle. This in turn insulated it from the need to reconcile science and revelation, and from the effect of modern literary analysis of the Bible. Orthodoxy has been mistrustful of rationalism as a tool for discussing a God who is essentially beyond our understanding. Orthodoxy looks rather to tradition, to the enrichment of its liturgy and to enhanced insight through meditation.

Nor is Orthodoxy inclined to a literal interpretation of the Bible, as are many in the Western Protestant tradition, and is more inclined to interpret it in an allegorical way. Indeed this was the attitude of mainstream Christianity for more than a thousand years.

In its struggle for salvation, humanity has had the disadvantage of **the Fall of man,** the separation from God caused by Adam's sin. Orthodoxy sees Adam as falling from a state of undeveloped simplicity and believes that after the Fall God's grace could still affect humanity from the outside. It doesn't believe in the Catholic and Protestant idea of an Original Sin which cut man off from God's help and grace. But as an Orthodox Christian you will believe that the Fall gave rise to a barrier which blocked the path to union with God's energies. Christ's death on the cross ended that. Some Orthodox believe the Word would have been made flesh even if Adam hadn't sinned and that

Christ came to show us the state we can attain through God's grace.

How does the idea of **grace** work for Orthodoxy? The idea doesn't intrude on mankind's free will. The two work together. God knocks but we have to open the door. Repentance is the key, helped by humility and prayer.

Love is at the center of Christianity. Orthodoxy recognises that our love of God can't be separated from our love of our neighbor, who we must love as ourselves. We can't do the one if we don't do the other. It is a whole.

A model of how our free will can make us Christlike is **Mary**, the virgin 'God-bearer'. She is the most exalted of God's creatures and is venerated but not worshipped. She is all-holy. Orthodoxy believes (not a compulsory belief) that on her death Mary was, as it were, resurrected in advance, and lives already in the age to come after the Day of Judgment, so being assumed into Heaven.

As a member of the Orthodox Church you will not believe in **Heaven** or **Hell** as a place, or in the usual Western idea of Hell generally. For Orthodoxy, Heaven and Hell are states not places. When we die there is only God. If we have lived well, God's presence is an experience of infinite joy. But if we come into that pure presence in an impure condition then we will experience it as torment. The Hell experience isn't so much a punishment visited on us by God as a consequence of our own behavior. And sin is not a legalistic act but a spiritual sickness.

Praying for and to the dead is part of this idea that alive or dead we are all members of the Church. Praying for the dead is in anticipation of their judgment at the end of time. Orthodoxy can be vague about just what happens between death and judgment, but has no truck with the Catholic idea of a temporary punishment in Purgatory. The dead can also be asked to pray for us.

The means for our salvation and for our transformation into

the divine likeness is the Church and the **sacraments**. These have been passed on with the apostolic succession. You will believe that the sacraments are vehicles of God's grace which we can access by our participation. The sacraments are baptism, Chrismation, the Eucharist (Greek for 'thank you'), confession (involving the forgiveness of our sins), holy orders, marriage and the anointing of the sick. Baptism is by immersion (three times) and can, if there is no alternative, be administered by a lay person, but only by one who has been baptized. Chrismation, a laying on of hands and anointing with oil blessed by a bishop, is usually done together with baptism, the idea being that the Holy Spirit thus descends on the newly baptized. In confession forgiveness isn't given at a distance but a hand is placed on the penitent's head. The Eucharist involves leavened bread and wine truly becoming the body and blood of Christ. Orthodoxy doesn't enquire how this happens, only God can understand it. A child will have its first communion (wine only) when an infant, after baptism and Chrismation, in the same ceremony. The celebration of the Eucharist and baptism stand at the head of the sacraments.

The Church permits **divorce**. If divorced by the Church (a state decree is not enough) you can remarry, but a maximum of three times is set. No sex outside marriage. No homosexual acts, but gays are to be treated with sensitivity and compassion. Many Orthodox theologians and spiritual fathers consider contraception within marriage to be acceptable. Abortion is forbidden.

The liturgy, the ceremonial and ritual of Orthodox worship, is at Orthodoxy's core. Remember, the word Orthodox means right teaching/worship. For the Orthodox, belief and worship are inseparable. Their doctrine is understood in the context of their liturgy, their divine worship. It isn't an intellectual understanding but a vision of how things on Earth are seen in relation to Heaven, a vision seen through participation in the liturgy. Worship leads, doctrine follows. If the faith interests you, go and see, go to Orthodox services.

God's presence is felt most clearly in worship with other people, particularly in the divine liturgy, the celebration of the Eucharist, the principal ritual otherwise known as the **Mass**. If you go to Mass in an Orthodox church the service will probably be celebrated by a priest who has a beard and who is married. The language of the service will be that of the country. Orthodoxy never settled on a common language for its services. The church itself will be full of holy images but all in picture form. The Orthodox Church found its solution to the commandment forbidding carved images by avoiding statues and confining itself to holy pictures, icons, and lots of them. Icons aren't just paintings; they are matter restored to its original harmony and beauty. There will be music, but probably no organ music, and a choir, and the liturgy will be sung or chanted. Singing by the congregation is a recent addition in many churches, or rather a return to ancient custom. There will be incense and candles and bright priestly robes. Unlike in a Catholic church, the altar is hidden by a screen, which is covered by holy images. There are doors in the screen, sometimes opened sometimes closed, and a platform in front of it. Much of the liturgy will take place there but some of it behind. If you are an Orthodox Christian you won't feel shut out. The screen with its images is a focus for your spiritual eye. You will look within yourself and use the methods of prayer which you have been taught as you dwell in this rich and traditional liturgy and its meaning. By the way, unless you are old or infirm, you will stand during the service.

Everything in an Orthodox ceremony has a special and traditional meaning, giving it a deep richness. For example, the immersion of baptism is performed three times as are many of the acts in the marriage ceremony, to symbolize and invoke the mystical presence of the Holy Trinity.

At home, depending on your devotion, you may say morning and evening prayers, and perhaps other prayers between. There are manuals of private prayers and even when alone you will pray as a member of the Church and with the Church, within the Body of Christ.

Orthodox rules of **fasting** may surprise a Western Christian. No meat, fish or animal products in Lent or Holy Week. Not everyone does it and there are get outs but it's still a significant feature, particularly for the devout. Dates of festivals may vary from those of their Western counterparts.

There is talk of **possible unity** between the Orthodox and the Catholic Churches, but this will require agreement on matters of belief. More likely is some unity with the non Chalcedon Churches. Anglican/Orthodox relations are good but the width of belief within Anglicanism makes unity unlikely.

The **Old Catholics** have their roots in the eighteenth century but took their present form after the late nineteenth-century pronouncement of papal infallibility, when they were joined by a significant number of Catholics who found that unacceptable. They have close relations with Orthodoxy, but unity is made unlikely by the fact that they are in full communion with the Anglican Church.

What next? Given its geography, Orthodoxy has had to cope with the power of Islam, in Russia with a Tsarist dictatorship which treated the Church as an arm of the state and then with the hostility of Soviet communism and so has had centuries of pressure which has tended to prevent it worrying too much about theology and the problems of addressing Western modern secular thinking. It has not been open to change but the future may be different and less inward looking. Perhaps Orthodoxy will have a renaissance, offering an old way in which scripture has been lived and experienced, an old but now new way which may be more in tune with the postmodern world.

As to **numbers**, I have quoted any figures above from Timothy (Bishop Kallistos) Ware's book *The Orthodox Church*. As he warns, these are to be used with caution and they are over ten years out of date, but they are a guide. Generally, he suggests there may be about three hundred million Orthodox Christians (adherents.com puts it at two hundred and forty million). There are about five million in the USA.

Note that both in the Ukraine and Romania there are significant numbers of **Greek Catholics**, of Orthodox belief but affiliated to the Catholic Church: in 1948 about 3.5 million in the Ukraine and about 1.5 million in Romania. Under the USSR they were forced to reunite with the Orthodox Church. Since 1990 they have re-emerged and there have been bitter quarrels, inter alia, about Church property.

Catholicism

The Catholic and the Orthodox Churches recognise one another's apostolic succession and for the most part have common views. Members of each Church can take communion in the other. Pope John Paul II spoke of the two Churches as 'two lungs' breathing together. I will concentrate on what differences there are between them. Bear in mind that Protestantism developed out of the Catholic tradition rather than the Orthodox one. If the Catholic Church is of interest to you, do note what is on offer now rather than get tied up in history, for the Church has changed considerably in the last fifty years.

Most notably, the Catholic Church is more **centralized** than the Orthodox, with the **Pope** at its head. For the Catholic Church the apostolic succession is also the basis of the Pope's primacy. The Church is often also referred to as the Roman Catholic Church. The word 'Catholic' means 'universal'.

The Church has **a hierarchical structure of clergy**. Each parish has a priest and is within a diocese, a larger geographical area with a bishop, occasionally more than one, in charge. Bishops are appointed by the Pope. Some bishops may have jobs which don't involve being in charge of an actual diocese. Archbishops are bishops who are in charge of a Province comprising the diocese of subordinate bishops. Cardinals, 'princes of the Church', are appointed by the Pope to assist him. Most but not all are Archbishops. Their most important role is to elect the Pope.

It is the Church which has authority, and which is the interpreter of revelation, of which the Bible is the major source. The Church has given itself additional authority (in 1870) by declaring the doctrine of **papal infallibility**. This does not mean that everything the Pope says is correct. It means that when he makes a special declaration, known as an 'ex cathedra' statement, he is preserved from error by God. Most people will be surprised to learn that technically only two ex cathedra statements have been made to date.

Do not get the impression that Catholicism prevents you in any way from direct contact with God. The Church emphasizes the power of **prayer**.

We have seen that Christians believe that man sinned in a way that made it impossible for his soul to be close to God. The Catholic Church calls the result of this **Original Sin**. It attaches to all humans – we have a wounded nature. Catholics say it had the effect of closing Heaven to us until Jesus Christ's sacrificial death, of God for love of man, opened up Heaven again.

As a Catholic you will believe that **Mary**, Jesus' mother, was not only a virgin but was born without Original Sin, and that she was physically somehow assumed into Heaven. Devotion to Mary is a notable feature of Catholicism. Her virginity and assumption into Heaven are required belief by virtue of two papal ex cathedra statements.

For most Catholics, **Hell** is a place of punishment. Many see it as a state, the pain of being knowingly separated from God. However, the harshness of the Heaven/Hell divide is softened by another, temporary, state called **Purgatory**. If you have not been good enough to go straight to Heaven, but not bad enough to be sent to Hell forever, you go to Purgatory until you have been punished enough to be allowed into Heaven, rather like being sent to Hell for a bit. Furthermore, you will believe that we can improve the Purgatory experience for the dead by praying for them and by having Masses (see below) said for them.

The **resurrection of the body** following the end of the world, Christ's return and the final judgment of everyone is part of Catholic doctrine, but it isn't much of a topic of conversation within the Church or in churches. Some Catholics take the whole thing literally, some don't.

As a Catholic you will, like the Orthodox, believe in seven **sacraments**: baptism, confession, the Eucharist or communion, confirmation, marriage, ordination, and the anointing of the sick or Extreme Unction. You will believe that the sacraments are vehicles of God's grace, which we can access by our participation. Baptism frees us from Original Sin and joins us to the Church. Confirmation, a laying on of hands and anointing with chrism, perfects baptism and gives additional grace from the Holy Spirit. In the Catholic Church it has become customary to defer confirmation until a person has reached the age of reason, usually taken as not earlier than seven. The actual age may vary; the teens are the most usual. An adult sponsor is required. Communion is the centerpiece of the celebration of God's sacrifice for us and involves transubstantiation or the turning of unleavened bread and wine into the actual body and blood of Christ during the Catholic ceremony of the Mass. Baptism can be administered by anyone if necessary. So can marriage if no priest is available. Otherwise the sacraments must be administered by ordained persons, although the actual distribution of the Eucharist can be by lay people. Confirmation is administered by a bishop unless there are exceptional circumstances.

On a day to day basis, your **Catholic spiritual life** will be one of private prayer, attendance at a weekly Mass at the weekend and an occasional and private confession, in a 'confessional' within a church, to a priest who can hear but not see you and who will give you God's forgiveness together with a penance which usually involves the saying of a number of prayers. You may pray to God in general or to Jesus. Or you may pray to your 'guardian angel' or to Mary or to a saint, for them to intercede with God. My Aunt Kath believed in the power of Saint Anthony to find lost objects and it certainly seemed to work when she lost her spectacles. Generally Catholic prayer will involve asking for something, saying thank you, directly or indirectly through Mary or a saint, loving God or being in awe of Him, and submission to Him. Meditative methods of getting closer to God are not usually practiced by the laity.

The Mass is the principal Catholic ceremony, and is a re-enactment of Christ's sacrifice. The priest and his altar server enter, and introductory prayers and responses are said. Next is a prayer of penitence. Then a chant of acclamation of God. Then a prayer of glorification of God. There are readings from the scriptures and the priest gives the sermon. That part of the Mass is followed by the liturgy of the Eucharist. The heart of this is the consecration, which involves the bread and wine being turned into the actual body and blood of Christ, a belief which Catholicism holds in common with Orthodoxy and which Protestantism does not accept. The Church sees Christ's body and blood and his soul and divinity as being inseparable from one another, so this idea is a sophisticated one in which the appearance of the bread and wine is unaltered. Prayers follow, including the 'Our Father', and then the rite of peace where the congregation offer each other a sign of peace. Following a litany of thanks the Eucharist is given to eat to those who wish to take communion. Attendees at Mass may or may not take communion. Those who do have a duty to have prepared themselves spiritually and this will involve not being in a state of significant sin, which in turn may require a previous visit to the confessional. After more prayers the priest blesses the congregation and dismisses them. A Mass can be a basic 'low' Mass or a 'high' Mass with additional ceremonial ritual, incense and a sung liturgy. As a Catholic you have a duty to attend Mass each weekend.

Christianity has been much influenced by **Greek thinking** and Catholicism, a Western Christian tradition, particularly by that of Aristotle. Accordingly, like Protestantism, Catholicism has sought to reconcile religion and science and to take a rationalist path. Thomas Aquinas, the great Catholic theologian of the thirteenth century, said that grace does not replace nature but builds on it and perfects it.

The Catholic Church accepts that **non Catholics can save their souls**. God's grace is available to all, even to those who don't believe in Him. The Second Vatican Council (of which more below), in its document *Nostro Aetate* says that " .. God caused the whole human race to dwell on the whole face of the earth. They also have one final end, God, whose providence, manifestation of goodness and plans for salvation are extended to all ..." It also says of other religions, "The Catholic Church rejects nothing which is true and holy in these religions. It regards with respect those ways of acting and living and those precepts and teachings which, though often at variance with what it holds and expounds, frequently reflect a ray of truth which enlightens everyone." So, if you aren't a Catholic or not a Christian, you can still achieve salvation through your own religion, but it will be through the Catholic God's grace.

Love is at the heart of Christianity. Pope Benedict, in a series of letters to the faithful, set out just how this works. The argument goes as follows. God loves us. That's why he sent Christ. We love God back in return for this, not just because he has told us to. As humans we need to both receive love and give it. Loving our neighbors as ourselves will ensure we can all become a 'we' with God, remaining ourselves yet becoming one. Prayer, which draws new strength from Christ, is an important help. We have free will, free will to do evil, and every generation has the task of guiding this will to good. It's only by encountering God that we can do this and see others as more than just other creatures. It's only by being close to God that we can truly be there for others. That's how it works. Political and social structures alone won't do it. For man, with his 'wounded nature', thinks he can cure this on his own but he needs God's help.

The analysis continues. The Church too, in its acts and very nature, must be full of love and of charity (which is love given). The Church influences society by forming consciences. Practical results of a proper social conscience would be the recognition that food and water are a human right and that the products of developing countries should be allowed to penetrate international markets. But progress needs to be more than just economic and technological and to be directed to every man and the whole man. Faith in progress as such produces selfishness. And the supremacy of technology tends to prevent people from recognizing anything that cannot be explained in terms of matter alone. For without God man neither knows which way to go nor understands who he is. We have to understand that our duties are to the human person and that we need more than a selfish search for salvation. We need to journey out of our inward looking self to liberation by selfless giving, a journey which points us to the eternal. That's what can govern the moral tenor of society. That's what can give an ethical foundation to the world's financial affairs. That's what can protect nature from reckless exploitation and protect the future of our descendants. It's down to truth and love.

In this way Benedict presents Catholicism as a Christian humanism. As St Thomas Aquinas said many years ago, the root of morality is what is good for humans and God is offended by those things which harm us.

A look at the **Second Vatican Council of 1962** and documents following it will give a sense of the current tensions within the Catholic Church. This Council of two and a half thousand members, principally bishops, and revolutionary in many ways, was initiated by Pope John XXIII whose short pontificate opened the door to new (some would say very old) ideas, and was presided over by his able but more cautious successor Paul VI. The Council emphasised the value of the previously Latin liturgy being in the vernacular. The priest now says Mass in the vernacular, the language of the country, facing the congregation instead of with his back to them. There has been a backlash against this by elements which regret the abandonment of centuries of tradition both as to the Latin Mass and other services and their associated musical heritage. Pope Benedict made concessions to this lobby, allowing the old forms to be used in certain circumstances. The Council also emphasised the importance of ecumenism. God might use other religions for salvation. An apology was given to the Jews. There was an emphasis on the importance of lay people in the ministry of the Church, and on the idea of the Church as the whole people of God, growing and developing rather than static and timeless. There was even discussion within the Council called by John XXIII as to the power of the bishops as a collegiate body, harking back to the early days of the Church, but this conversation was firmly put in its place by subsequent Popes. Indeed the papacy has held back the development of many of the ideas discussed at the Council, but much still bubbles below the surface. We have to see what Pope Francis's papacy brings.

A significant development in Catholicism, independent of the Vatican and found in other Christian Churches, has been '**liberation theology**', emphasising the need for justice for the poor. Bear in mind that the Church is particularly strong in Africa, South America and parts of Asia. Liberation theology was not popular with the Polish Pope John Paul II, who seemed to associate it with communism. You have seen how Benedict dealt with the issue, emphasising the need for social justice side by side with his condemnation of Godless liberalism.

If you are thinking about Catholicism you are likely to dwell long and hard on the issue of its attitude to **sexual matters**. I have already referred to this. The Church sticks to celibacy of the clergy both as an ideal and as a matter of financial practicality, hardly something to concern you unless you want to be a married priest. For many years the Church failed to get to grips with the issue of child abuse by sinful clergy but seems now to have taken a strong hand on that. Divorce is out but in some circumstances a marriage can be nullified, declared never to have existed. The Church holds its positions on abortion and homosexuality in common with many other religious organisations. But it is largely on its own when it comes to the issue of contraception. In 1968 a papal commission of experts which had sat for five years was going to publish a report concluding there was no good reason to ban contraceptive devices. Paul VI ignored their work and instead the Church got an encyclical *Of Human Life* confirming the ban. Millions of Catholics cheerfully ignore this, and you might have to decide whether you could happily be one of these. Perhaps there will be another commission and another papal response one day.

Protestantism

From about the fifth to the fifteenth century, you didn't have much of a choice if you were a Christian. There were the non Chalcedon Churches, the Catholic Church, Orthodoxy and, if you were feeling brave, heresy. However, the Protestant Reformation of the sixteenth century changed all that. I will not go into the historical details of the Reformation. Suffice it to say that modern Protestantism developed out of the Western and Catholic tradition and that it covers an immense range of views.

Generally, Protestants believe in the Trinity, in the virginity of Mary, in Original Sin, and in the fact that Christ's crucifixion had an effect on the burden of Original Sin and opened the way to Heaven for mankind, and in grace, prayer and the end of the world scenario.

As for the **number** of Protestant denominations, there are literally thousands. Certainly enough to ensure a multitude of complaints that some are missed out here.

Protestantism believes that **the Bible** is the only source of religious truth and what makes it so difficult to generalise about Protestantism is its belief that each individual has access to this truth directly, rather than being told by a Church what the truth is. Nonetheless, some groupings, having freely established their own thoughts, do require you to agree with them if you wish to join. You can't join some groupings if you believe the Bible is largely allegorical, nor can you be a Christian Scientist if you are keen on modern medicine.

In order to direct yourself to the most suitable Protestant grouping you will need first to consider a number of further issues and decide where you stand on them.

First we need to revisit the idea of **grace**. Remember, grace is a connection with God, a sort of current, power, that you can get spiritual strength from.

The question is, who can have access to this grace?

Firstly, you have to choose whether it is available to absolutely anyone who seeks it; even if they don't know they are addressing a Christian God.

Or perhaps you think grace is available only to Christians. Exclusivity is not an uncommon idea in religions. This idea will place you on the conservative wing of Protestantism.

Or maybe you think grace is available only to certain Christians, of which more shortly.

Secondly, you need to consider the nature of this grace. If you have the chance of it, can it be resisted, can you ignore it and go your own primrose path way? Or is it irresistible?

Thirdly, let us revisit the idea of Original Sin. Remember, Original Sin manifested itself from the act of humankind which separated us from God and got us chucked out of Paradise. It is common ground within Christianity that this separation could only be overcome by Christ's death on the cross. The supplementary question you have to face here is whether Christ's sacrifice was such that humans can now overcome Original Sin on their own, or whether something else is required from God, such as His grace or His selection, or both.

These questions may seem academic, even odd. But they are questions which separate many Protestant denominations. Better to look at the underlying issues first before diving into the frothy stuff at the top.

So, read that lot again, several times. Think about your choices. Then read on.

Before you do read on, a reminder about **the Bible**. This is important to all Christians, who regard it as the source of religious truth. But as step two you will also have to decide whether, for you, it is the only source of religious truth. And for step three you will have to choose whether you believe in the literal truth of what is in the Bible. Finally, having made your choice you have to decide which bits of the Bible to select, and how to interpret the words, or alternatively whose selection to adopt. So, some more decisions for you.

You may wish to bear in mind that the literal interpretation of the Bible is a relatively modern phenomenon. Traditionally the Bible was a book to seek revelation in, to be reread in the light of circumstances as they arose, as a source of guidance and inspiration. The wider emphasis on the literal meaning of the words of the Bible developed after the Reformation. Bear in mind that where the Bible is translated from its original Hebrew or Greek the translators' choice of words may have affected the meaning.

You must now consider a subset of ideas which, in various combinations, may lead you to or away from a number of Protestant denominations.

These ideas are:

the idea that our lives are predestined,

the idea that only certain people selected by God will go to Heaven,

the idea that our behavior does not earn us a place in Heaven but our faith.

Let us deal first with the idea that things are **predestined**, that the course of events is preordained. As a Christian you will have to take a position here. The problem arises from the fact that Christians believe God knows everything. But if He knows everything then He knows what is going to happen. You have to decide whether you want to make a jump from that to say that, therefore, God has predestined all actions by everyone. The Orthodox Church, Catholic Church, the Anglican Church and many other Christians do not take that view. They say that God gave men free will and that knowing what will happen is distinct from making it happen. You may feel that if you abandon the idea of free will you give yourself a bigger problem when it comes to explaining how God allows evil behavior to happen. However, a significant number of Protestant denominations believe in predestination.

That idea can then link in with the idea that only certain people selected by God, for reasons only He knows, will go to Heaven and that this selection is not a matter of good works on the part of the person, but simply God's choice. This is sometimes called '**election**', and those chosen are the '**elect**'.

This in turn is sometimes associated with the idea that belief in a particular approach to God, that is to say membership of a particular denomination, is a characteristic of those who are chosen by God to be saved. This idea usually involves a moment of conversion to the denomination. In some denominations that is referred to as being '**born again**'. Have faith, believe and you will be saved. It is not so much that believing saves you, as that belief is the mark of someone who God has chosen to save. Such believers sometimes refer to themselves and their co-believers as 'saints'.

The believers of these interlinking ideas support them by carefully chosen and literally interpreted quotations from the Bible.

Now we get back to the issues of **Original Sin and grace**. By now you will have thought about these issues and be ready to form a view which can be applied to this context.

As I have said, some believe that Original Sin is such that man cannot overcome it on his own, notwithstanding Christ's sacrifice; that only God's selection can overcome it, for the chosen, who believe, and that God's selection cannot be resisted. Note that in such a view if someone does seem to resist then they cannot have been really chosen.

Some believe that God chooses who can be saved, but that the chosen person has free will to resist it and choose sin.

I had better raise the issue here of **good works**. For if you believe in election, good works will not be enough to get a person to Heaven. Only being chosen does that. If that bothers you, avoid this stream of Protestantism. On the other hand many groupings that believe in election concentrate on good works as being the sort of behavior a chosen person would get involved with.

If these ideas appeal to you, you will direct yourself to this wing of Protestantism.

I have tried to arm you with knowledge of the main issues which distinguish and divide Protestant denominations. It is difficult for a guide to direct you within such a varied sea; but perhaps it can give you the ability to guide yourself in a situation where there can sometimes be a greater variation in belief within one denomination than between one denomination and another.

If you wish to decide what you believe and then choose your faith, you will need to get to grips with these ideas, and then ask the appropriate questions. Or perhaps you will take a denomination off the shelf and find out later what you've signed up to.

Another issue that you need to consider is **Church organi-sation**. In particular whether there is a central structure, and whether there is a clergy, for some denominations make do without formal clergy. This is mentioned here as a subsidiary matter. There are many who would regard it as more important.

If you are interested in Christianity it will not be long before you come across the word '**Evangelicalism**'. Evangelicalism is not a denomination but a description of various characteristics that a denomination or a group of Christians may have. In particular there is an emphasis on sharing one's belief, by missionary work, or just by personal encounters. In this sense the word can be applied to a wide range of Christians. For example, some Catholics might so describe themselves. However, the word is usually associated with a central focus on Christ's death as the only means for salvation, with a belief in the Bible as the primary or only source of religious authority, and with an emphasis on the moment of conversion, of being saved, or born again. This group of characteristics is shared by a number of Protestant denominations, by some groupings within denomina-tions, and by some nondenominational congregations.

The word '**nondenominational**' is a self-description used by churches (individual congregations) which consider themselves independent from other congregations. This self-defined separation may be one of ideas or simply of organisation. Individual nondenominational churches may in practice cooperate with one another.

Calvinism is a school of theology which formulated the doctrine of predestination; that Original Sin enslaves mankind, that some people are chosen by God to be saved and cannot resist this choice, and that God's grace is only applied to those people. Calvinism forms the basis of the Reformed tradition. So if you see a church with the word '**Reformed**' in its title, you know it is Calvinistic in its thinking.

Another expression is '**nonconformist**'. This word applies to non Anglican Protestant Churches. And if you see the words '**free church**', they will refer to Churches independent of the Church of England or the Presbyterian Church of Scotland.

Two other expressions you will meet are **High Church** and **Low Church**. These describe two approaches to worship. High Church denotes an emphasis on ritual and ceremonial and the sacraments. Within the Anglican Communion it describes a ritual of worship close to the Catholic form. Low Church denotes a simplicity of worship, without ritual or vestments. These alternative terms are applied principally within the Anglican Church, but also within some other Protestant Churches, including the Lutheran Church, and the Methodist Church in the USA. Most other Protestant churches could be described as Low Church.

Thus, **worship** in Protestantism can be very varied, ranging from what in appearance seems very like a Catholic Mass, to prayer meetings with no clergy, no special clothing and no ritual, to services with or without music and/or singing, to evangelical meetings or services seeking direct contact with the Holy Spirit.

I will now try to give a thumbnail sketch of the better known Protestant denominations, concentrating on what makes each different.

The Anglican Church is the largest Protestant Church. It consists of thirty-eight self-governing provinces which are in communion with one another. It considers that its bishops are part of the apostolic succession, seeing the pre-Reformation Church as the Early Church or Undivided Church. The Catholic Church, for example, takes the contrary view, that the apostolic succession was broken in respect of the Protestant Churches. So a Catholic is not permitted to receive communion from an Anglican priest, whereas an Anglican may take communion from a Catholic priest.

The Archbishop of Canterbury is a focus of unity within this communion, and he is the head of the Anglican **Church of**

England. This Church is 'established', a sort of state Church in that its head is the English monarch.

The Church of England and much of Anglicanism is a broad Church with space for most, if that's what you're looking for. Much will depend on which parish you attend and the views of the vicar. There are High churches and Low churches. In some you may have difficulty believing you are not in a Catholic church. In others you may find an evangelical approach. In others a liberal approach. The Church accepts divorce, and elements within it accept woman priests and same sex relationships, although these are issues which could tear the Church apart. However, note that many of Anglicanism's Third World provinces take a more rigid view. As in many Protestant denominations an important church service of Anglicanism is its version of the Mass, often referred to as Holy Communion or the Lord's Supper. Like all Protestants, Anglicans don't believe in transubstantiation, the turning of bread and wine into the body and blood of Christ.

If you live in the **USA** and you are an Anglican you will belong to **the Episcopal Church**, which separated from the Church of England in 1789 so its clergy would not have to accept the supremacy of the British monarch. This church tends towards the more liberal end of Anglicanism.

Methodists believe that God's grace is available to all Christians. They (mostly) do not believe in salvation by predestination, but in free will by God's grace. But you have to be a Christian and salvation always involves Christian mission and service to the world. Here enters an important aspect of Methodism which may attract you. It emphasises charitable and social work, and helping the poor. Love of God is always linked with love of your neighbor. You will seek Christian perfection, or 'perfect love'. If you like singing, consider that hymns are important in all branches of Methodism. If you are female, note that woman can be ordained ministers and become bishops.

The evangelical **Baptists** get their name from their requirement that people who join their Church be baptised by immersion in water, as opposed to pouring over the head, or sprinkling, and that that baptism should not take place until the person is old enough to make a profession of faith. They don't believe this is the only legitimate form of baptism, just that it is the form you must accept if you want to be a Baptist. Nor do they think baptism is necessary for salvation but that it is simply a symbolic ritual. As a Baptist you will believe the Bible is the only authoritative source of God's truth and that individuals are free to interpret it, but note that many Baptists do not take the Bible literally. Their individual churches are for the most part autonomous, rather like Congregationalist churches. They have pastor teachers and deacons and sometimes elders but believe in a priesthood of all believers. A basic idea is that each member has liberty to choose what their conscience dictates and is responsible for that only to God. There is a great variation between individual churches. Some take a Calvinistic approach and some don't. If you like sermons you will welcome the Baptists' emphasis on the weekly sermon. Baptists are particularly strong in the southeast quarter of the USA. The website of American Baptist Churches USA lays claim to five thousand eight hundred Baptist congregations.

If you join the **Lutherans** you will believe that it is your faith alone which will give you salvation and that the Bible is free from error. All who trust Jesus can be sure of salvation. However, faith itself is a gift of God, put there by the Holy Spirit via God's grace. It is a sort of predestination for the faithful without explicit damnation for the rest. You will see Christianity as a single church and faith. But good works on their own won't get you to Heaven, though if that is your destination you will undoubtedly do good works. You may enjoy the emphasis on liturgy and music. There will be images in the church. Holy Communion, still called the Mass and which follows the pattern of the Catholic

Mass, is the main act of worship, but many churches are moving from traditional liturgy to 'contemporary worship'.

One of the Reformed churches is the **Presbyterian Church**. There are many differences of view within this family. There are conservative elements and liberal ones. Some contemporary groups do not emphasise the Calvinist element by which the Church is best known. Presbyterian government is based on elders, who are ordained, and who convene as a Kirk Session. Above these are Presbyteries covering an area. Above that is a Synod of a number of Presbyteries and above that a General Assembly. The idea is that all members are equal under God and all who hold office do so by election of the people. Some groups exist outside this structure. Although it is faith that is paramount, most Presbyterians emphasise that faith is exhibited by good works. Within the UK the Presbyterian Church traditionally dominates Scottish Protestantism in the form of the **Church of Scotland**. This is not an established state church like the Church of England, but it is recognized by various Acts of Parliament. There are other independent Presbyterian denominations.

Congregationalism also falls within the Reformed tradition, yet has within it a great diversity of opinions. This arises from its basic structure. Congregationalists believe that every local church is a miniature of the entire Church of Christ. They believe this is the Biblical pattern of church government and a protection against abuse of liberty by those in authority. At the same time this freedom exists under the responsibility of each member to govern themselves under Christ. If you are interested in this, it will be a question of picking which local church, which may have a Calvinist approach or not. Congregationalists have a long tradition of toleration and have tended to the liberal part of the mainstream.

There are a number of branches of the **Mennonites**. The **Amish** is the one likely to be most familiar to you. The

Mennonites tend to be concentrated in the USA or Africa. Their Churches have a wide range of view. They are committed to pacificism and have a strong emphasis on voluntary service and disaster relief. As a member you will accept the primacy of Jesus' teachings as set out in the Bible and will value the ideal of a religious community. You will accept the discipline of the Church. There are liberal Mennonite groupings but they are in the minority. Conservative Mennonites emphasise traditional life and dress.

Pentecostalism is a rapidly growing denominational family of an evangelical nature. This movement lays emphasis on the Holy Spirit, of speaking in tongues, of a moment of conversion, sanctification, being born again. Members tend to be conservative on religious issues. If you join you will not be a Calvinist in your thinking, but will believe that anyone can believe in Jesus and be saved. Water baptism is the outward sign of conversion but the real thing will be your spiritual experience of the baptism in the Holy Spirit, your direct personal experience of God. The preaching of the gospel, which is incapable of being wrong, will be important to you.

The Brethren are often called **the Plymouth Brethren**. The Brethren arose in the early nineteenth century, partly as a reaction to denominalization. Its originators resolved just to read their Bibles and do without clergymen. Every Brethren church is independent. The services are run on unstructured lines. The idea is one of verbal and group inspiration from the scriptures, with evangelical witnessing. Some Brethren believe in election, some don't. As Brethren, you will attend the Breaking of Bread communion service. This is unstructured. 'Brothers' get up and pray, or suggest a hymn, or expound upon scripture. The purpose is worship rather than prayer or exhortation. Women usually cover their heads, and they don't speak, (though they do at ladies' meetings). There will also be one or two preaching meetings on Sunday, and usually a midweek prayer meeting.

The Exclusive Brethren, also called **the Closed Brethren**, are an offshoot. They usually believe in election. They are called Exclusive because they believe that members should only mix with other members when engaging in eating, drinking, entertainment and even business (they usually run family businesses). As an Exclusive Brethren you will endeavor to mix exclusively with your fellow brethren and you will usually attend daily prayer meetings and Sunday communion.

Certain groups call themselves **Restorationists**. Their idea is that they are restoring a Church that was somehow lost at some time in the past. So some prefer the word Restorationist to that of the word Protestant. This grouping covers denominations with otherwise different views. It includes some groups of Quakers and Baptists. However, in practice, many worshippers in Churches within this category may never have heard of the word Restorationist. Some Restorationist Churches concentrate on the Second Coming of Christ, and on the end of the world, which they believe to be ongoing or imminent.

So, one Restorationist church is that of the **Seventh Day Adventists**, and if you join them you will expect the Second Coming soon. The time is not known, but it is imminent. It could be tomorrow. So it is essential to be ready for it. Indeed, the process of preparing Heaven and judging those who will live forever (or not) has already begun. On your death you will be in an unconscious sleep. At the Second Coming the righteous dead will come alive, in the First Resurrection, and will go to Heaven with the righteous living, where they will live with Christ and the saints for a thousand years and the unrighteous will die. At the end of the thousand years, the unrighteous dead will be resurrected, in the Second Resurrection, and with Satan and his angels will all be consumed by God. The universe will thus be freed of sins and sinners forever. God and the righteous will dwell on a new earth eternally in a state of love, joy and learning. You will believe in salvation by faith alone, by your choice (a choice available to everyone), and in the infallibility of the Bible. As a Seventh Day Adventist you will have to observe the Sabbath strictly (but from Friday sunset to Saturday sunset, not on a Sunday) and to observe the highest standards of Christian taste and beauty. Your dress will be simple and modest. Your body is a temple of the Holy Spirit. No alcohol, drugs or tobacco for you. You will engage in whatever brings your thoughts and bodies into the discipline of Christ. You should only marry another Christian, and not divorce other than on the ground of your spouse's adultery. Your baptism will be by immersion, but will be a necessary and symbolic ritual, not a sacrament necessary for salvation.

Or you could become a **Jehovah's Witness**. If so, you will have to believe that the battle of Armageddon is imminent, after which there will be a thousand-year reign of Christ on earth. Your God will be called Jehovah, the Old Testament name, but you will believe in the entire Bible. You will not believe in the Trinity, but that Christ is God's creation, only a perfect man, and is inferior to Him. Some say that Jehovah's Witnesses should not be categorised as Christians because of this. Nonetheless you will believe that Christ's death was necessary to atone for humanity's sins. You can have everlasting life, but only if approved by God. Believing is essential but not enough, for by your behavior you can fall from grace; so good works are essential too. You will have no clergy, and your baptism, just a ritual, will be by total immersion. You will note that your soul ceases to exist at death, and that there is no Hell, another exception to our rule of thumb initial route to Christianity. However, if you believe and are good you will have eternal life, by physical resurrection on earth. Your belief will be that from 1914 Jesus became King of Heaven. Satan and his angels were expelled to earth, hence the post 1914 horrors. Soon 144,000 faithful followers of Christ will join Jesus in Heaven. During this thousand year period of the Kingdom of Heaven the dead will be resurrected and Jesus will judge everyone. Those approved will receive eternal life. And then Jehovah will rule again. Wickedness will be eternally destroyed. As a Jehovah's Witness you will attend five meetings a week at your local Kingdom Hall. You will not celebrate Christmas, Easter, or any of the usual Christian holidays, but you will celebrate the memorial of Christ's death at Passover. You will not salute a nation's flag, or serve in its armed forces or have a blood transfusion or smoke. You will pay self-imposed tithes. You will not use images in your worship. You will obey the Bible's rules on morals. Most familiar to the public will be your obligation to give public testimony to the scripture's truth. If you are a woman you are unlikely to have much responsibility in the Church, despite the fact that a significant proportion of the preaching work is done by women. Generally, the Church has conservative views.

The **Mormon** Church or **The Church of Jesus Christ of Latter-Day Saints** (LDS) is another Restorationist Church. Mormons believe that God the Father, Christ and the Holy Spirit are distinct, albeit interrelated, divine beings and that the Father and Christ have glorified bodies of flesh and bone. Because of this, many Christians say that Mormonism is not part of Christianity. However, it is undoubtedly Christ centered and although there have been recent suggestions that it could be regarded as a fourth Abrahamic religion, I include it in this chapter. Be aware that there is no comprehensive official Mormon theology.

In addition to the Bible, the Mormons have their own revealed religious book, The Book of Mormon. This was revealed by an angel to one Joseph Smith in the 1820s. The Book opens at about 600 BCE, telling the story of the prophet Lehi who, foreseeing the destruction of Jerusalem, flees with his family on a trip which eventually takes them to the Americas. Lehi's son, Nephi, has a vision of Christ's coming, which the Mormons await. In due course, after much teaching and history, the Book recounts how Christ, following his crucifixion and resurrection, visits the Nephites and appoints apostles among them, just as in the ancient Christian Church. Today, the LDS Church is led by a prophet and twelve apostles.

Mormons don't believe in Original Sin. We are punished for our own sins. Adam and Eve had a choice, and took a courageous one. Without it there would be no human race, nor the possibility of some humans dwelling with God for eternity (2*Nephi* 2.22). Our souls exist before we are born and we have to live as mortals in order to be able to return to God in Heaven. We exist to have joy (2 *Nephi* 2.25) and we have joy by understanding we are God's children and following his teachings. As for Satan, God made and (ultimately) controls him. When he can be dispensed with it's the outer darkness and the bottomless pit for him.

The way to salvation (enabled by Christ) is by faith, repentance, baptism by immersion, the laying on of hands for the gift of the Holy Spirit (usually right after baptism), and participation in other sacraments (Mormons call them ordinances) necessary for salvation, including marriage for eternity. Mormons believe in worshipping God according to their own conscience, in obeying the law, in being chaste, benevolent, true, virtuous, and doing good to all men. If you are a Mormon, then it's no alcohol, drugs, tobacco, coffee or tea for you. And love of money is targeted: "And behold, their treasure shall perish with them also." (2 *Nephi*,9.30). Although plenty of Mormons have no problem chasing wealth.

Note that for Mormons revelation comes after prayer and enquiry, not before it. And they do not believe in predestination, although some tasks may be 'foreordained'. We have the choice between good and evil. So works are essential, but works with the correct inner thoughts behind them.

What are the afterdeath options for Mormons? First stop is the spirit world. If you have lived your life well you will go to the spirit paradise. Otherwise, it's the spirit prison. This is temporary and will last until the second coming of Christ. But we can get out and into a paradise if we repent sufficiently and accept the gospel, which is preached in the spirit world. It's our choice. That's one reason why Mormons baptize their ancestors to give them a helping hand in the spirit prison should they be there. And note that a spirit has a choice whether to accept such baptism. At the second coming we are joined to our perfected body and judged for the final time. Then it's off to one of three paradises or Heavenly kingdoms unless you are still in spirit prison. In that case you may go to the lowest level of paradise or, for a minority, it's outer darkness.

Outer darkness is for the very few who have committed the most grievous sins and have not repented them. Such are "... cast out and consigned to partake of the fruits of their labor or their works, which have been evil, and they drink of a bitter cup." (*Alma* 40.26). Perhaps they relive their evil actions again and again. Conversely good acts are 'restored' to their makers. "For that which ye do send out shall return to you again, and be restored ..." (*Alma* 41.15).

Those who haven't heard Christ's teachings aren't judged by them. The crux is that you must live faithfully and repent of your sins. Those who have heard Christ's teaching are so judged. The reward is to live in the fullness of God's presence. And remember that everyone will get the chance to hear the Mormon version of things in the spirit world.

A hundred years ago Mormons substituted water for wine in their 'sacrament' ritual of the breaking of bread in remembrance of Christ's body. Mormons take the sacrament most Sundays, so renewing their baptismal covenant and helping their spiritual strength. They try to pray in their families and they pray individually. Prayer should be only for what is right. Provided it is right God will provide. All are welcome to Sunday services, although the special temples are only for members.

Mormons are best but wrongly known as polygamists. Some

Mormons, often the most elite, did practice polygamy until about 1900. Since that time the policy of the church has been to excommunicate anyone who practices polygamy. It is now confined to small break off groups.

As to numbers, mormonnewsroom.org.com claims there are fifteen million Mormons.

Everyone has heard of the **Quakers**, or **The Society of Friends**, and again some may protest that they shouldn't be in the Christian section. Quakers believe that the experience of God is available directly to everyone. You don't need a Church or organisation or sacraments to connect with God. You have your own 'inner light'. Quakers are group oriented, and direct themselves outwards. So although Quakerism has a mystical approach it translates that into action. Quakers respect the Bible but believe it is subordinate to the inner spirit. Holiness exists everywhere, in every activity of your life. Quakers are best known for their belief in pacifism. There is no creed of Quakerism, and there are such people as Quaker atheists, although that is a controversial issue within Quakerism.

The **Church of Christ, Scientist**, or the **Christian Science Church**, was founded in the nineteenth century by Mary Baker Eddy, and believes that in view of God's goodness sin, disease and death were not created by him. Potentially that gives rise to problems: who did create them? Ms Eddy had a neat response: they were not truly real. So this Church believes that disease and adversity can be cured through prayer, via God's grace. An interesting aspect is that Christian Scientists may use other medical systems if their faith does not give the required result. Most believers won't do that, but outsiders may feel less discouraged to join by virtue of this apparent openness.

Unitarians have a wide range of views, so wide it is difficult to give a summary which won't offend some of them. Unitarianism grew up in the Christian tradition. Some Unitarians are Christians, but these are now a minority. Most Unitarians would probably term themselves Humanists. Many would regard themselves as agnostics or atheists. There are probably as many Buddhist as Christian Unitarians. Unitarians can include pantheists and neo pagans. Most choose no theological label. So I have dealt with Unitarianism also in the chapter on secular belief systems.

Unitarian Christians don't believe in the Trinity, hence the word Unitarian. Jesus, important and preeminent as he is, is not actually the Son of God, although his teaching has a divine character, spirit and foundation. Nor do Christian Unitarians believe in Original Sin or in Hell. Some Christians say you can't be both a Christian and a Unitarian. The two main Christian Unitarian organisations are the Christian Universalist Association and the American Unitarian Conference. Unitarian Christianity emphasises that human nature is as God created it and not spoiled by Original Sin, that no religion has a monopoly of truth, and that the Bible, while inspired by God, is written by humans and so subject to human error. The emphasis is on individual conscience. If all this attracts you bear in mind that Unitarian Christians are spread throughout different denominations and that this is not a distinct Church or denomination, so you may have to search to find a suitable church to attend. You will get help from Unitarian Christian organisations and their websites and journals.

Other Issues

You are likely to come across a number of other issues that are controversial as between and also within denominations. As an outsider you may be surprised at the passions these issues can rouse. Be ready for them. Women priests are one example. Another is the celibacy of the clergy, which applies to the Catholic Church and to Orthodox bishops. This doesn't depend on theology but economics, sugared with a covering of praise for the spiritual virtues of celibacy. Until the eleventh century it was not uncommon for priests to marry, but the Catholic Church got increasingly fed up with priests' children regarding the Church's land as part of their inheritance, and so enforced celibacy. Another issue is the method of baptism, whether by sprinkling water over the head, pouring water over the head, or by total immersion.

As to **numbers**, the following figures derive from the website www.adherents.com. It is in the nature of things that the precise numbers of followers of some Churches are disputed, but this table gives some guide to very approximate numbers. Please regard it as better than no guide. The figures may vary from ones quoted in the text above.

Branch	Number of Adherents
Catholic	1,050,000,000
Orthodox/Eastern Christian	240,000,000
African indigenous sects (AICs)	110,000,000
Pentecostal	105,000,000
Reformed/Presbyterian/Congregational/United	75,000,000
Anglican	73,000,000
Baptist	70,000,000
Methodist	70,000,000
Lutheran	64,000,000
Jehovah's Witnesses	14,800,000
Adventist	12,000,000
Latter Day Saints	12,500,000
Apostolic/New Apostolic	10,000,000
Stone-Campbell ("Restoration Movement")	5,400,000
New Thought (Unity, Christian Science, etc.)	1,500,000
Brethren (incl. Plymouth)	1,500,000
Mennonite	1,250,000
Friends (Quakers)	300,000

Chapter 19

Islam

To consider Islam, you have decided:

- that spirit exists,
- that there is a creator God,
- that He is good,
- and all-knowing,
- and all-powerful,
- and eternal,
- and knows you personally and is interventionist,
- and that you have an immortal soul,

The very core of your belief as a Muslim will be that **there is no God but God and Muhammad is his prophet**. The word for God is Allah, which includes the definite article. He is not 'a God' but 'the God'.

What sort of God is this, besides being the only one and all-powerful? Well, we can't comprehend Him but we can understand His attributes. He knows everything, which includes every intimate detail of your every thought. He is compassionate and merciful and will forgive you your sins if you are repentant. However, He can also be very angry, notably with those who don't follow the 'straight path'. This God has friends and enemies and you will be a friend. If you are His enemy, watch out.

'Islam' means 'surrender' and that is what you must and will do to this your God. However, your submission is to be a rational choice, not an act of blind faith. Faith is a result of enquiry not a substitute for it.

The word 'tawhid' is also central to Islam. **Tawhid** means the unity or oneness of God. Through God everything is interconnected and symbiotic: humankind, individuals, nature, all emanating from a single will; that of God. We are trustees of God's creation. Everything should be in a state of harmony and grace. For us this harmony means acting in permitted ways and not acting in ways which are not permitted. For the purpose of creation is for us, through God's guidance, to bring about a moral order on earth. Thus, if you become a Muslim you will say goodbye to the Western distinction between the sacred and the secular. Muslims see almost all aspects of individual and group life as being guided or regulated by Islam.

This all amounts to being obedient to our inner and innate nature. There is **no Original Sin in Islam**. We have a natural predisposition for good.

As a Muslim you will be part of the **umma**, the Islamic community. It is said that the Muslims are like a human body. If one part is in pain, the whole body suffers.

Muhammad, who lived from 570 to 632 CE, is God's prophet. Not the only prophet, for there have been others such as Abraham, Moses and Jesus, but the latest, last and most important one. Islam has come to see Muhammad as perfect and sinless, albeit human and capable of making mistakes, and that is how you will regard him.

The Koran is a recital of God's words, revealed to Muhammad via the Angel Gabriel over a period of thirty years. It is God's final revelation to man. Muhammad, like most people of his time, was said to be unable to read and write, and the words of the Koran were initially preserved orally and only written down later, that task being completed by about 650 CE.

The Koran consists of some 6,200 suras, or chapters or verses, with the longest tending to be at the beginning and the shortest at the end. Their order is different from the order in which they were revealed to Muhammad. The Koran isn't a narrative like the

Bible, but a series of themes. Given its oral beginning it is perhaps not surprising that the Koran seems designed to be recited aloud rather than read. The beauty of its language is only really apparent in its original Arabic. If you can't understand Arabic, that will be a loss to you as it is for the seventy-five percent of Muslims who are non Arabic speakers. The Koran has stood up to modern scholarly analysis better than the Bible.

Not that the Koran scorns the Bible. It sees the Gospels and the Torah as previous revelations of God, albeit ones which have been tampered with and misinterpreted: there is no fall of humanity, Original Sin, Son of God or redemption in Islam; Adam is restored to favor by Islam's God and becomes the first prophet.

You will see the Koran as a divine text which contains absolute truths. It has come to be seen as uncreated, on the basis that God's word cannot be created. As such, it cannot be imitated. Reading the Koran or listening to it being recited will itself be an act of devotion. In this chapter I use the translation by A J Arberry.

However, don't think all you need to do is to get a copy of the Koran and read it. You'll need other help to understand it as a whole. And you won't find much about Muhammad himself in it. His name is mentioned only four times.

Needless to say, there are differences of opinion within the Muslim tradition as to how the Koran should be interpreted. There are seeming contradictions within the text and it is accepted that one verse may abrogate or cancel another. Given that the Koran was revealed to Muhammad over a period of many years, it is often argued that a later verse should have priority when contradiction is perceived. Later, we'll look further at problems of interpretation. For now, bear in mind the difficulties that a divine and unchangeable text may present to those who seek to reconcile Islam with modern Western values.

The power of the Koran is assisted by the fact that it is

compact, has a single source and is written in the only major classical language still in current use.

Like Judaism and unlike Christianity, Islam is a religion of **orthopraxy** rather than orthodoxy. What you do matters more than what you believe. Theology has a minor place. Theological speculation is dismissed as pointless and divisive guesswork. That is not to say that in the past perceived heresy has not sometimes been savagely punished. Nonetheless, once you have taken on the primary belief in Allah and submitted to Him, what matters most is that you should obey His will. We are called by God to take action, to be moral and live the good life. It is the moral law which is our guide to that action.

Unlike Christianity, Islam doesn't start with ethical principles and work onwards from those. Instead it has a structure of law which God has determined on the basis, it is assumed, of what He considers to be good and evil. Sin involves parting from these ways of God. Note that both duress and necessity are acceptable reasons for breaking this law.

The structure of moral law which sets out the rules by which Muslims should live is known as the **shari'a**. At this stage in the chapter I use the word with great caution for it is one greatly misunderstood both outside and within Islam. At this stage do note that the shari'a is distinct from the law of whatever land you may live in although many Muslim countries have elements of the shari'a within their law. I will explain the shari'a in detail later on.

The object of these rules and categorizations is to direct you to the good life, to the moral ways of living in a moral community. This means that these rules guide us to avoid going to **Hell** and to getting us to **Heaven**, ideas which are very alive and well in Islam. After death you will undergo a twofold judgment. First, in your grave, angels will ask about your faith. If you don't answer correctly about God's oneness and Muhammad's identity you will suffer torment until the Day of Judgment. On the Day of

Judgment all living things will die. However, death as well as life, is impermanent for Islam. For all humans will then be resur-rected, judged individually, and sent to Heaven or Hell. So in both Heaven and Hell you will have a physical body. Some Muslims believe that the stay in Hell can be a temporary purgation. If you aren't a Muslim I'm afraid it's Hell for you, a good reason for being a Muslim. Both Heaven and Hell are well described in the Koran. It's bliss or torment. Some Muslims believe in the literal descriptions of Heaven and Hell in the Koran, others that these are metaphorical. If you die a martyr, in 'the path of God', you don't have to wait for resurrection and the Day of Judgment, but go straight to Paradise. Some Muslims desirous of accommodating to Western values may seek arguments to make Paradise more inclusive. For example, it can be argued that it is only God, who cannot be known in His entirety, who decides who will go to Heaven. But the general view is that unbelievers won't go to Paradise.

Are there **mechanisms which will help you avoid Hell and get to Heaven**? The first and essential one is to believe in Allah. If you don't, hard luck! If you do there are a number of other ideas to choose from, separately or in combination. One is that belief is enough. A lot of Muslims believe this, subject to penalties for sin. Some believe it unconditionally. An increasing number of Muslims believe that good works are also required. Most Muslims put their hope for forgiveness of their sins in a combination of God's mercy and the possible intervention of Muhammad with God, all encouraged by prayer. One sin is unforgiveable, that of believing there is another God besides Allah.

Another mechanism is that of **predestination**. After all, if God is-all powerful isn't everything his doing? Although the Koran and the stories about Muhammad refer to the free choice of humans there is a strong strain of predestinationism in Islam. The words 'it is written' are a cliché of daily life. The Koran

(Q16:95) even says of God '... He leads astray whom He will ...'. This line of thought is softened by the idea that by our actions we somehow 'acquire' our predestined fate. Predestination is a majority view within Islam but many current Muslim thinkers disagree with the idea.

Another issue which arises from the all-powerfulness of God is that of **evil** and how it came to be. The penultimate chapter of the Koran (Q113) says, 'I take refuge with the Lord of the Daybreak from the evil of what He has created ...' For Islam, both good and evil are elements in a struggle which suits God's purpose. Humans were evicted from the Garden of Eden not just as a punishment but so they could assist God in creating a moral and beautiful world.

According to classical Islam, **our actions fall into five categories**: obligatory, recommended, permissible, disapproved and forbidden. This links in with the system of reward and punishment in the next life. Obligatory actions are rewarded if done and punished if not done (for example, prayer and payment of debts). Forbidden actions are punished if done, but you are rewarded if you avoid them (for example, breach of contract and theft). Recommended actions are rewarded if done, but there is no punishment if they are omitted (for example, helping the poor). Disapproved actions are not punished if done, but you are rewarded if you avoid them (for example, unilateral divorce by the husband). Permissible actions bring neither reward nor punishment. Take time to work all that out.

In your daily life your desire to act as God would wish will be supported by the structure of the **Five Pillars**. These are: witness to faith, prayer, charity, fasting and pilgrimage. It will be your duty as a Muslim to observe the Five Pillars. These rules of ritual behavior are additional to and separate from general rules of behavior. We need to talk about them in detail, because they will have such an effect on your life.

Witness/testimony to faith, or shahada, involves repeating two phrases, 'There is no God but God' and 'Muhammad is the messenger of God'. You have to say this in Arabic, and really mean it. The intention is all important, for it turns the act from a mere ritual into a proper act of devotion. The shahada is the act which signifies a convert becoming a Muslim. You will also say it on waking, before going to sleep at night, on the birth of your new baby, and in the presence of the dying so that, if possible, these are the last words they hear.

As for **prayer**, you are probably already aware that you will have to pray five times daily: at daybreak, noon, mid-afternoon, sunset and evening. First you ritually wash, then you face Mecca and recite sections of the Koran, which you yourself, within limits, may select. Doing this, you could note the utility of Islam's traditional emphasis on learning the Koran by heart. While thus praying you move from standing to bowing, to half-sitting, and then to prostration. There may be variations according to which legal school of Islam you follow. For Friday prayers at noon you will go to the mosque, unless you are sick or tending the sick, or are fleeing oppression or are a woman. These Friday prayers will be led by a prayer leader, an imam, who will probably also give a sermon. There are other, non compulsory, ritual prayers which you may undertake. By ritual prayers I mean ones which follow a formal pattern of actions and words. Again, intention is paramount. You are not supposed just to mouth the words. In prayer you face God one-to-one. Its purpose is to make you grow morally and spiritually and to bring you closer to God.

In addition you may make private prayers of request: for forgiveness, guidance, health, passing exams and so on. You may recite passages of the Koran to yourself. In parts of the world the Koran may be chanted. Michael Cook of Princeton University refers to '... a scriptural saturation of daily life which it is hard for most inhabitants of the Western world to imagine ...'

Throughout the Koran there is an emphasis on helping the poor, orphans and widows, something to be done discreetly. Our belongings are on loan from God and indeed are potentially a moral liability. As a Muslim you should engage in regular giving. In Islamic societies this **charity** or **zakat** has been precisely structured and sometimes formulated as a tax for social purposes. The conventional sum is 2.5 percent of one's wealth per annum. There is also a voluntary donation called sadaqa.

Fasting applies to the ninth month of the Islamic calendar, Ramadan. Since the Islamic year is ten to twelve days shorter than the conventional year, Ramadan moves backwards in the conventional year by those ten to twelve days per year. During Ramadan you may have no food or drink (or cigarettes) between sunrise and just after sunset. The purpose of this fasting is to make you sympathize with the poor, as well as to appreciate the blessings of earth which God has given us humans. Lots of little rules also apply. And don't eat or drink in front of someone who is fasting. That's very rude. You may read the entire Koran during Ramadan, one section for each of the thirty days. The end of Ramadan is marked by a principal Muslim festival, Eid al-Fitr, sometimes referred to as Eid. You may fast at other times, to make amends for moral or ritual failings.

Finally, there is the **pilgrimage** or **haj** to Mecca. This is compulsory once for every adult who can afford it. If and when you go, it will involve seven days at Mecca during the first half of the last month of the Islamic year. For a Muslim, the haj is a lifetime event. It is an act of worship and sacrificial effort. For younger Muslims nowadays it is often also an assertion of religious identity.

These Five Pillars, together, provide a structure which will permeate your daily life. That is true in particular of the daily prayers during which you will recite extracts from the Koran.

So, how far have we got? **The theme of your life as a Muslim** will be submission to God, which practically will mean to live humbly and appreciate the life and nature we have got. You will lead your daily life within a structure of ritual observance that constantly puts the words of God's sacred book, the Koran, before you. You will have available a structure of rulings which will tell you what course to take in most of the situations you find yourself in. You will be surrounded by a tradition which has a strong social conscience deriving directly from God's word. You may or may not be in a country which acknowledges some of these rules in its state law.

Thus **your daily life as a Muslim may vary considerably depending on which country you live in**. In Saudi Arabia you will live within a narrow and legalistic interpretation of the religion, subject to considerable restrictions if you are female. In Indonesia you'll find yourself in a more tolerant and liberal situation, in a country influenced by other traditions. In Somalia female circumcision will be assumed to be part of your faith. In Turkey you will live in a Muslim country with a secular state. In Western countries much will depend on the extent to which your family is adapted to the local culture there.

An issue within Islam, which has come to the fore again in modern times, is the question of just **who is a Muslim** and whether mere belief is enough to qualify. Historically, there have been a number of approaches to this. An early splinter group, the Kharijites, argued that sinful acts such as adultery made you a non believer. The grouping faded away, but this line of thought remained, as it were, on the shelf, ready to be picked up later, notably by modern fundamentalists. A counter argument was that only God knew what a person's spiritual state was. The view which became that of the majority within Islam was that the decider was the initial profession of faith. If you made that first step then you were a Muslim. Your faith was then perfected through works. If you sinned, you were still a Muslim, but not such a good one as someone who did not sin. On this basis, you can be a believing sinner and there are degrees of faith. A variation on this idea is that there is a third category beside that of believer and unbeliever, that of the hypocrite, who professes belief but doesn't follow the rules.

You will be familiar with the word '**jihad**' which you may understand to mean holy war. Jihad means 'struggle', and its most important application in Islam is to the personal struggle to live in the moral way God has intended for human beings. Jihad became politicized in the Muslim world following colonialism, but its original meaning was neither political nor military.

Your **mosque** is a place of prayer for both men and women, although women pray in a separate area from the men and may have a separate entrance. Children also attend to pray and are taught Islamic studies in the mosque. The mosque will have no chairs and you will sit on the floor. Nor will there be any pictures, for anything that could encourage idolatry is forbidden. Many women pray at home rather than at the mosque and an Islamic home will often have a separate room for prayer. A mosque may be used for other activities.

There is no priesthood in Islam. The **imam** is the prayer leader at the mosque. He may also deliver the Friday sermon and teach the children. Generally, in Western countries the imam has a wider role. In the UK each mosque elects its imam from those it considers to have the necessary learning, piety and other qualities.

In Islam, as with many religions, culture, custom and religious belief blend and bind with one another in a way which makes it difficult to see where one stops and another begins. This can give rise to problems when believers of one country move to another which has different attitudes. In the West there are **issues of integration** in some Muslim communities. These focus on family and moral matters. Some less integrated Muslim communities in the West have imported from their country of birth an imam with little knowledge of Western society and sometimes of narrow education, and that can accentuate the problem of non integration.

Sexual morality is very important in Islam. Sex is a blessing from Allah. The family is a fortress, and sexual morality an important part of its defense. Equally the family is the protection of sexual morality. Promiscuity is out. Privacy between unrelated people of the opposite sex is discouraged (and forbidden in some countries). Early marriage is sometimes seen as an answer to the dangers of moral temptation.

The Muslim world has always contained the usual proportion of **gay people**. They have lived like anyone else for centuries without there being any disciplinary action against them. They have merged into society without demanding their own identity. In parts of the Muslim world they may display their nature publicly. Yet modern fundamentalism has harsh thing to say of and to gays and Islam condemns homosexuality. If you are gay you may consider this an issue in your choice.

If you are going to marry a Muslim, do note that **a husband's family should not require a dowry and that the husband should pay a dowry to the wife**. If he divorces her or if she has grounds to divorce him she can, in most circumstances, keep it.

As for **mixed marriages**, a Muslim boy may marry a Jew or a Christian but a Muslim girl may not. Most schools permit a non Muslim woman to maintain her faith after marriage to a Muslim man.

Arranged marriages are a matter of culture and custom rather than religion. **Forced marriages** shouldn't happen but do.

There are a number of methods of **divorce**. One is khul, a divorce at the request of the wife, done by negotiation, perhaps through an imam, and involving the return of the dowry to the husband. Another is tafriq, a judicial divorce on various grounds, including where the continuation of the marriage would harm the wife's health or interests. The one likely to be most familiar to you is talaq where a spouse may declare three times that they no longer wish to be married. The idea is that the parties should refrain from intimacy for three menstrual cycles, corresponding with the three pronouncements. If they do the

divorce is finalized. Sometimes men make the three pronouncements in one go. This isn't based on Islamic scripture but it has
become established in some countries. The wife will keep the
dowry the husband paid her and any other property she has.
Note than within the marriage she has no duty to spend these
monies other than on herself. In most Muslim societies remarriage has been the norm for divorced women.

Popular newspapers and some Muslims may talk of a
Muslim's right to have up to four wives but in practice that is
misleading. The Koran (4.1) refers to marrying up to four wives.
However, the matter is not quite so simple. The Islamic experts in
the law, the jurists, always agreed that monogamy was preferable
and the practice was and is not common. Those in favor of it
argued that it could give protection to women who otherwise
would have none, that it could prevent immoral temptation, that
it could deal with the situation where a wife could no longer look
after or give sexual satisfaction to her husband, that it could be an
answer to a husband's involvement with another woman, so
avoiding both adultery and divorce. However, some scholars
point out that the reference in the Koran to having more than one
wife is in the context of men marrying their orphan wards. The
Koran also says that wives must be treated justly and then goes
on to say that men with more than one wife will not be able to do
that. At 4.1 the Koran says, 'but if you fear you will not be
equitable then only one (wife), or what your right hands own; so
it is likelier you will not be partial.' In practice, many Muslim
states don't favor **polygamy**. The Ottoman Empire gave a wife
the right to a judicial divorce if the husband took another wife, a
provision which spread elsewhere. Tunisia made polygamy a
criminal offence on the grounds that no man can be just to two
wives. Other Muslim states have taken measures to curb
polygamy. Turkey has been trying to stamp out polygamy since
1926 without success.

Islamic rules concerning marriage are designed to secure

women and children economically, and to ensure that children are the offspring of the man who pays for them.

While we are on the issue of marriage, you are likely to come across unpleasant remarks concerning the fact that **Muhammad had many wives**, and that one was very young. Muhammad took at least twelve wives into his household in his last ten years. All but one were widows. Marriage gave a woman protection. Sometimes it would serve a political purpose. One wife was young. Some say thirteen, some say as young as six. The usual age for marriage then was between eleven and fifteen, but the bride might be younger. The crucial thing was whether menstruation had begun, and in a really young marriage any sex would await that. Chaucer's Wife of Bath married at twelve. Louis XV of France was engaged to a three-year-old. Muhammad's young wife continued to live at her father's house for some years.

As for **abortion**, the fetus is not considered a human being until the spirit enters the body. Depending on the interpretation of sources, that is held to occur either after forty-two or one hundred and twenty days. Until then abortion is permitted, but afterwards only if the mother's life is at risk. Preventive contraception is OK if both parties agree. There is debate as to whether the morning after pill is allowed. The coil is not permitted, as an interference with the body. All Muslim boy children are subject to **circumcision**, but converts can choose.

As a Muslim, you will observe certain **food rules**, the principal ones of which are that you should not eat pork and that you should only eat meat from animals which have been slaughtered by having their throats cut while a prayer is said. As for drink, alcohol is forbidden. So generally are drugs. We should not injure our bodies, which belong to Allah. Smoking seems to have escaped prohibition. So does chewing Qat, a plant containing stimulants.

Whether you are female or male, you may have a particular concern about **female Islamic dress**. It's certainly a story in

Western newspapers and is seen as a divisive issue. It may involve the burqa, a head-to-toe cloak, with or without an unveiled gap over part of the face, or a covering which fits over the head and neck, covering the hair but exposing the face, or just a headscarf. The Koran has but one reference to veiling, using the word 'hijab', which at that time referred to a screen or curtain. The custom of veiling the whole body was initially a Byzantine upper class practice, which Islam picked up with its expansion. The issue only started to stand out from the general principle of modesty in dress in the last century and has since gained increasing support within much of Islam. For many it has become an issue of identity politics.

In the West such dress is often seen as backwards looking. However, you don't have to view it in either the way of Western secularism, or in the way of the Taliban. It can be quite compatible with modern gender values. You may see it as a statement of your religious identity. A woman may see it as a protection, and a freedom to avoid being looked at sexually. You may take the view that it overcomes class differences and encourages a sense of Islamic community. You may, if you wish, just see it as a cultural thing, which may give rise to clashes of culture. Such dress doesn't necessarily have to go hand in hand with sexual inequality although in many places it may. Surveys have shown a significant proportion of veiled woman as having progressive views on gender. Some Muslim feminists support it. You might say that veiling is as veiling does. Do you do it because you want to or because you are made to? Or to make a point? What is the balance between your reasons and the reasons of those who may object?

As for **womens' rights** generally, many Muslims will say that women have equal rights with men, but different ones. Islam gave women property rights that Western countries didn't give until much later. But it is a fact that some countries with large Muslim populations have a culture which gives women inferior status, and that this is reinforced by Islamic conservatism and more so by fundamentalist views.

Human life is sacred to Muslims and **suicide** is a sin. **Euthanasia** is forbidden. The issue of the **death sentence** has been and is hotly debated by Muslim jurists.

As to **work**, Islam disapproves of idleness and of ways of earning a living which harm others. There is no disgrace in menial work.

Islamic law forbids the lending of money at interest. This has been much evaded. Relatively recently, forms of interest free Islamic **banking** have been developed.

There should be no **racism** in Islam. Here's a passage from Muhammad's Farewell Sermon. "No Arab has superiority over a non Arab; a white has no superiority over a black, nor a black over a white, except in piety and deeds." However, in practice, racism is alive and well in the Islamic world.

A quick word about **Satan**. Satan is a created being and represents temptation. He is not a rival to God and lacks the powerful associations that Christianity attaches to him. His influence is everywhere, he is an evil whisperer, but he will not succeed. These are the inferences when Iranian clergy refer to the USA as the Great Satan.

Like all religions Islam has its large share of sinners. Unlike other religions, it doesn't leave it to God to punish them, but may prescribe **earthly punishments**. This is the bit of shari'a law that non Muslims think of when they hear the word 'shari'a'. It will only be of relevance to you if you live in a country where such penalties are enforced by the state. There are certain offences, called hadd offences, usually offences against God, where a severe punishment is prescribed as a deterrent. Examples are: amputation for theft, flogging for drunkenness or sexual transgression including fornication, and death for apostasy and publicly witnessed adultery. Note that homicide is a private wrong, prosecuted only on the demand of the next of kin, graded from intentional murder to accident, and giving the next of kin the right to damages instead. Thus where shari'a penalties are enforced, the family of a murdered person can overrule a judge's sentence of death, as an act of forgiveness, or may accept financial compensation instead.

Formulated in earlier days, these punishments can be a bit of a problem for those in Islam who wish to engage with the modern. Some of the punishments are specifically set out in the Koran (the penalty for apostasy is not in the Koran nor is the death penalty by stoning for adultery). Historically, courts would avoid such penalties if possible. Professor Wael Hallaq, a leading scholar and practitioner of Islamic law, to whose works I am indebted, says (in his *Shari'a*, p311-2) "It would not be an exaggeration to say that ... the only offences that required ... capital punishment or mutilation – aside from highway robbery – were, short of confession, nearly impossible to establish." Stealing an item of small value, or for hunger, would not incur the punishment. And note that Muslims disagree as to whether these are automatic penalties or merely maximum penalties. An ancient account has the Prophet saying that his mercy prevails over his wrath. Many Muslims will emphasize that. But fundamentalists won't.

The practical effect of this aspect of shari'a depends on which country you are in. Most Muslim countries do not enforce the shari'a's penalties. Such penalties are confined to countries such as Iran, parts of Pakistan, and Nigeria. Remember also that this is but one aspect of the shari'a.

Muslims might have another riposte to criticisms of the punishments of the shari'a. They might ask you to consider which crimes and pain might be absent from a society with no alcohol, no drugs and no sexual 'freedom'.

Let's consider **how the rules of the shari'a were arrived at. The Koran is the start**. But the Koran does not contain all the answers as to how life should be lived and organized. Of its more than six thousand verses only about five hundred relate to what we should or should not do. Islam has three other sources of authority for the laws that may be said to govern Islamic behavior. These are hadiths, qiyas (analogy) and ijmah (consensus).

Hadiths are the sayings of Muhammad obtained from accounts of his life and reports from his contemporaries about his acts and sayings. Collectively they form the **sunna** of the Prophet or 'example', for every Muslim to emulate. Each hadith can be traced through a chain of transmitters and those which have been accepted as genuine are set out in a number of compilations, classified by subject. Thus, if you had a legal question, that is to say if you wanted to know what should be done in a particular circumstance, the jurist or Islamic scholar advising you looked at the Koran and then the hadiths to see if the answer could be found there. However, the Koran and the hadiths only cover a limited number of situations on which a ruling might be required.

Majority Islam got over this problem by allowing the use of **qiyas**, or systematic reasoning from the texts. The principal though not only method was **analogy**. This method sought to find some common basis between the case in question and a case that was regarded as accepted law, and to make some deduction leading from the one to solve the other. The idea was that the law has God's purpose in it and so it is possible to draw conclusions from the law on one situation as to what the law should be in another similar situation. The deduction would be made by an individual jurist, or Islamic scholar.

The test of the qiya would be whether it was generally accepted. The general acceptance was called **ijmah** or '**consensus**' and for most Muslims this was the fourth basis of Islamic law. A hadith has Muhammad say that his community will never agree upon an error. Ijma/consensus also enabled some things, like circumcision, which only rested on Arab custom, to become a requirement. Note that the consensus was that of the jurists, scholars of Islamic law. The major part of Islamic law is based on qiyas and ijmah and is the product of the views of Islamic scholars of many centuries ago.

In developing this structure the Muslim jurists came to accept three guiding principles which were: **necessity, equity or fairness, and public welfare**: principles which were applied cautiously.

This method of interpreting Islamic law was known as **ijtihad**. This was the exertion of mental energy to arrive, through reasoning, at a considered opinion. The law was thus a synthesis of revelation and reason. Note that the jurists didn't see this as a process of making law but of discovering law which already existed. The idea behind this was that our intellect, or rather the jurists', bridged the gap between God and our human reality.

Note that a **fatwa** is merely a legal opinion given by a qualified Islamic cleric. Its authority would depend on its quality of reasoning and on the cleric's learning.

Also note that this method of applying law was **different from the doctrine of legal precedent** that we are used to. The shari'a court didn't regard some previous case as binding. There was instead a mass of rulings which a jurist would pick from in order to form his own opinion tailored to the particular circumstances of the case he was dealing with.

The next step in understanding the shari'a is to appreciate how it fitted, blended with, society. The shari'a depended on a truly **pious society**. The sanction of the law after death was greater than its sanction in life. There used to be examples of people confessing to capital crimes in order to avoid Hellfire. Shari'a courts attached great evidential value to the very fact that people gave an oath in support of their evidence. That's because to give a false oath was to face Hell. This was a bottom up system, not top down.

An Islamic ruler was expected to rule in accordance with Islamic principles. That's one reason why it's difficult to separate

Islam and politics. But the political authorities didn't create the shari'a they administered. It was the jurists, the Islamic scholars, who made the law. Equally, the shari'a has never exclusively governed an Islamic state. There was always tension between the shari'a and the ways and needs of the center of power. So while personal law such as marriage, divorce and inheritance was a stronghold of shari'a, both commercial and criminal law tended to be affected by the needs of the political authorities. And Islamic law has always been supplemented by local customary law.

Thus the shari'a blended with and was founded on a truly pious society. It was the product of independent jurists, legal scholars. It was administered by the political authorities but not created or controlled by them. Equally, the jurists did not seek or have political power. The purpose of Islamic law was not to control or discipline, objects which we would identify with law, but to help people live in peace with themselves and their neighbors. It was interested in all human acts with no distinction between the moral and the legal, from major ones to minor issues that you might consider as merely manners.

In addition, although the shari'a's social context was a **patriarchal** society, this patriarchy tended to a mild form which gave many legal rights to women, rights which were used frequently and effectively by them. A woman's evidence was worth less than a man's. Yet Ottoman court records show women successfully using the law in all its spheres and often being preferred as guardians of minors. In some cities women were parties in about forty percent of property transactions and many were administrators of family and other charitable trusts.

I've gone into all that detail because to understand **what now remains of the shari'a** you need to understand what it was in full and what has been lost – which is most of it.

What's left? In the words of Wael Hallaq the shari'a has been "dismantled" and has become "a textual entity offering little more than fixed punishments, stringent and ritual requirements, and oppressive rules under which women are required to live." (*An Introduction to Islamic Law*, p2.)

How did that happen? First the period of colonization and then the growth of the nation state.

Prior to colonization judges were employed by government but the law was developed by the jurists who the judges depended on for guidance. The jurists developed teaching circles, which developed into law colleges which were charitable trusts within which the teaching circles operated. In time, within the Ottoman Empire, legal education became absorbed into government bureaucracy and the legal profession into the administration of the Empire. And in some areas, such as public order, the law itself was added to by the government.

Under colonization, within the British Empire, Islamic legal texts were translated and Islamic law codified, so losing the flexibility that had been a principal feature. And it was separated from the customary law that it had been entwined with at a daily level. The imposition of the doctrine of precedent made the system yet more rigid and, excepting family and some property law, British-made law ruled. A similar process took place within the Dutch Empire in Indonesia, which did include the influential and flexible customary law but codified it and gave it primacy. In its later days the weakened Ottoman Empire became subject to Western influence, the Sultan put himself and his legislative council above the shari'a, the shari'a courts became an arm of the state and the law was codified. Egypt was nominally under the Ottoman Empire but autonomous and became an indirect colony of European powers. It introduced Mixed Courts, and codes based mostly on French law. The shari'a courts' jurisdiction became limited to family matters. When Britain occupied Egypt the shari'a was further marginalized. In the French colony of Algeria, French law dominated and by independence the shari'a was confined to family law.

Post colonialism took things a step further. There were still independent jurists to offer their opinion, but once the nationalist elites held the levers of power they were as keen as the colonial powers to use them. The law had become an instrument of control.

The colonial powers had for the most part left alone the law of personal status: child custody, inheritance, gifts and so on. But the post colonial nation states used legal devices to shape these remaining areas of Islamic law as they wished, separating them from their roots and from the methods traditionally used by Islamic law.

Colonialism left another legacy, making the shari'a in some countries an issue of **political identity**, something which the new nation states had to struggle with and still do.

Fundamentalism then sought to return to the roots of Islam and considered its texts with little regard to traditional Islamic interpretation.

Another factor which has affected such of the shari'a as remained is that the general level of **education** of Islamic jurists has fallen and their standards tend to be low within fundamentalist circles.

To summarise.

- The shari'a was a flexible all-embracing system of law administered but not created by or developed by political rulers, and depending on a pious society.
- It has never wholly and exclusively ruled any Muslim state.
- It was largely destroyed by colonial powers followed by the modern post colonial states.
- The area of family law was the last to go and elements of this aspect of the shari'a remain in many Muslim states, but divorced from their roots and from the traditional methods of their interpretation and application.

- Although the context of the shari'a was always a patri-archal society it gave many rights to women, but the restructuring of its family component in modern times in terms of the nuclear family has reduced their position. Where fundamentalist views reign, women have been oppressed.
- If the shari'a were to be restored it is difficult to see how it could actually work.

We now need to look at the **divisions within Islam**, and how they came to be. You should first bear in mind that within Islam some differences of opinion may be regarded as equally probable expressions of God's will. For example, Sunni Islam (of which more below) has four different schools which have different views on some aspects of diet, marriage, guardianship, female rights and inheritance. Local and regional custom also have their place.

However, that doesn't explain major differences within the faith. So let's look next at **how different views can arise**, how the revealed words of God can have led to diversity. First, there are some contradictions within the Koran and that gives scope for arguments. The doctrine of abrogation enables a later statement to overrule the earlier, although scholars are usually reluctant to take that path. Verses may be interpreted without reference to the rest of the Koran or to the life of Muhammad. The Koran may permit different interpretations. An up to date example is its use of the words 'straight path'. In Q36:4 God assures Muhammad that he is on 'a' straight path. It has been argued that this implies there is more than one straight path, quite a significant argument. Some hadiths, the anecdotes about Muhammad's life, contradict one another. Some are regarded as strong and some as weak, and opinion may differ as to which is which. There may be arguments as to whether hadiths have been properly reported. For those who say that later contradictory words supersede earlier words, there is scope for arguing about the historical order of the verses of the Koran or of hadiths. There is controversy as to whether recurrent hadiths can abrogate something in the Koran.

Let us take **two examples of differences of interpretation**, for which I am indebted to Michael Cook's book on the Koran. The Koran says, '... Men are the managers of the affairs of women for that God has preferred in bounty one of them over another, and for that they have expended of their property. Righteous women are therefore obedient, guarding the secret for God's guarding. And those you fear may be rebellious admonish; banish them to their couches, and beat them. If they then obey you, look not for any way against them; God is All-high, All-great.' (Q4:38). It's in the Koran! How do you get round that? Traditional approaches have been as follows. It's not about relations between men and women, but about husband and wife. It does limit the husband's authority a bit. It doesn't limit a wife's property rights or her social and political freedom. Limits on beating are found in traditional Muslim literature. It's a last resort. It's better not to do it. Modernists do their best, difficult in view of the words of the Koran, to bend scripture to accommodate Western values. Fundamentalists seize the stark words.

Another example relates to toleration. The 'sword verse' says, '... slay the idolators wherever you find them ... But if they repent, and perform the prayer, and pay the alms, then let them go their way; God is All-forgiving, All-compassionate.' (Q9:5). But later the Koran says, 'No compulsion is there in religion. Rectitude has become clear from error.' (Q2:256). You can see how this explains how different Muslims can come up with very different views on toleration.

Tom Holland in his readable book *In the Shadow of the Sword* at page 335 points out that the tenth-century scholar Ibn Mujahid established that there were seven equally valid 'readings' of the Koran and that the idea that there is one single text dates from a Cairo edition of 1924 which became the global standard.

And a word of warning. **If you read the Koran in translation** be aware that what you read may vary according to the translator. I have followed the translation by A J Arberry which seems favored by academics. However, the Penguin Classics translation by N J Dawood, for example, has some interesting differences. I have referred to Q16:93 where God 'leads astray who he will' raising issues of predestination. However, Dawood says God 'confounds who He will', which is not the same. In Arberry Q113 refers to the 'evil' God has created. Dawood refers to 'mischief' instead of 'evil,' again a softening of an important point. These are not insignificant differences, so just be a bit careful to double check before you start quoting words from the Koran at someone.

From time to time, in the West, we see people on our TV screens saying that this or that Islamic tendency isn't '**true Islam**'. That's a favorite comment about fundamentalism. But the fact of the matter is that there are a number of streams of thought within Islam and whether one or the other isn't 'true' is itself a matter of opinion and perhaps faith. Hopefully, the above paragraphs will help you appreciate how such variation can be.

Since the decline of the caliphate in the tenth century (of which more later), Islam has been in the care of its learned men, its scholars, the **ulama**, that word being the plural of 'scholar'. So this is a religion with no 'Church', **no central body**. The ulama have had great influence in Islamic countries. They have been a brake on those in power, in a sort of constitutional balance. But as we have seen, they have not held political power other than in Iran, a modern and single exception. So majority Islam lacks a structure that can command universal support and provide leadership.

There are **three major traditions within Islam**: Sunni and Shi'a, and then Sufi, which cuts across the first two traditions. The majority tradition, broadly described above, is **Sunni**. The name comes from the sunna, the examples of the life of Muhammad, the model for all Muslims. An important characteristic of Sunni Islam is that there is no clear pecking order among its clerics. It has been said that any such qualified person can declare whether something is against Islamic law. "All qualified jurists are correct" is an Islamic saying. At the same time this operates within a most conservative tradition.

For centuries the common view has been that in Sunni Islam the development of the law ended long ago, that the 'gates of ijtihad are closed'. Recent scholarship suggests otherwise. Be that as it may, it's evident that the great majority of Sunni rules represent the views of clerics from long ago.

Westerners will be aware of the conflicts between Sunni and **Shi'a** and may be puzzled about the difference between them. We need to start with a short history lesson. The Shi'a arose initially out of an issue of leadership. On Muhammad's death in 632 CE his companions concluded that the Islamic community, which then consisted of a confederacy of tribes, should have a single ruler and they chose Abu Bakr, a companion of Muhammad as his successor. On his death another companion, Umar ibn al-Kattab was chosen as second caliph. Umar estab-lished an electoral council which after his death elected as third caliph Uthman ibn Affan, one of Muhammad's early converts. In 656 CE he was assassinated by disaffected Muslim soldiers who acclaimed Ali bn Abi Talib, a cousin and son-in-law of Muhammad as the new caliph. A grouping centered on Muhammad's favorite wife Aisha attacked Ali for not avenging Uthman's death but was defeated.

An effect of Muhammad's teaching had been that as tribes turned to Islam they ceased to attack one another, and directed their traditional system of raiding elsewhere. This coincided with a time when the two great empires, Byzantine and Persian, were exhausted by conflict with one another. The upshot was that by the time Ali was acclaimed caliph an Islamic empire had itself developed, to include Iraq, Syria, Egypt, part of Persia, Palestine, Tripoli, Cyprus, and elsewhere. (Note that religious conversion to Islam spread at a much slower rate than the political expansion.) Muawiyyah, a member and then head of the powerful Umayyad family, had been appointed governor of Syria by Uthman, his kinsman. As kinsman, Muawiyyah had an obligation to avenge Uthman. Muawiyyah had power which Aisha did not, and after an abortive negotiation he deposed Ali. Although Ali eventually accepted this, many of his more ardent supporters did not, and he fell out with some of them. In 661 CE one of them murdered Ali. Ali's son, Hasan, was then paid off by Muawiyyah. However, when on Muawiyyah's death his son Yazid succeeded to the caliphate of an Umayyad dynasty now akin to an absolute monarchy, there was a small rebellion centered on Ali's second son, Husain. On an unequal battlefield Husain and his followers died, Husain holding his infant son.

This was the beginning of the Shi'a, that word being a shortened version of 'Shi'al Ali', or 'the party of Ali'. A principal Shi'a festival, Ashura, commemorates Husain's death. Men and women process and beat their chests and men flagellate themselves, mourning for an abandoned Husain.

Followers of Ali came to believe that he had inherited some of Muhammad's qualities. Within Islam their opposition generated theological discussion and development around the issue of leadership and issues such as free will, predestination, and the question of who was a Muslim. The word 'imam' means 'leader' and Ali was seen as the first Imam of the Shi'a. His descendants successively became Imam. The Shi'a ignore the first three caliphs, seeing the succession from Muhammad as running through the Imams. As time passed, there became a tendency for Muslims who protested against whoever was the reigning caliph to refer to themselves as Shi'a. By the time of the Tenth Imam hostility between the Shi'a and the leadership of the weakening Abbasid Empire (the Abassids had taken over from the Umayyad dynasty) was such that the then Caliph placed the Imam under house arrest. After that Imam's death the Eleventh Imam continued to live, and died, as a prisoner. However, it was said that his son, the Twelfth Imam went into hiding. From this the belief grew that he had been hidden by God and would return one day, far distant, bringing an era of justice. Shi'as believe that on Judgment Day the martyred Husain and the Imams can intervene with God on their behalf in the same way as Muhammad.

Thus the role of the **Imam** is central to Shi'ism. The Imam is sinless, infallible and perfect. He isn't a deputy but a substitute for the Prophet in the Prophet's absence. He isn't an instrument of revelation like the Prophet, but when he conveys what the divine law is he is infallible. After the Imam went into 'hiding', the learned men, the ulama of the Shi'a, used their own insights to work out the will of the Hidden Imam. And they regarded ijtihad, the further development of Islamic law as a process which could continue.

So while consensus still has its place, for the Shi'a it is the Imam's will that underpins Islamic law. As for arriving at what that will is, the Shi'as have their own interpretation of parts of the Koran and have their own, four, additional collections of hadiths. They use reason but are averse to the method of quiya or analogy which the Sunni majority use. They tend against the idea of predestination.

You are probably aware from your knowledge of current affairs how the roots of hostility between Sunni and Shi'a have flowered. The Shi'a cause has traditionally attracted those who have felt that the worldly rulers of Islamic countries have betrayed Islam's message of unity, peace and social justice. Shi'ites have had a tendency to feel persecuted. Out of that grew the Shi'ite idea of 'taqiyya', that they could legitimately conceal their true beliefs. The Shi'ites add the words 'Ali is a friend of God' to the shahada, the declaration of faith. Above all, the Shi'ites hold to the right to still independently interpret Islamic law, something which the Sunni has until recently thought closed.

The Shi'a clergy don't speak with one voice, but unlike the Sunni they do have a hierarchy. Within the qualified clergy an internal consensus promotes senior clergy to the rank of Ayatollah. From these the clergy choose five or six to be Grand Ayatollahs. Theoretically every Shi'a, clergy and lay, chooses a Grand Ayatollah as religious guide. The Grand Ayatollahs may have diverse views on both religious and political matters, so there is plenty of variation.

The main body of Shi'ites is referred to as **Twelvers**, after the twelve Imams. There is a Shi'ite grouping which holds that the last Imam was Isma'il the son of the seventh Imam. They are called **Seveners** or **Isma'ilis**. They have a number of subgroups one of which terms its Imam the Aga Khan. Other Shi'ite offshoots are the three million Yemeni **Zaidis** (who accept five Imams) and the **Alawis** of Syria. The Druze of Lebanon and the Baha'i Faith derived from Shi'a groups.

There is more detail in the differences between Sunni and Shi'a. If this is of particular concern to you, you will need to treat this as a first introduction and follow it up with further reading.

That brings us to **Sufism**. This is the mystic tradition within Islam. It sits side by side with both Sunni and Shi'a Islam. Sufism emphasized the need for its practitioners to have a master to guide them. This in turn led to the development of the Sufi orders, groups each led by a particular master or shaykh, accepting the law and ritual of orthodox Islam but concentrating on teaching and exercises to enhance spiritual advancement and achieve mystic experience. Sufis tended to be more tolerant of other religions and more relaxed about the inclusion of women. Sufis displayed reverence to those they regarded as saints. Sufi chants have sometimes been accompanied by music and dance. The whirling ritual dance of the Mawlawiyya order led to them being described as whirling dervishes. In pre-modern times many adult urban males belonged to Sufi brotherhoods.

The central idea of Sufism is that of spiritual unity with God, to return to a pre-creation state, to experience the pure and original message of the Prophet, to annihilate the ego. Yet this experience is not a lonely or separate one. The Sufi can have a normal Muslim existence in his community, in a state of both inward and outward piety. For Sufis, Heaven is not the usual Islamic Heaven, but is a union with God.

In times and places Sufism has been very influential and at others it has suffered opposition. The Wahabbi movement which began in the eighteenth century attacked Sufism and modern day fundamentalism is hostile to it, a contrast between spirituality and ideology. Generally Sufism has been a source of periodic spiritual renewal within Islam, as it has been and is for the individual. Modern Sufism offers a combination of inner exploration and voluntary association. It is more woman friendly. It is associated with music and poetry. For many people it may offer a depth of spirituality that a Westerner might feel is absent from orthodox Islam. Yet it has been seen as backward by modernizers and has greatly declined in the modern world although it is still influential. If you are interested in Islam you may find it a rewarding area of enquiry.

Wahhabism is a form of Sunni and was founded in the eighteenth century in what is now Saudi Arabia by Muhammad ibn Abd al Wahhab. He criticized any practices he saw as deviating from pure and original Islam. Wahhabism sees Jews and Christians as being as bad as atheists and polytheists, is hostile to mysticism and is ready to treat those Muslims who disagree with its views as unbelievers. It is dominant in Saudi Arabia.

Now I will discuss the problems Islam has in adjusting to modernity and also the issue of fundamentalism. That means venturing into matters outside religious ideas.

An important issue today is that of **the interlinking of religion and politics**. The West has separated these. Turkey, a Muslim country has attempted to do that. The Shah's Iran tried to do so. But the issue is a difficult and contentious one for Islam. Islam is a way of life. It permeates every aspect of a believer's daily life. It is about bringing a moral order on earth. It is committed to social justice. It seeks a harmony between everything, a harmony coming from the will of God, which should be obeyed. It is difficult to separate politics out from such a world view.

To understand Islam today you have to grasp this, and **the cultural and political obstacles that Islam has had to face in coming to terms with this modern world**. In Islamic countries the modern has tended to be embraced by intelligentsias and political elites. It has been espoused by (often ultimately unsuccessful) nationalist leaders and veil-ripping feminists. Its secular aspect has sometimes been brutal. The hearts and minds of the faithful have too frequently been left behind. Furthermore, the Industrial Revolution was slow to reach Islamic countries. When it did, those countries did not experience it as the crest of a wave of their own making but more as a foreign and colonial tsunami. What was organic growth for the West was something more artificial for the Islamic countries. Post colonial resentment and a reaction to the apparent political and military failure of many Islamic countries has encouraged a tendency to look within the faith rather than to seek to adjust to the outside. In some Muslim countries a feeling of impotence accompanies awareness of a powerful past.

Nor has the structure of the religion made theological and legal reforms easy. There is no institutional hierarchy to provide a mechanism for change. Individual jurists may each present their own view. The majority Sunni tradition long ago closed down the development of Islamic law, freezing an edifice of law which was once dynamic. Although Shi'a Islam does have a clerical hierarchy, it speaks with different voices. All these structures operate within a most conservative tradition. Some might say that the clerical establishment has a vested interest in the status quo. Within Islam there are large numbers of people who have not been exposed to modern Western style education. All this prevents the subtle alteration of inherited conceptions that a traditionally minded society needs to smoothly adapt itself to change.

Don't get the idea that the problem of adjusting to modernity is just down to Islam. People of **the West** take for granted trends of thought and attitude that may mean different things to other societies. Their primary orientation for action is the future and they may not appreciate that it isn't necessarily backward to look back when considering what action to take. They concentrate on the individual but ignore the alienation that can come from separating ourselves from a sense of a collective entity. They concentrate on choice and liberation and ignore the idea of fate that is so important within other societies. They fail to understand how threatening their secularization can seem to those outside their box and how unnecessary that is.

These are issues that echo within a Western society which increasingly questions its own values, which is becoming disillusioned about the limits of science and the use of economic prosperity as a touchstone. Islam is a growing religion, growing faster than any other. It must be getting some things right. Do those who sneer at it do so from an ivory Western tower?

We next need to look at **political Islam, which some refer to as Islamism, and Islamic fundamentalism**. Political Islam is the idea that society should be Islamicized and that this process should involve political control. Fundamentalism is a return to what are perceived as the roots of a religion, to seek reform and renewal. It considers the Islamic texts, particularly the Koran, without regard to their subsequent interpretation by scholars. It junks hundreds of years of Islamic scholarship. Political Islam and fundamentalism generally go hand in hand but they are distinct. Some fundamentalists are apolitical, concerned only with inner piety. Some advocates of an Islamic state don't agree with matters such as the more severe punishments of the shari'a. Many advocates of an Islamic state seek a state that is both fully modernized and fully Islamic. Within those who are both political Islamists and fundamentalists there is another divide, between those who countenance violence, even against innocents, to fulfill their purpose, and those who do not.

A problem of political Islam is that it hasn't been able to find a model which works well. The Saudi regime is much criticized by a fundamentalism that it has subsidized. In Iran, the Shi'a Ayatolla Khomeini used the principle of ijtihad to innovate and established a theocracy on the grounds that in the absence of the Hidden Imam the ulama, the religious teachers, were justified in seizing power. But that regime sometimes looks fragile.

You will be familiar with calls to 'restore the **Caliphate**', so I will explain the background to that. The caliphs or 'deputies' were Muhammad's successors. The caliphs came to exercise power like an absolute monarch. Following the political disintegration of the caliphate's Abbasid Empire in the tenth century the development of Islamic thought came under the guardianship of the ulama, or learned men, and separate from political rule. The caliphate, in name, technically continued, but with only symbolic authority. You can argue whether the caliphate up to this point was the sort of institution that fundamentalists want to 'restore', or whether it had become a setup in which Islam was a tool in the hands of the ruling power. The final resting place of the caliphate was the Ottoman Empire, and the caliphate ended after the demise of that empire following the First World War.

The caliphate that fundamentalists look back to is that of early times. Yet the shari'a in those times was supplemented by local customary law and was subject to political pressure from the caliphs. It can be argued that the caliphate which the fundamentalists want to restore never existed.

Islamic fundamentalism is a modern phenomenon. Some people see it as a reversion to a medieval creed, but that is not generally the case although there are some medieval scholars who could be described as fundamentalist. Wahabbism, founded in the eighteenth century, is fundamentalist. The idea of theocratic government, rule by clerics, put forward by Ayatollah Khomeini is not a reversion to the past but a modern idea and one which puts the Jurist-in-Charge, exercising the functions of the Hidden Imam by proxy in his absence, over and above the shari'a. The modern state rules.

It is in the last sixty years that Islamic fundamentalism has taken off. It is sometimes argued that that growth is a product of a Western aggressive secularism. Western culture is very intrusive. If you live by traditional Islamic values you will find things that are offensive to you, such as blasphemy, immodesty, disrespect for marriage and family values, coming at you from all directions: TV, radio, newspapers, magazines, advertisements. It's in your face. You yourself may not mind this sort of stuff, but try to envisage what it is like for someone who does. How would you feel if someone kept coming into your living room, using the word 'nigger' and advocating sex with children? You would probably end up getting a bit unreasonable about it. Consider the offence you feel at such words, and appreciate that that is how many Muslims feel about some things that you may find acceptable. Their fears may be compounded by advocates of secularism who see themselves as missionaries.

One of the ancient lines of thought that fundamentalism has picked up is that of the long extinct **Kharijite** grouping of early Islam (mentioned already under the issue of who is a Muslim). To the Kharijites, the Koran was everything and only the Koran. Its words were not to be interpreted by reference to the hadiths or otherwise. Those who fell short of total adherence to it were to be treated like unbelievers.

It is much easier to treat your opponents harshly if you dehumanize them first, and the manner in which fundamentalists see the distinction between true believers and the 'kafirs' (unbelievers) assists that.

The thinking of fundamentalist groups tends to **black and white views**. They concentrate on the literal meaning of passages which they select from the Koran, ignoring traditional interpretation where they choose. Pure Islam is the cure and everything else is barbarism. Force may be a legitimate way to enforce the cure. And the focus is on what it sees as corruption within the Islamic community just as much as on the corruption outside.

Both political Islam and fundamentalism have been influenced by the analysis of the Indian Mawdudi in the 1930s and later, and by the Egyptian Qutb, spokesman for the Egyptian based **Muslim Brotherhood**. The Brotherhood was founded in 1928 and was a major force in Egypt in the 1940s and 1950s. It sought to purify Islam of Western corruption through revolutionary social action, and regulate life totally. The Brotherhood emphasized that Islam was a total way of life and couldn't be separated from politics. The Brotherhood was a great success. It was committed to social justice, and ran schools, hospitals and even factories. These ideals were to operate only within the moral principles of Islam. When a few of its members descended to terrorism the Brotherhood was suppressed in Egypt. However, this model has spread and proved popular elsewhere, particularly with the better educated young. It is not necessarily wedded to all fundamentalist views. For example, the Brotherhood did not support the severe shari'a penalties. They wanted an Islamic state but a fully modernized one. As the results of the Arab Spring develop so we will see how the Brotherhood itself deals with that.

The idea of a return to the pure life of the first Muslims, and confining the law to the Koran and hadiths, or even just to the Koran, is sometimes referred to as **Salafism**. 'Salafi' means 'pious forebears'. The Taliban come within this category. Many Salafis wear beards and clothing in the style of early Arabs. Some people who are not Salafis do this too.

I make two final points about Islamic fundamentalism, particularly the more extreme forms. I repeat that it's no good just declaring that it 'isn't Islam'. There are significant numbers of fundamentalists. They justify their acts by their faith. You may not like their views, but they are coherently linked to the Koran. They are a type or types of Islam. To say they aren't is just confusing. The second point is that fundamentalism presents a particular problem for mainstream Islam. As a Muslim, how do you on the one hand deal with those who shout their Muslim status but act in a way you see as inappropriate to Islam, and on the other hand deal with those who attack Islam as representing such extreme views? Non Muslims need to appreciate this dilemma, just as Muslims need to appreciate that unless they stand up publicly against aggressive fundamentalism the outer world will identify them with it.

How can the problems of Islam's adjustment to the modern world be overcome, bearing in mind the fact that the Koran is God's unchangeable word? Those who attempt this adjustment are known as **modernists**. They do go back to the Koran, but to interpret it in the light of scientific reason, a tradition strong in parts of early Islam but long quiescent. Some of them disregard the hadiths as incorporating the ideas and attitudes of Muslims of over one thousand years ago. Some of them repudiate the traditional methods of interpretation. But they are still stuck with unequivocal statements inconsistent with Western values, the very words of God, written in a living language, which precludes the softening that translation can sometimes offer.

Since there is no church structure or hierarchy to decide on doctrinal matters, looking at modernism means looking at a range of ideas supported by a variety of Muslim theologians. Some see a new wave of ijtihad as being required. One idea is that what matters is not the form of the Koran but the divine guidance it gives. That opens the door to interpretation. Another is to say that the Koran was installed in Muhammad's heart and then spoken through his but human faculties. Another is to say that the Koran uses striking literary expressions to reveal religious truths. Another idea is that the jurists were wrong to read the Koran literally and should have concentrated on the moral idea behind the words. Modernists oppose the literal interpretation of the Koran. Some feel its meaning should be construed and reconstrued according to the historical context. But most are reluctant to go down that road which they see as having led to the self-destruction of parts of Christianity.

This is a most difficult time for Islam. Modern communications, which have pushed the underside of Western secularism into the faces of the faithful, have made them more accessible to popularist preachers, sometimes of little training, who seek to interpret Islam's texts themselves. Mass education has led to a decline in the prestige and authority of traditionally trained clerics, who can find themselves attacked on both sides. On one by those seeking a path to the modern, on the other by those seeking to return to what they see as pure Islam. All this takes place in a world in which many Muslims live under governments which they see as lacking moral or spiritual authority.

What is Islam's future? To what extent can the gates of ijtihad, of development of the shari'a, be opened again? Perhaps the decider and driver will be the demands of the younger generation of Muslims and of Muslim women and the way will involve a concentration on inner spirituality.

So there you have it. One of the biggest and fastest growing religions in the world. One of the most successful in the world. The only religion in the world which has a grouping, and one with substantial support, which justifies murder in the name of its faith. A religion based on an idea of social justice, yet awash with tyranny. A religion which froze its development hundreds of years ago. A religion whose inflexibility contrasts with the early adaptability and relative toleration which enabled it to accommodate so many different cultural systems. A religion present throughout the globe yet dominated by its Arabic roots and its minority Arab population. A religion which permeates your daily life with spirituality and concern for others and yet which in places is reduced to a mindless following of rules and legalism.

If Islam has an attraction for you the big practical question for you is one of geography. Where would you propose to practice the faith? Rural Pakistan? Indonesia? Iran? Egypt? Turkey? Bosnia? Europe or the USA? Your daily life may be very different according to your choice.

Finally, the matter of **numbers**. adherents.com suggests there are about 1.5 billion Muslims. Eighty to ninety percent of these are Sunni. There are about 80 million Shi'ite Twelvers, predominantly in Iran which has been a Shi'ite state since the sixteenth century and southern Iraq. Indonesia is the country with the most Muslims. More Muslims live in India than in Pakistan. Less than one quarter of Muslims live in the Middle East. The country with the largest Arabic speaking Muslim population is Egypt. The majority of Arabic speaking Muslims live on the African continent. Muslims are the second largest faith group in Europe and the USA. Figures are, as usual, extremely approximate.

Chapter 20

Sikhism

To consider Sikhism you have decided to believe:

- that spirit exists;
- that there is a creator God, just one,
- that it is good
- and all-knowing
- and all-powerful
- and eternal;
- that you have a soul, which is essentially part of God;
- in reincarnation
- and in karma.

Sikhism was founded by Guru Nanak who was born in 1469 and died in 1539. He expressed his teachings in 974 hymns. Guru Nanak's authority was passed on down a line of nine successive Gurus, who added further teachings in the form of hymns. The fifth Guru consolidated these into a collection known as the Adi (first) Granth (AG). This also included verses by non Sikhs. Subsequently, verses by later Gurus were added. The tenth and last Guru, before he died in 1708, conferred Guruship on the scripture, which was and is known as the Guru Granth Sahib. Sikhs believe that God decided to communicate with humanity by means of the Gurus and that this scripture is divinely inspired. It is more than a mere book and is referred to as **Sri Guru Granth Sahib**, a form of address to a person. This is sometimes shortened to **SGGS**. Note that any quotations I give from Sikh texts derive from translations referred to in the various works of Owen Cole.

Sikhism is thus **a revealed religion**, albeit one which evolved over a period of more than two hundred years. Sikhs do not treat their revelatory material in the same way some devotees treat the Bible or Koran, arguing over the literal meaning of words.

When you consider the chapters on **Hinduism and Islam** you will see how many ideas of each can be found in Sikhism. Some people have described Sikhism as a mixture of the two religions. However, it is now generally accepted that Sikhism has to be considered in its own right, and cannot be properly understood by reference to ideas found in other religions, or as a blend of these.

As a Sikh you will believe that there is **one creator God**. The fact that Sikhism is one of the monotheistic religions tends to be overlooked.

You will believe that **God is impersonal**, that He does not intervene in the world or manifest Himself in human form. The SGGS says, "Only your functional names I have been able to describe. Your oldest name is Eternal Reality."(AG1083).

You will believe that **God, His nature beyond our comprehension, is self-revealing**. It is for God to choose how much He reveals. It will be sufficient to enable your spiritual development and liberation, but you will have to exercise your free will to make that happen. For Sikhs, the Guru Granth Sahib contains a divine message to facilitate this.

God is immanent in all things. In other words, He is present in all things. The SGGS says, "God lives in everything, and dwells in every heart, yet is not blended with anything." (AG700). Being present in all things, God is, therefore, available to everyone. So there are many ways to this God, and the Guru Granth Sahib gives advice on how Hindus can be better Hindus, and Muslims can be better Muslims.

This God is just, and not capricious.

Evil is what happens when the ego takes over, God having given humankind free will. And it is a product of duality, of separation from God. "Duality clings to mortal man" says Guru Nanak (AG132). The answer is to realize, with effort and God's grace, that there is really no duality; that the temporal will merge with the eternal.

Undeserved **pain and catastrophe** are tests of courage and faith.

All beings have spirit, **a soul**, attached to them. Indeed the SGGS (AG176) makes reference to the possibility of soul being connected to vegetable or inanimate matter. This soul is a bit of God. The desired objective in life is for the soul to be liberated, so it can become unified with God.

Sikhs believe in reincarnation and in karma. For them, karma is a process whereby every action has consequences for the perpetrator, perhaps in a later life. As Guru Nanak says, "One receives in accordance to what one does" (AG662). One consequence will be the nature of one's next life. A human is best. If you aren't good, you may find yourself as a rat, for example, and it's very difficult for a rat to improve itself spiritually. You will just have to wait until your karma has worked itself out and you get another shot at a human. You will then have your chance to exert your free will, and not to behave like an animal. The Gurus say, "You are blessed with being born human, it is an opportunity which has been given to you to meet your God." (AG378). Good karma may see you born into the Sikh community.

Haumai is the problem that has to be overcome in our life, that is to say **I-am-ness**. Haumai consists of putting yourself at the center of life, and it can live within an outwardly good lifestyle as well as within an overtly evil one. It is a more sophisticated idea than mere selfishness. Being altruistic isn't enough. A verse of the Guru Granth Sahib says, "In haumai one fails to perceive the real nature of liberation. In haumai there is worldly attachment and doubt, its shadow. By acting under the influence of haumai humans cause themselves to be born repeatedly. If haumai is understood the door of liberation can be found but otherwise there is argument and dispute." (AG466). It is a question of what takes you away from a higher devotion, to God. Attachment to matters which do that, however apparently worthy, involve haumai. It can reduce us to the level of animals, albeit sometimes well-behaved and intelligent ones. And it can let love become lust and self-respect become pride.

As a Sikh you will believe that your spiritual development and the consequent removal of ignorance can lead to **spiritual liberation**. Your soul will then merge with God. It will in one sense live forever, but by disappearing into God. This is the ultimate objective of your life.

Since we live here and now in the immanent presence of God, it is possible, albeit uncommon, to achieve liberation while still in the human body.

There is a strong element of **panentheism** here. We merge with God. But we, as it were, live in Him, still separate in some way. Guru Nanak's Japji prayer says, "Some will be seated near your throne and some far away."

The question is, how to get liberated? The answer is to become God centered, not man centered. The means are our **free will and God's grace**, His focus of attention on you. You need both. However, God's grace is available to everyone. Meditation is a way of getting access to it. Guru Amar Das says, "Humanity is brimful of the nectar of God's name." (AG378). You will receive grace when you are ready for it.

This path to liberation involves traveling spiritually through **five realms** or stages. These are the realms of duty or piety, of awareness or knowledge, of endeavor, of grace and of truth. There is much discussion among Sikh scholars as to what these realms involve. In particular, a Sikh will seek to avoid the five evils, of lust, greed, attachment, anger and pride.

You can see from this analysis how, as a Sikh, you will be able to view other religions as ways to the same God. Sikhs believe that truth can be reached through other religions, but lies beyond them. In the same way the Guru Granth Sahib says, "I am neither a Hindu nor a Muslim. My body and soul belong to the one called Allah by Muslims and Ram by Hindus." (AG1136). The point is that **Sikhs see God as transcending all other concepts of God.**

Guru Nanak prescribed a daily formula of 'nam dan ishnan'. **'Nam'** is 'the name of God', that is the means by which divine reality is conveyed and in which it is contained. It will be the object of your daily meditation. It is what the Sikh turns toward and away from the ego. It is by meditation on nam, with your effort and God's grace, that you may overcome the effect of karma. You will dwell on nam and on the Guru's words. The technique of meditation which this involves is called 'nam simran'. It will be at the center of your spiritual life.

'Dan' means giving. "Those who meditate on God do good to others." (AG263). The process of this meditation goes with a life of service, working, sharing the proceeds with others. There is a long Sikh tradition of building facilities for the sick.

'Ishnan' means bathe. For Sikhs, cleanliness is most important. You will bathe every day and always before going to a place of worship. However, note that this is not a ritual. Sikhism does not approve of ritual. Nor is the bathing connected with the idea of pollution. The emphasis is more a product of tradition, a hot climate and common sense.

Thus, **private worship** will usually involve meditation. Also, the scriptures may be sung, chanted or read at home; although the ceremonial care that the Guru Granth Sahib requires means that many Sikhs won't have a full copy at home since they won't have a separate room to devote to it. Hence the increasing popularity of the internet, Punjabi TV, CDs and tapes for hearing the scripture at home.

The Sikhs' place of worship is called a **gurdwara** (meaning the doorway to the Guru). **Communal worship** takes place there, usually in early morning or in the evening. There is no fixed day for worship. Some overseas communities may find Sunday the most convenient day. Excerpts from scripture will be read or sung. Such singing is known as 'kirtan'. Music plays an important part in Sikh worship. Stories of the Gurus may be told, texts explained, spiritual advice given. When worshipping in the gurdwara you will cover your head. There are no rituals. "Rituals are chains of the mind", said Guru Nanak (AG63S). The **language of worship** is Punjabi, even in communities outside India.

On special occasions there may be a continuous forty-eight-hour reading of the whole SGGS. This is known as an **akhand path**. The last Guru's last words are said to have been, "Whoever wishes to hear the Guru's word should wholeheartedly read the Granth or listen to the Granth being read". Such a reading may take place on a festival. It can also be a prelude to a personal event such as a wedding, funeral or anniversary. On such domestic occasions the reading may be a broken one, perhaps taking seven to ten days.

Your worship will never involve **images**. Immanence (God being present in everything) does not involve pantheism (God and everything being a unity). And Sikhism turns its back on such Hindu practices as praying before images, though a Sikh might worship in a Hindu temple if none other is available.

Guru Nanak said, "God cannot be told what to do. God's own will determines His actions." (AG2). This suggests that your **worship** will not be about asking for things. However, the important Ardas prayer asks the Gurus for help, protection, and forgiveness, and victory in battle, which does seem to leave the door open for requests.

A principle of Sikhism is the unity of the human race, and hence the **equality** of all humans. All sit equally on the gurdwara floor. As a woman, Sikhism considers you have equal standing to men in the gurdwara and may do anything, for example leading worship, that a man would do. However, social attitudes can fall behind this ideal, and even more as regards the general status of women.

Guru Nanak condemned the idea of **caste**. "God's light pervades every creature", he said (AG469). He saw caste as divisive, a spiritual view rather than a social one. In practice, Sikhs have been largely unable to shake off the mindset of caste.

A reason for everyone sitting on the gurdwara floor is that the place of honor is occupied by the scripture, the **Guru Granth Sahib**. That is on a throne, and so honored by the congregation. When you bow to the SGGS you are praising God, whose word it contains. You will hope that God's word nourishes you. Pictures of the Gurus are kept well away from the Guru Granth Sahib, perhaps not even in the same room, so nothing can be seen which might in the eyes of the young or uneducated rival the scripture.

You will also get physical nourishment at the gurdwara, for an aspect of Sikh worship together is the meal the congregation eats together after worship. In overseas communities it is usually eaten after congregational worship ends. In large Indian gurdwaras where worship continues throughout the day it may be given before leaving, whenever that is. Food is vegetarian, since many members may be vegetarian, although vegetarianism is not compulsory in Sikhism. This meal or **langar** reaffirms the equality of everyone, particularly in a society where there has been a tradition that sharing food with others of lower status can lead to ritual pollution. The organization of the langar is done by members of the congregation. In helping you learn to serve humanity. Washing-up is just as much worship as singing.

Most **Sikh festivals** celebrate life events of the Gurus. Sikhs also have a festival on the same day as four Hindu festivals (including Divali and Holi), originally a device to wean them from Hinduism.

There are no Sikh priests or permanent officials. Members of the community are appointed for a while to certain duties. A gurdwara will be run by a committee. The committee may appoint a **granthi** to look after the gurdwara day to day and to look after and read the Guru Granth Sahib. They may appoint more than one if the community is well off. In practice almost all granthi are men.

A **sant** is the name given to a person of knowledge and enlightenment who has gained a reputation as a teacher and spiritual guide. Such a person can have many followers and be influential.

There are **no monks or ascetics** in Sikhism, no seeking a path of inner individual spirituality. You won't find God in your heart unless you can see Him in everyone else's. Nor is celibacy held a virtue.

Sikhism is based on life as a householder, helping other householders. Right living is the key to our relationship with God. The SGGS is full of references to individual conduct. Guru Nanak said, "We must be traders in truth." (AG939).

Sikhism is thus **centered on the family**. God is found at home. The home is in the community.

The Sikh marriage ceremony sees **marriage** as the union of two souls. There are aspects which are cultural rather than religious. Traditionally there is less emphasis on the private aspect between the two parties and more on the close connection it involves between two families. Arranged marriages are usual, and early marriages are not uncommon.

If you become a Sikh, **the extent to which traditional culture may affect your life** will depend a lot on where you live. Life in Pakistan will be different from life within the Sikh community in India and even more within one in the West.

A few words about Sikh names may be helpful. Most forenames can belong either to men or women. However, the last name is Kaur (princess) for a woman or Singh (lion) for a man. There is also another surname, which can be indicative of caste. People of higher caste may be more tempted to use that one with their last name to distinguish themselves from the multitude of Singhs and Kaurs. Sometimes those of lesser caste promote themselves by adopting a name associated with a higher caste.

Sometimes the name of a person's village is used instead.

As to **ethical matters**, the faith has no objection to and encourages transplants, seeing a dead body as discarded. It objects to artificial insemination by a donor but not to in vitro fertilization. Divorce is not approved but is more common than it was, overseas anyway. Abortion is condemned but nonetheless a fact arising principally from a desire for male children. Circumcision is rejected as interfering with the human form. Differences between Sikh views in India and overseas in Western communities are what you would expect. However, there is an increasing tendency abroad to embrace traditional Sikh heritage as a matter of identity.

As to **work**, in the words of Owen Cole, to whose books on Sikhism this chapter is much indebted, 'no task is ignoble but some work is unworthy.' Selling tobacco or alchohol, prostitution, professional begging or gambling, for example.

Sikhs have **a martial tradition.** The Gurus said that without power righteousness does not flourish and that when other methods have failed it is permissible to draw the sword. They set out rules for a just war. There should be no hatred or desire for revenge, no looting or rape, no seizing of territory and only minimum force.

The most important Sikh rite is that of **initiation, or amrit sanskar**. Initiation is a personal commitment to the religion. Some Sikhs undertake it when young, but most who undergo it do so in adulthood. Most Sikhs get initiated but some don't. Initiates are called **Khalsa Sikhs**, the Khalsa being the community of initiates.

If you are initiated, you must observe **five rules of personal dress**. You must not cut your **hair** or body hair. You must wear a **comb** and a **thin iron wristlet**. You must wear a **one sided sword**, a requirement which can be satisfied by an ornament in the shape of a sword. You must also wear a **hacka**, trousers or underpants which do not come below the knees and which are tied with a drawstring. The idea behind these rules was to distinguish Sikhs from their Hindu or Muslim contemporaries. In addition to these rules, you must also wear **a turban**, even if you are bald, except that woman can wear a scarf instead. There are also rules of behavior. Chucking out offences are: eating meat killed by Muslim custom, committing adultery, and using tobacco. If chucked out, you can be reinitiated once, twice or perhaps even three times. Minor offences are: dying your hair or plucking grey hairs out, seeking a dowry for your child, and using alcohol or narcotics.

So, **there are various categories of Sikhs**. Initiates are known as Amrit-dhari Sikhs or Khalsa Sikhs. Lapsed initiates are termed Patit. Sikhs who don't seek initiation are called Khes-dhari Sikhs. Uninitiated Sikhs may keep their hair uncut and wear a turban. A minority of Sikhs cut their hair because they do not consider it to be an important issue and these are termed Sahajdaris. Sikhs who are clean-shaven and who cut their hair other than on principle are known within the Sikh community as 'Mona' (which means bald, clean-shaven or with trimmed hair) though some people disapprove of the term. Within the Sikh community the recognition of Monas as true Sikhs is a matter of controversy.

As to **numbers**, these are disputed but there are certainly over twenty million Sikhs in India and eighty percent of those live in the Punjab. The total abroad may be two perhaps three million. The biggest communities abroad are in Canada and the USA and rather more in the UK. The waves of migration to the UK tended to be of particular caste communities and because of this there is a tendency for UK gurdwaras to be associated with a particular caste, another point you should bear in mind should you be in the UK and should this faith attract you.

Sikhism is not a missionary religion and is usually regarded as an ethnic religion, although its founder had a far wider vision than that. Sikhs are not supposed to marry non Sikhs, a rule frequently unobserved in America. However, Sikhism does accept converts. These tend to be attracted by sants, inspirational teachers who have a following. For example, Yogi Bhajan of 3HO, the Healthy, Happy, Holy Organization in the USA has some thousands of Western followers.

A question a Sikh convert is likely to ask is: **who is in charge?** That question does not have an easy answer. The Sant Samaj is a coalition of prominent religious leaders. The SGPC is the Sikhs' most powerful elected body, administering the gurdwaras. Decrees which have moral authority can be issued by the elected heads of certain major gurdwaras in India. The Akali party is the political voice of Sikhism. There is a Sikh Code of Conduct, agreed in 1945 after fourteen years of drafting, but which does not define how gurdwaras' committees should be elected. The answer to the question 'who is in charge', albeit one which lacks practical definition, has to be that the Guru Granth Sahib is in charge.

Chapter 21

The Baha'i Faith

To consider this faith you will believe:

- that spirit exists;
- that there is a creator God, just one,
- that it is good
- and all-knowing
- and all-powerful
- and eternal
- and it cares for you individually and is interventionist;
- and that you have an immortal soul
- which is in some way in God's 'image'.

If you join this faith you will believe in the evolution of religious history by means of a succession of messengers from God. Previous messengers include Abraham, Krishna, Moses, Jesus, the Buddha and Muhammad. This revelation from God is thus progressive. There will be other future messengers although not for about another one thousand years. The most recent messenger, who founded this faith in nineteenth-century Iran, was one Baha'u'llah. Hence the name Baha'i Faith.

We each have a duty to recognize God through His messengers. Our purpose is, through recognizing God, being obedient to Him, by service to others and by prayer and spiritual practice, to become closer to God. When we die our place in the spiritual world is decided by how we have lived. Heaven and Hell are states of nearness or distance from God.

Baha'u'llah says that humanity has now reached the stage where all peoples can be united into a peaceful and integrated global society: "The earth is but one country and mankind its citizens."

A common summary of Baha'i principles is as follows:

- Unity of God. There is only one God, so great that he is beyond our comprehension.
- Unity of religion.
- Unity of mankind. World federal government is desirable. Diversity of race and culture is to be tolerated and appreciated.
- Equality between the sexes.
- The end of all forms of prejudice, whether of religion, race, class or nationality, for these are all impediments to unity.
- World peace.
- The harmonization of religion and science.
- An independent search after truth, unfettered by superstition or tradition.
- Universal compulsory education.
- The introduction of a universal additional language.
- Obedience to government.
- The elimination of extremes of wealth and poverty, and the pursuit of social and economic justice.

This list strikes many contemporary chords. You will direct your spiritual life to these ends. Useful work is a form of worship. Monasticism is off the agenda. Your spirituality must find itself in your ordinary daily life. Note that for all the progressive agenda, involvement in politics is forbidden. The Faith is committed to obedience to established political authority.

As with most religions, Baha'i has rules for its members. If you are over fifteen you must pray every day. You must not gossip or backbite. If you are fit, you must fast from sunrise to sunset from 2 March to 20 March. No drink, no drugs, no gambling. And no sex except between husband and wife in marriage, so if you are gay avoid this religion unless you are happy to be celibate. If you wish to marry you must have both parents' consent, even if one of them is not a member of the Faith. Divorce is discouraged but permitted.

The daily prayers are done in private. Communal gatherings take place about every three weeks, and on the nine holy days (on which work may not be done). Texts are read, there may be sermons, and food is served on feast days. Baha'i meetings are usually held in individuals' homes but may be in rented halls. Worldwide there are just eight Houses of Worship.

The Baha'i Faith plans for its own growth, with a centrally organized missionary system. It has a system of education through self-perpetuating study circles, and has launched a large number of grassroots based social and economic development projects. It has close relations with the United Nations.

The Faith's organization is run by elected representatives. There are National Spiritual Assemblies and a supreme Universal House of Justice. The Universal House of Justice was first elected in 1963 and now has permanent headship of the Faith. It is regarded as being divinely assured.

Let's have a look at the roots of the Faith, and how it has grown, for that may give some guidance about the future. The Faith developed out of 'Babism' in the mid-nineteenth century. The Bab was a member of a Shi'ite sect in Iran who declared himself to be first a messenger of the Hidden Twelfth Imam and then the Imam himself. Babism was inclined to exclusivism and sometimes fanaticism and was suppressed. Baha'u'llah, a prominent Babist, sought to revive Babism and then moved on to declare himself a messenger of God and found the Baha'i Faith. The Faith thus has Islamic roots. Its rules, found in Baha'u'llah's Kitab-I-Aqdas (Most Holy Book), are a sort of shari'a, designed to regulate society at all levels. In practice, however, much of this law is not acted on or even known in non Islamic countries. And most members of the Faith now come from non Islamic countries. The Baha'i Faith has endured with fortitude much persecution in Islamic countries and only 300,000 now live in Iran.

The majority of the Faith's devotees are now found in India (40%), Africa (20%) and Latin America (16%). That growth is postwar and many of those converts are from the poorer classes. Total members currently may be about five million. Britannica says the faith has a presence in 247 countries. Nonetheless, the Faith's organization is mostly run by Iranians, Americans and Europeans.

The Faith makes much of its own unity. Preservation of that is an overriding concern. There have been divisions in the past. Those who rebel against the central authority of the faith are excluded.

Remember, this is a revealed religion. It is changed from time to time as fresh messengers from God arrive, but another one isn't due for a thousand years, which over time may cause some inflexibility as social attitudes change. For all its progressive agenda, the Faith has a conservative attitude to such matters as homosexuality, cohabitation, abortion, alcohol, euthanasia and capital punishment. Since 1983 it has accepted social action as an aspect of its development plan. Yet its commitment to obedience to established authority may be a source of future tension within its ranks.

Time will tell how this plays out. Do you want to be a part of this dynamic process?

Further Reading

Writing this short chapter has been one of the more difficult bits of the book and I have tried to work out why. How should I write the chapter? My first thought was to list all the books I had read and say which I liked most. But I think that can all sit on the website for the book at dyngod.com. Go there. There are material and links to help you to follow your quest or your curiosity. And I will try to keep it up to date.

What I have found writing this book is that there are some religious texts that are short and accessible and which can give a real feel for a religion and that is what I will center on here. It is a personal assessment and I miss some religions out.

For Buddhism: The *Dhammapada* is a no-nonsense collection of teachings of the Buddha. Skylight Paths Publishing print a usefully annotated copy. The Dalai Lama's *My Spiritual Autobiography* is easily read and has a subtle and profound simplicity. It is printed by HarperOne in the USA and Ebury Publishing in the UK. I have quoted from it.

For Confucianism: *The Analects* is a collection of sayings attributed to Confucius. Read them and then reread the chapter. Penguin books have a translation by D.C.Lau.

For Taoism: The *Tao te Ching* is one of the world's most translated texts. I quote from it in the chapter on Taoism. Get a copy.

For Judaism: The most interesting book I read for the chapter on Judaism was a series of extracts from the *Zohar*, a principal text of the Kabbalah tradition. This was published by Skylight Paths Publishing. But remember, this isn't mainstream Judaism.

For Hinduism: The *Bhagavad Gita*, of which there are many translations, would be a good follow on to the chapter on Hinduism. The *Upanishads* are interesting and on the website I have a section on these, including extracts.

For Christianity: Read Pope Benedict's encyclical *Deus caritas est*. I think this is as good a statement of Christian humanism as you could find and applies to Christianity as a whole, explaining in detail just what the idea that God is love means. So don't be put off by the fact that it is written by a Pope. You can find it on my website.

For Sikhism: Owen Cole and Piara Singh Sambhis' book *The Sikhs* published by Sussex Academic Press is well laced with extracts from the Sikh sacred text, the Guru Granth Sahib.

For Jainism: Any Jain texts I have read have been hard work. The Jain Library at www.jainlibrary.org has a mountain of stuff from books for children upwards.

For Islam: I didn't read anything that particularly struck me, other than to say that I think Wael Hallaq's book *An Introduction to Sharia Law* is modestly titled and masterly. But you might find some of the collections of hadiths, stories about Muhammad's life, interesting. These stories were collected by early Muslim clerics and I particularly liked the account of one such collector who traveled long and far to interview a man said to have evidence of a particular hadith. On arrival he saw the man beating his camel. The cleric went home without interviewing the man. When asked why, he said: "How can you trust the word of a man who beats his camel?"

Finally, read anything by Karen Armstrong. I am a great fan of her scholarly and readable books.

Afterword

That's it. I hope you enjoyed the book and found something different in it. I tried to find something like it in the bookshops, couldn't, and started writing it myself out of frustration.

Who writes books on religion anyway? Ask yourself the question and I think you may have an answer as to why they don't deal with questions you want to ask. So, who are they?

People who want to convince you of a point of view. Not for me.

People who have made their living from the study of a particular religion. These writers are well qualified, and are ideal to deal with that religion and associated ones. But their ship has a lot of ballast to one side, their knowledge is thin in terms of some religions and this can produce a lack of balance.

Publishers know this and sometimes attempt to get over it by having specialists write on each religion, with an editor to impose an apparent coherence. There are a good number of such splendid works but by definition they cannot have a 'voice' and they tend to lack inner coherence. The imposition of a uniform layout for each religion can be unproductive. For example, if you are dealing with Judaism you need to spend much more space dealing with the rules of daily behavior than with other religions.

And most such books don't spend the time I have spent on how the belief system 'works' and how the ideas fit together. Many commentators treat religions as cultural artefacts. But they are living organisms of thought, affecting the way people think, feel and see the world. That's how I see religions and how this book treats them. Some people call this a 'doctrinal' approach.

I did approach a former Professor of Comparative Religion of a major university and asked him to vet the book. I have immense respect for this man and he was very fair to me. He is averse to the doctrinal approach, and said, "Given your wishes/aims I think you have done a good job, it is just that I do not agree with your aims and wishes." Well, I think that may be the view of other academics, a reason why I couldn't find a book like this in the bookshops.

Religion, particularly comparative religion and the God debate are quite hot topics, but it is not an easy area in which to get published. You have to have something different. But that isn't enough. As a major international publishing house told me, "… it is very difficult for books by relatively new authors to achieve the necessary level of sales required in this sector of the challenging market."

Having got to the end, I think you are entitled to ask what my own views are. Thus far I have tried to keep them out of the way.

I was brought up as a Catholic and was an earnest disciple, a pillar of the One True Church in my heavily Protestant Grammar School, serving at Mass up to the ripe age of nineteen. At Cambridge University the Scottish eighteenth-century philosophers plus the new delights of fornication did in the foundations of my cradle faith and by my thirties I had abandoned Christianity.

Strangely, since then I have combined a very limited range of belief with a great interest in belief systems as a whole. I have no abiding faith, no belief that I 'know'. I do believe in the absolute value of 'good' and have a fairly firm conviction that there is some sort of existence after death and that how we behave in life (in terms of the 'good') will affect what happens afterwards. That's it really. I quite like the idea of reincarnation but am open minded about it. I am inclined against the idea of God but am open minded about that. In so far as I have doubts about such beliefs as I have, I adopt them as a working hypothesis on the basis that if there is nothing afterwards I have nothing to lose by believing otherwise.

What about my views on the belief systems set out in this

book? I have an instinctive reservation about systems that claim exclusivity and that are intolerant of other systems, damning non members. For me, that means Islam, aggressive secularism and parts of Protestant Christianity. I also hesitate at missionary systems, which I would identify as Islam, Christianity and aggressive secularism. I ignore political dimensions which are not inherent in the system itself, examples being Sinhalese Buddhists in Sri Lanka and the BJP Hindu based party in India.

If I were to pick a God system, I would incline to one where my soul could be unified with God after death. And I am tempted by reincarnation, since it solves the problem of why bad things happen to us. Those inclinations lead me towards Hinduism.

I am impressed by systems that don't have get-out-of jail free cards. Zoroastrianism and Jainism are the best examples of that. I'm in a minority here. Forgiveness is popular in the Abrahamic religions. And Buddhism has its quick fix corners.

I like the Jain idea that all matter has a soul. And as a system it's great, but just impossibly austere.

To me Sikhism has a great deal to offer. Reincarnation, union with God, meditation, non missionary, tolerant of other religions, no something for spiritual nothing. But I don't identify with its cultural and ethnic stuff, which I find difficult to separate out.

If you were to twist my arm and say I must make a choice which otherwise I would not make, I would settle for mainstream Buddhism. It's tolerant, logical, flexible yet uncompromising, very different, an ideal adjunct to a modern life with its modern stresses and strains.

As to whether secular humanism can provide for spirituality without spirit and find common ground with religion: I wonder.

We will see what is what in due course. At the age of seventy-two I look forward to finding out.

CHRISTIAN
ALTERNATIVE

Throughout the two thousand years of Christian tradition there have been, and still are, groups and individuals that exist in the margins and upon the edge of faith. But in Christianity's contrapuntal history it has often been these outcasts and pioneers that have forged contemporary orthodoxy out of former radicalism as belief evolves to engage with and encompass the ever-changing social and scientific realities. Real faith lies not in the comfortable certainties of the Orthodox, but somewhere in a half-glimpsed hinterland on the dirt track to Emmaus, where the Death of God meets the Resurrection, where the supernatural Christ meets the historical Jesus, and where the revolution liberates both the oppressed and the oppressors.

Welcome to Christian Alternative... a space at the edge where the light shines through.